AXIS

OF

EVIL

AXIS
OF
EVIL

The War on Terror

edited by

Paul Moorcraft

Contributing editors
Gwyn Winfield and John Chisholm

Pen & Sword
MILITARY

First published in Great Britain in 2005 by
Pen & Sword Military
an imprint of
Pen & Sword Books Ltd
47 Church Street
Barnsley
South Yorkshire
S70 2AS

ISBN 1 84415 262 6

Typeset in Sabon and Gill Sans by
Phoenix Typesetting, Auldgirth, Dumfriesshire

Printed and bound in England by
CPI, UK

Pen & Sword Books Ltd incorporates the imprints of Pen & Sword Aviation,
Pen & Sword Maritime, Pen & Sword Military, Wharncliffe Local History,
Pen & Sword Select, Pen & Sword Military Classics and Leo Cooper.

For a complete list of Pen & Sword titles please contact
PEN & SWORD BOOKS LIMITED
47 Church Street, Barnsley, South Yorkshire, S70 2AS, England
E-mail: enquiries@pen-and-sword.co.uk
Website: www.pen-and-sword.co.uk

Contents

About the editors   viii

Introduction
New wars, old conflicts? – Paul Moorcraft   1

One   **Aftermath of 9/11**
Feith in the future – Douglas Feith, the US Under
      Secretary of Defense for Policy   6

Two   **War against Saddam**
      DISSENTING VOICES
      Fighting the war – George Galloway MP   10
      The father of the house – Tam Dalyell MP   20
      A liberal dose of realpolitik – Sir Menzies Campbell MP   23
      War, Church and State – Dr Rowan Williams,
          Archbishop of Canterbury   29
      The Road to Baghdad – Paul Moorcraft   32
      In the Bunker – Tariq Aziz, then deputy Prime Minister
          of Iraq   35

      THE 'OFFICIAL' LINE
      The beginning of the war – Geoff Hoon MP, the UK
          Secretary of State for Defence   39
      British air power – Air Chief Marshal Sir Peter Squire   45
      Virtuous intervention – and good luck – The Rt. Hon Lord
          Hurd of Westwell, former Conservative Foreign Secretary   49
      Pearls of Wisdom – Richard Perle, former US Assistant
          Secretary of Defense for International Security Policy   53
      CBW genie out of the bottle? – Professor Richard Holmes,
          Cranfield University   59
      Last Chance Saloon – Peter Rodman, US Assistant
          Secretary of Defense for International Security Affairs   62

CONDUCT OF THE WAR – OVERWHELMING IRAQ

An Overview of land, sea and air operations – John Chisholm 66
Desert Rat – Brigadier Graham Binns, 7 Armoured Brigade   71
Allied amphibious assault – Major General Jim Dutton,
    Commandant General, Royal Marines   79
Holding the Red Card – Rear Admiral David Snelson   86
Engaging the enemy more closely – Lieutenant Commander
    Mike Leaney, Lieutenant Commander Andy Swain and
    Captain Roger Robinson-Brown   94
Showdown in the sun – Chief Warrant Officer Stacy
    Jeambert, 1st US Marine Division   98

LESSONS LEARNED

Ruler of the Queen's Navy – Admiral Sir Alan West,
    First Sea Lord   104
Up Tempo – Lieutenant General Claude Christianson,
    Chief of Logistics, US Army   110
Red lessons – Lieutenant General Ronald Keys, deputy
    Chief of Staff for Air and Space Operations, USAF   118
The lessons of Iraq for the British army – Brigadier R.A.M.S.
    (Mungo) Melvin, the Director of Land Warfare   124

Three **Imperial Overstretch**

Policing the World – Dr John Mackinlay, War Studies
    Department, King's College, London   133
The Long Haul – Richard Lee Armitage, the US Deputy
    Secretary of State   141
High-intensity warfare – but only with the Yanks – Paul
    Keetch MP, the Liberal Democrat defence spokesman   146
'I wasn't going to cut your throat' – Lord Guthrie,
    former UK Chief of Defence Staff   149
Teaching UAVs to Dogfight? – General John Jumper,
    Chief of Staff, USAF   156

AFGHANISTAN

Afghanistan: a personal perspective – Paul Moorcraft   162
Commanding the 'peace' – Major General John McColl,
    British commander, ISAF   165
Building work ahead – Gwyn Winfield   168
Any old iron – Colonel Richard Davies, Commander UK
    PRT, Mazar-I-Sharif   171
Divide and Rule – General Mohammed Attah, General
    Abdul Dostum   175
Tracking the Taliban – Donald Rumsfeld, US Secretary
    of State for Defense, Lieutenant General David Barno,
    Commander US forces, Afghanistan   179
Not West Belfast – Colonel Mike Griffiths, British army   183

Iraq
A war of unintended Consequences – Lindsey Hilsum,
    Channel Four News International Editor   186
Re-inventing the wheel – former US Ambassador Timothy
    Carney   192

Four   **The Broader Middle East Conflict**
Sudan: the bin Laden connection – Paul Moorcraft   199
The West Bank: can there ever be peace? – Paul Moorcraft   210
Israel's 'War on Terror' – Brigadier General Eival Gilady,
    Israeli Defence Force   215
Battles in a twice-promised land – Brigadier General
    Gershon HaCohen, Israeli Defence Force   220

Five   **The Global War on Terror**
NATO: Modernization versus marginalization – George
    Robertson, then Secretary General of NATO   227
The Rumsfeld Question – Dr Paul Cornish, Director,
    Centre for Defence Studies, King's College, London   232

Six   **Homeland Security – the UK example**
Battle of Britain Mark 2 – Paul Moorcraft, Gwyn Winfield,
    John Chisholm   238
Chasing shadows – Patrick Mercer MP, the Conservative
    Shadow 'Minister for Homeland Security'   244
Eternal vigilance – Nick Raynsford, the Minister
    responsible for UK resilience   251
Heart to Hart – City of London Police Commissioner
    Dr James Hart   257
Finessing the terrorist threat – David Veness, Assistant
    Commissioner, specialist operations, Metropolitan
    Police   263

Seven   **Future Shock**
Paper Tiger: real teeth – Gwyn Winfield   270

Conclusion
A new Hundred Years' War? – Paul Moorcraft   278

Index   289

About the Editors

Dr Paul Moorcraft is a former senior instructor at the Royal Military Academy, Sandhurst, and the Joint Services Command and Staff College, UK. He worked in the Defence Procurement Agency and in communications in the Main Building, Ministry of Defence. He also spent nearly twenty-five years working in thirty war zones, often with irregular forces. He has taught at ten major universities, including a distinguished visiting professorship in the US, and is the author of a range of books on military history, crime and international relations as well as being an award-winning novelist. He returned to work in the MOD (Whitehall and Iraq) during Operation Telic in 2003. Until October 2004 he was the editor of the Defence Division of Surrey House Corporate Communication. He is now the director of the Centre for Foreign Policy Analysis in London.

Gwyn Winfield was the publisher of *Defence Review* for four years. He is now the publisher of the Defence Division of Surrey House. He has expertise in land forces, armoured fighting vehicles and main battle tanks, with a special knowledge of NBC issues. His interest in NBC has led to detailed investigations and interviews with the leading policy makers and technologists in the UK, France, Germany and the US. Gwyn Winfield is one of the leading NBC commentators in the UK. Recently he covered events in Kosovo, Macedonia, Oman and Afghanistan. He is a regular speaker at NBC conferences and recently presented a BBC television documentary on the subject.

John Chisholm is an authority on naval warfare and extreme weather operations. He is the chief reporter of *Defence International* and *Resilience* magazines.

Introduction

New wars, old conflicts? – Paul Moorcraft

Avalanches of books have been written about the conflicts that followed from al-Qaeda's strategically bold attack on 9/11. But none contains so many differing views from so many senior politicians, military commanders, academics and journalists who were closely involved in the events that this book covers – from the West's retaliation against the Taliban in Afghanistan to the chaos of post-Saddam Iraq.

The implicit theme of the book is whether the causes of – and the course of – these conflicts are exacerbating the rift between Islam and the West – Samuel Huntington's so-called clash of civilizations. The professor's theory could indeed become a self-fulfilling prophesy, unless compromises are reached, especially in the Arab-Israeli conflict. Otherwise, the current 'war on terror' could endure as long as the Cold War. Like the former Soviet-American saga, the current global antagonism is being dragged into an ever-accelerating cycle of action and reaction.

The West is often perceived as trying to impose its systems on a hostile Islamic world, while sacrificing some of its own civil liberties at home, and imposing death, Abu Ghraibs and cultural and economic imperialism in the regions it penetrates. Though few can persuasively compare the freedoms of American citizens with those of Saddam's dictatorship or North Korea's eccentric Stalinism, a dangerous blurring of ends and means is evident. President George Bush's Manichean division of 'for us or against us' ignores the fact that many Muslims are convinced that contemporary Anglo-American policy is evil; that its pre-emptive strategic option based on dodgy dossiers and incorrect

1

intelligence on weapons of mass destruction is part of a crusade against Islam, not Islamic terrorists. Bush cries freedom, but to many outside America his methods are morally equivalent to those states said to be members of the 'Axis of Evil'.

Such political themes are implicit, however. Although a wide range of opinion is considered, this book is explicitly concerned with the practical political issues of why the West went to war and how these wars are being fought. The term 'Axis of Evil' includes, according to the US demonology, North Korea and Iran. This book concentrates, however, on the political and military campaigns in Afghanistan and Iraq, though there are chapters on related conflicts in Israel/Palestine and Sudan.

The narrative of the book raises the following major questions:

1. The topic endlessly debated in military staff colleges: what is the Clausewitzian end state of any military campaign? What were the precise end states of attacking Afghanistan and Iraq? Regime change alone cannot justify a long war against *stateless* enemies fighting asymmetric war. What precisely must be achieved in Iraq or Afghanistan – beyond some vague and perhaps impossible notions of democracy – before foreign troops can be withdrawn?
2. Is this a war on a culture or a method? After all, terrorism is simply a means, not an ideology, as in the Cold War.
3. Therefore how can you defeat a method which goes back millennia?
4. Can this war ever be won? Even if it can, will victory – however defined – take longer than the Cold War?
5. Is this a single war, or is it a series of separate conflicts? Is the Arab-Israeli struggle central or peripheral to, say, the war on Osama bin Laden, no matter how much the Saudi warlord says they are related?
6. This book describes in some detail the military campaigns, but all successful counter-terrorism is based upon long-term social engineering – political, economic and social change. In this context, can Islamic discontent be seen as a crisis of modernization, not faith?

Many of the book's sections are based upon interviews by the three editors: Paul Moorcraft, Gwyn Winfield and John Chisholm, who have worked extensively in the conflict zones, especially Afghanistan and Iraq. Some of the essays and interviews are based upon the work done for two magazines, *Defence International* and *Resilience*, which the editors produced. Other interviews and essays have been commissioned especially for this book. Although *Axis of Evil* spans three years –

September 2001 to September 2004 – the original words of the key participants, whether senior politicians or military commanders, have been left in their historical context. The date of each interview is noted, and occasionally additions to update the record, where necessary, have been included.

But the record speaks largely for itself. Sometimes the experts were plain wrong. For example, the overconfidence of the neo-conservative position as espoused by Richard Perle, or the interview with Tariq Aiz in Baghdad shortly before the war broke out. This writer was convinced the Iraqi deputy Prime Minister was lying about weapons of mass destruction (WMD). His denial of WMD possession offers an illuminating historical perspective for those in the West who were convinced that Saddam had these weapons or was about to develop them.

Axis of Evil provides an intriguing narrative from the military commanders as well as the pronouncements – some of them ill-judged – of the politicians who led them to war.

The first contribution is from Douglas Feith, the US Under Secretary of Defense, who gave his views soon after the 9/11 attack. Then the book encompasses the critics of intervention in both Afghanistan and Iraq, most notably George Galloway MP and the Archbishop of Canterbury. This section is contrasted with the 'official' line from, for example Geoff Hoon, the UK Secretary of State for Defence.

The section on the conduct of the war consists largely of lessons learned by senior British and American officers who were closely involved with the campaign on land, sea and air as well as the crucial logistical support. Some hitherto unpublished nuggets of information can be gleaned, for example, from the account of the Royal Marines' amphibious operations. The American generals are typically more open and frank in their admissions of failures, especially in logistics. On the other hand, Lieutenant General Ronald Keys explains what the Iraqis should have done to have had a fighting chance of delaying the mighty American war machine.

But once the Taliban and Saddam regimes were toppled – if not perhaps totally defeated – what next? The editors made a number of trips to Afghanistan to look at imperial overstretch first hand. The British led the first international security force in Kabul. Its commander, General John McColl, was interviewed in early 2002. Later, Gwyn Winfield travelled to examine the role of British provincial reconstructions teams in the country. He also interviewed Donald Rumsfeld, the US Secretary for Defense, who was visiting Mazar-I-Sharif.

Much of Afghanistan has reverted to control by warlords; the Taliban and al-Qaeda are resurgent in the south and in the tribal border areas. Opium production has shot up, a notable British failure. And an increasingly virulent insurgency is growing in Iraq.

Dr John Mackinlay, an expert on peace support operations, compares the roles of British and American troops in what he calls 'imperial policing'. Lord Guthrie, the former Chief of Defence Staff and commander of the British SAS, gives his only interview since leaving office. He contributes a wide-ranging view on such issues as UK military overstretch. Richard Armitage, the US deputy Secretary of State, is robust in his defence of US policy in both Iraq and Afghanistan. But Lindsey Hilsum, the international editor for Channel Four News, writes on the devastating unintended consequences of occupying Iraq. In perhaps the frankest interview in the book, Timothy Carney, a former US ambassador and a member of the reconstruction team in Iraq, outlines the series of US bungles in the first days of the occupation. The contribution from General Jumper, the Chief of Staff of the US Air Force, paints a far more rosy picture of American power. From the UK political perspective, opposition spokesman Paul Keetch MP castigates the repercussions of overstretch of British forces.

Beyond Iraq and Afghanistan, the wider issues of the Arab-Israeli conflict are discussed in the context of the siege of Jenin, from where this writer provided an eyewitness account. Generals of the Israeli Defence Force give their perspective on the intifada. Sudan, the epicentre of an international crisis in 2004, is examined in the context of the growth of Islamic extremists, particularly in the context of Khartoum's support for Osama bin Laden.

Also in the wider context, the then Secretary General of NATO, George Robertson, considers the relevance of the organization to asymmetric conflict. Dr Paul Cornish of the Centre for Defence Studies, King's College, London, analyses the war on terror and attempts to provide a scorecard of the results.

The British homeland security front is discussed in the context of resilience preparation. Patrick Mercer MP, the Tory shadow Homeland Security Minister, lambastes British preparation for 9/11-style attacks. Dr James Hart, the Commissioner of the City of London Police, talks about London's defences, while David Veness, the Assistant Commissioner of the Metropolitan Police, offers a powerful insight into counter-terrorism strategies.

So what of the future? The concluding section examines the current threats from nuclear, chemical and biological attacks. The final essay asks whether a compromise with Osama-type activists is possible and, if not, how long will the new wars of the West continue? Years, decades or another hundred years' war? Or will the wars of 2001-04 – in the framework of an historian writing at the end of this century – merely constitute a brief, if unruly, adjunct to the end of the long civil war in Europe (1914–1990)?

ONE

Aftermath of 9/11

Feith in the future – Douglas Feith, the US Under Secretary of Defense for Policy, on the immediate aftermath of 9/11. He was interviewed by Gwyn Winfield in November 2001. Feith was considered one of the more media-savvy neo-conservatives.

GW: *Can you define the changes in foreign policy since 11 September?*
DF: I don't know if I can say anything non-obvious. We are focussed on the threat posed to the US by terrorist organizations, by the states that provide a territorial base and financial and other types of support. We are concerned in particular about the coincidence of the countries that are seeking WMD [Weapons of Mass Destruction] and missiles.
GW: *In other aspects, then, US foreign policy can't have changed that much, as I am sure that on 10 September your policy would have been against states that had violent ambitions towards the US and a lot of those states are ones we would have recognized as states of concern before that as well. Have there been any real changes, or is it just a new flavour for an old policy?*
DF: I think you're right in that a lot of these concerns we have, we had in one form or another before 11 September. But 11 September has changed a lot. We were not happy with the Taliban and we were not happy with the Taliban harbouring al-Qaeda before 11 September, but we were not taking military action in Afghanistan before then. The recognition that this problem is so urgent and so important that it requires an active US policy employing the range of tools of US national power, and the active cooperation of numerous friends of ours around the world and the use of intelligence, financial and military tools from the US and from the coalition, count as new. We are approaching this subject not as an

6

attempted threat but as an actual threat that requires us in self-defence to take immediate action, including military action.

GW: *Moving onto the secondary point, how does this affect UK policy? The UK, for example, is the only one still contributing to the no-fly zone in Iraq and there is a long history of cooperation, so what developments on UK policy have we seen?*

DF: We have a unique relationship with the UK that gets drawn on, re-affirmed and re-energized every time we wind up in a problem and find ourselves shoulder to shoulder with the UK. This is another item on a long list of events in recent history when we and the UK wind up being allies and partners and working together. We are very happy with the UK.

GW: *Has this overshadowed other allies' response, whether they could have done more?*

DF: No, we are pleased with the response we have got from NATO in general and with the individual members. It is impressive to think that this is the first time in history that NATO as an organization has invoked Article 5. Friendship is not a zero-sum game; just because we are especially happy with the UK doesn't mean that we are not happy with others.

GW: *But in the UK there seems to have been some confusion over whether allied troops were asked for. Germany, for example, saw this as a major issue but the pace seems to have stalled, confusing some and upsetting others. So where has this confusion come from?*

DF: My sense is that some people had unrealistic expectations about how smoothly some of the cooperation could be organized under extremely difficult circumstances. We were not ready for 11 September, we didn't have plans in place, we didn't have an organization in place, and we didn't have an alliance mechanism in place. We got attacked, not only in a surprising fashion, but also in a completely shocking fashion and we had to plan a war almost overnight and not merely a war but a war unlike any other that we have participated in. Many people have commented on the peculiar characteristics of this war against terrorism. It is not standard. It requires you to think a lot of things through for the first time. Militarily, we have to think through our entire homeland security just as a case of first impressions, and while we are at it we have all these issues of the coalition and diplomacy and how we deal with the extremely impressive outpourings of offers from people all round the world; some of which were allies, some of which were friends and there were different types of contribution to the war effort, intelligence, military and other. While we are doing this planning for a war, and planning for territorial security for the first time, and getting all these offers, we have to respond to them and we have to work out how to make use of the assets that are available to us from other friendly countries. And it took some working out. Some people thought it was going to go smoothly and that as soon as somebody came forward with an offer we would know exactly whether we could accept it, or if we are going to accept it and when we were going to accept it and how we are going to fit it into our war effort and when – and that is just un-realistic. There was some improvising and some people didn't get the answers as quickly as they wanted, and some people still don't have answers to some of the offers they have made, but we are doing the best we can.

GW: *This seems to have also crept into the usual smooth running between the US and UK with confusion over troops . . .*

DF: Look, it has crept in between different offices of the Pentagon. This is a big project and not everything goes smoothly. People who have lived through this year tend to think that 11 September was three years ago, because of all that has been done and we have expended three years of emotional energy between 11 September and now. The fact is it was only a few weeks ago; but, in that time, look what was planned and executed.

GW: *What is the parallel in US history? Vietnam, Korea, World War Two?*

DF: No, it is hard to imagine. I didn't live through Pearl Harbor, but I am not sure that Pearl Harbor was as complete a surprise as the attacks on the World Trade Center and the Pentagon. Pearl Harbor happened in the context of an ongoing world war, people understood America might get involved. This idea that we were going to be fighting a war against international terrorism was not at the forefront of people's minds.

GW: *Do you accept critics' opinion that this is a war that has been fought for some time, but only now that the US has suffered casualties do they appreciate the fact?*

DF: Yes, there is something to be said for that. In retrospect, historians may well conclude that we were at war a long time before 11 September but one side didn't wake up to it until the attacks occurred. It is an intellectual construct that could be argued for.

GW: *Does the current situation have a long-term effect on NATO's forward-deployment policy? Will it mean any changes to NATO, especially ideas of Russian involvement?*

DF: I don't think we are going to make major changes to NATO. We don't have a forward deployment policy as such. NATO doesn't deploy outside of NATO on a permanent basis and I don't think that is going to change or create a fundamental change in the relationship. As with the Russians, what we are trying to do is find ways of improving relationships between NATO and Russia without changing NATO's character.

GW: *Iraq has made a number of comments about renewing its sovereignty over Kuwait and has fired mortars in, as well as refusing to let inspectors in. President Bush has made some belligerent comments. Does this mean that Iraq is top of the list, above countries such as Sudan and Somalia?*

DF: We don't list things that way. Iraq is a problem country and the things that you have cited illustrate that this is widely recognized. One of the points that President Bush has made is that there are a lot of problem countries. We have to address all of them if we are to deal with this problem globally. We are not going to say: 'Our resources allow us only to hit our top two or three priority countries and we will leave the rest alone'. We have to tackle this globally.

TWO

War against Saddam

Dissenting voices

Fighting the war – George Galloway MP, senior vice chairman of the Parliamentary Labour Party Foreign Affairs Committee, powerfully challenged accepted wisdom on Iraq and Saudi Arabia and much else. He was interviewed by Paul Moorcraft in 2002. Galloway was the most vociferous critic of the government, especially in eloquent speeches in the House of Commons.

PM: *How do you defend a man who gassed his own citizens at Halabjah?*
GG: Let's start from first principles. I never visited Iraq before the Gulf War, and I would not have been welcome if I had. I was outside the Iraqi embassy demonstrating for human rights in Iraq, when British ministers and businessmen were inside [Iraq] trading and doing arms deals. In the 1970s I was one of the founding members of CARDRI (The Campaign Against Repression and for Democratic Rights in Iraq). I was an opponent of Saddam Hussein before most people in Britain had ever heard his name, and when the British state was doing all it could to arm and strengthen him. So I have nothing to defend in terms of my attitude to the regime in Baghdad. I am not defending Saddam Hussein. I feel that my work is in defence of the 23 million Iraqi people who are not Saddam Hussein, and who did not elect him. Indeed, we are the ones who helped to choose Saddam in that the British brought the Ba'ath party to power in the first place. The complicity of the British and American embassies in Iraq in the takeover by the Ba'ath is very well charted.

So I am on very sure ground when I say that the British and Americans

10

helped to choose Saddam, the Iraqi people did not. But they are being starved and bombed to death, and now face an onslaught the like of which has not been seen for almost thirty years since the crazed bombardment of Vietnam. This is because of a dispute between Saddam and the powers who helped to make him.

The question of Halabjah is a red herring. Saddam almost certainly committed the crime (although for eighteen months the United States government claimed it was Iran who had gas-bombed Halabjah). Britain had continued to supply Saddam long after Halabjah. Of course, this was not the first use of chemical weapons against the Kurds in Iraq – the first person to do so was Winston Churchill in 1924. As Colonial Secretary, he dropped mustard gas bombs on what were termed in the House of Commons as 'rebel northern tribesmen'.

So the perfidy of Saddam's use of chemical weapons against the Kurds has to be seen in that context, and the context of the Iran-Iraq War. If I was to calibrate the big mistakes Saddam has made and the crimes he has committed, the attack on Iran in 1980 was his biggest crime and is the one that can be most directly linked to the current tragedy. But Saddam attacked Iran at our behest. Saddam attacked Iran to please the Americans who were terrified at the prospect of Islamist revolution which Khomeini had unleashed. In order to defend the very conservative monarchies and imperialist satraps who are now the very 'neighbours' that Britain and America pay and aid in support of their policy.

I cling to the old-fashioned notion that the only people who have a right to change the government of Iraq are the people in Iraq. One day they will do so, but this is less likely when they're worried about whether they've got anything to eat tomorrow, whether their child, if she falls sick, will be dead in a fortnight, and all the other horrors that go with the twelve years of siege we have imposed on Iraq, which have effectively frozen politics in Iraq and left Saddam in a stronger position today than when this policy started.

PM: *Do you get on with Saddam personally?*

GG: I've only met him once, and then with a large group of people. [Galloway subsequently met Saddam in August 2002.] I don't really have a relationship with him . . . . The problem for the West is this: in Arabic there is a saying identical to the English 'In the land of the blind, the one-eyed man is King.' Saddam is many, many bad things. But the Arabs and the Muslims see him as at least a man with one eye. In a region where the corrupt kings and puppet presidents, installed and buttressed in many cases by us, are seen as incompetent, corrupt, thieving slaves,

Saddam looks like Saladin. In fact, we have helped make a rather second-rate, tinpot dictator an Arab hero, just as we did with bin Laden.

If you say to me: Saddam, with all his monstrous carbuncles and warts, or one of these corrupt kings or puppet presidents, whose idea of governance is to steal their people's money and invest it and spend it in the West, and be called upon to betray anything resembling an Arab cause – I'd choose Saddam. But, much more importantly than me, the Arabs choose Saddam.

PM: *You mentioned starvation in Iraq. It's a common question: what about the money allowed in for food, but diverted instead to weapons?*
GG: It's simply untrue. You don't have to take my word for it. You can rely on the testimony of the two UN undersecretary-generals, whose job it was to administer the oil-for-food programme: The Irish Quaker, £250,000-per-year UN civil servant Denis Halliday, or the German conservative, Hans von Sponeck. Both resigned their positions as the head of the UN's humanitarian programme in Iraq, claiming that we were perpetrating genocide against the Iraqi people under the banner of oil for food.

PM: *Why not the official line? You're a member of the Labour party . . .*
GG: It's mendacity. We have a militarized mendacity. The men who know about these things – von Sponeck, Halliday, or Scott Ritter, the former arms inspector whose job was to blow up Iraq's weapons – these are the men who know, are in a position to know, and have no conceivable axe to grind, unlike the propagandists of the British and American governments.

PM: *But it's* your *government . . .*
GG: I am in outright opposition to my government's policy in the Middle East. I am having a reasonable run of success in persuading my fellow citizens that I am right and they are wrong. So there is no diversion (in oil for food). How could there be? Iraq doesn't get any money from the oil-for-food programme. The money is in New York in an escrow account controlled by the United Nations. Iraq never sees the money. Iraq sells oil, 25 per cent of the proceeds of which are sliced off the top for the so-called 'compensation fund', given to cash-strapped Kuwait and other fat-cats claiming money off the programme. The rest is paid by the UN in New York to suppliers who deliver the supplies. So Iraq doesn't get any money from oil for food. If there's smuggling on the margins it's small, small beer. The oil-for-food programme, since its inception in 1996 (bear in mind that there was no oil-for-food programme between 1991–96, with all the aggregate or cumulative

suffering that it caused), has provided the rich sum of thirty cents per day for every Iraqi. Not exactly a beanfeast.

PM: *Why are we getting such a different picture about Iraq then?*

GG: There's no excuse for people not knowing the truth, because the Internet is chock-full of alternative points of view. For four years now I have been producing a daily digest called the *Iraq Sanctions Monitor*, which 10,000 people a day read. We have meetings two or three times a week on these subjects. We've got Ritter here [in the House], we'll have von Sponeck here early in the next term. The work of people like [John] Pilger and so on – anyone who wants access to the truth can find it.

The Americans have abandoned all pretence at finding a pretext for invading Iraq. They tried linking Iraq to 11 September – they gave up. They tried linking Iraq to the anthrax attacks that followed – they gave up. They promised us dossiers on weapons of mass destruction – they gave that up too. Now it's simple: they intend to change the regime in Baghdad, even if it means an invasion by 250,000 Western crusaders of an Arab Muslim country. One part of me wishes them on, because as somebody who's interested in revolution in the Middle East, nothing could be a better basis for revolution than 250,000 crusaders invading an Arab Muslim country, while Afghanistan and Palestine are in flames. The only thing that draws me back from wishing them on is that tens of thousands of innocent people will lose their lives. In the chaos that will follow, we may get not new, progressive, nationalist governments in the Middle East, but bin Ladens and Khomeinis, which I don't want to see.

PM: *Some in the intelligence community believe there is a correlation [between Saddam Hussein and 11 September].*

GG: I've seen no evidence of this, and logic points in the opposite direction. The Iraqi dictatorship is a secular, socialist dictatorship . . .

PM: *But they both hate America.*

GG: It is the victim of Islamic fundamentalism. The dagger at the heart of the government in Baghdad is the 60 per cent of the population who are Shi'ites, fundamentalist Islam of the Khomeini variety. We in the West have supported Islamist terrorists against Iraq – explosions that take place in Baghdad, car bombs and so on, are paid for by the Liberation of Iraq Act 1998, passed by the US Congress. The fact that both hate America . . . Iraq, for twelve years before 11 September, did not strike, using any agents or surrogates, any Western targets – even when, in the Desert Fox bombardment in 1998 during Ramadan and Christmas, we were setting their country on fire. So why would they choose to strike on 11 September. It's absolutely illogical.

13

PM: *It looks like there is going to be a major attack on Iraq. What are you going to do about it?*

GG: We've built a big movement in Britain. We've had three demonstrations of 100,000 people in Trafalgar Square since 11 September, and we have another on 28 September [2002], the day before the Labour conference meets in Blackpool. It will be the most important demonstration in Britain probably since the Grosvenor Square demonstrations in 1968. I believe it's going to be mammoth, bigger than we've ever had before and as big as the Poll Tax demonstrations.

We have 161 MPs who have signed Alice Mahon's motion against war on Iraq. We have the editorials of some of the most important publications in Britain, left and right (the *Mail on Sunday*, the *Guardian*, the *Financial Times*) on our side. We have a much more informed public, and a clear majority – as tested through opinion polls, the letters pages, the phone-ins – do not think this is a good idea. There are many people in the Foreign Office and even in the Ministry of Defence who also are extremely worried about this. Amongst our 161 MPs we have former defence ministers, former foreign ministers. And there are many more outside the 161 who will make their position clearer as (military) action becomes more imminent.

Mr Blair had better beware. He will split the Labour Party from top to bottom. He will split Parliament. And he will split the country if he performs what would be the ultimate act of obeisance to George W. Bush, a man who is widely regarded in this country (indeed across Europe and increasingly in the United States) as – how shall I put it politely? – not the wisest war leader that any British Prime Minister ever followed down the descending staircase to disaster.

PM: *You're not 'on-message' . . .*

GG: I reject the whole concept of being 'on-message' . . . If we're not to be a parliament like the rubber-stamp Parliament in Baghdad . . . they're all 'on-message' in Baghdad. The leader gives out the message, and the members of the Parliament all parrot it. I don't think the British people deserve a Parliament like that. This is a democratic Parliament, a hard-won democracy, one which we defended, for a time, alone in 1940–41 while the Americans were watching on newsreel, when we stood alone with the barbarians at the gates. If the barbarians had managed to invade and subjugate us, and if the Japanese had not attacked Pearl Harbor, the United States would never have been at war.

So I am aware of the value and preciousness of this parliamentary democracy, and I fully intend to play my part in it. The government have not had the courage to place a substantive motion in any of the wars they have fought since Mr Blair came to power, because they don't want the country to know that there are MPs, on all sides, who disagree with the wars they have fought. This will be the least popular war that Mr Blair will ever fight; like Mr Eden at Suez, it ultimately has cataclysmic political implications for him. I'm not alone – there are 161 of us. I want nothing from Mr Blair, and he can take anything from me.

PM: *So you've given up any hope of becoming a minister?*

GG: I want nothing from him. He has nothing that I want, and he cannot take anything away from me.

PM: *What if you were deselected?*

GG: If I were deselected, I would stand as an independent and win. They know that. I have a fantastic support base in my constituency. Indeed my constituency is much larger than just my parliamentary constituency, as my postbag shows. I have the support of the Muslims in this country, the Left in the country, many parts of the Christian Church (I have fantastic support from the clergy and the laity in the Catholic Church). I have a big constituency amongst progressive people in this country. An attack against me by Mr Blair would be a foolish thing. To be fair, neither he nor the whips have ever asked me to stop saying things I say, to stop doing things I do, or to start saying things or do things they want me to do. They have behaved honourably towards me personally.

PM: *You recently encouraged Scots to boycott Israeli goods – is that working?*

GG: Very well. Our boycott campaign is proving remarkably successful. You will see that the DTI [Department of Trade and Industry] succumbed to our campaign demand last week by declaring that goods from the West Bank and Gaza Strip could not be classified as made in Israel, and are therefore not part of the free trade agreement between the EU and Israel. This means that the fruit and vegetables and other agricultural produce that are made on the most obscene basis, on illegally occupied land using stolen water, can no longer be sold here.

The columns of the newspapers are full of the academic boycott. There's a defence of it in the *Guardian* by the two chaps who wrote their manifesto for it. Our campaign is aiming to establish in the public mind that it is as immoral to buy Israeli goods as it was to buy goods from apartheid-era South Africa. A recent opinion poll showed that 65 per cent of the British people were more sympathetic to the Palestinians than the Israelis.

PM: *So therefore you do not support in any way Bush's statement on the removal of Arafat?*

GG: This is another area where Britain and America are parting company. The British know the Middle East rather well (after all, they were the people who divided it up and created the State of Israel).

PM: *I was surprised at the number of people who mentioned Balfour in Jenin (when I was there during the recent siege).*

GG: Balfour's was the original sin in which this whole tragedy was born. One people promised a second people the land of the third people. The anti-Semite Balfour promising the Zionists (who then represented a tiny fragment of Jewish opinion) the land of the Palestinian people without consulting any of the parties involved. But the British know that the Palestinians, after all these decades, are not going to accept a man inches from imbecility, in Washington, choosing their leader. They're the last people in the world who are going to accept that. There are few more politicized people in the world than the Palestinians. The idea that they will allow this dolt to choose their president is absurd. In fact it [Bush's statement] gave Arafat a shot in the arm, and his popularity (which declined for a number of reasons after the siege ended) will climb if and when an election for the Palestinian Authority and its presidency is able to take place. Clearly, while there are Israeli tanks on every street and a curfew most of the time, it's absurd to talk about an election.

PM: *What about the suicide bombers?*

GG: The suicide bombers will continue as long as the occupation lasts, because the Palestinian people are virtually defenceless. They have virtu-ally no weapons . . . .

PM: *Are you condoning this?*

GG: . . . And so in despair the Palestinians, in significant numbers, are ready to turn their own bodies into weapons which destroy themselves and as many others as they can take with them. It's absurd to ask me if I condone or don't condone something. The people who have to answer for what the Palestinians in despair are doing are the people who put them in despair. British people, above all, given the authorship of this tragedy, are the least qualified to condemn the only methods that some of these young people have concluded they have to strike back. Mrs Blair had it absolutely right before she was bludgeoned by the backlash against her comments. Where young people have lost all hope in any political progress, it's not surprising that some of them, having concluded that life is worse than death, are ready to kill themselves.

PM: *Arafat could have got what he wanted in terms of a political deal; it was so close at Camp David and Taba II.*

GG: I don't agree with that. Oslo was a big enough compromise. I

16

supported it, but a lot of my friends were very angry because it did represent the betrayal of large numbers of Palestinians whose interests are not catered for by Oslo, but I supported it. In my mind I concluded that it was thus far and no further. The idea that Oslo, which represented this joint compromise, could be then compromised on ad infinitum is a sliding scale to disaster. Taba II was the best of the offers made, as Arafat says, by a government which had only days to go and could not deliver. So why should Arafat have agreed to further compromises on top of Oslo, for a proposal by [Prime Minister] Barak who only had days to go in power? It was evident that the Israeli public did not support Barak's line by then, that they preferred Sharon. On the eve of the poll Barak said: 'If you vote for Sharon tomorrow, you're voting for war.' They voted for Sharon, they voted for war and they got it. If Sharon were to fall from power tomorrow, he will fall not to [Shimon] Peres but to [Benyamin] Netanyahu, who is worse than Sharon. So in my opinion the Israelis want peace, like the Northern Irish Protestants want peace. The question is: are they ready to pay the price that's required for peace, the price in terms of compromise and justice. I'm afraid that the answer, in the case of the Israeli public opinion, is still no.

PM: *Would you admit that perhaps you are wrong about Afghanistan? A few weeks ago I was out on patrol with ISAF [International Security Assistance Force], going around the schools they had opened. They have done some good on a limited pro-tem basis.*

GG: No, I don't consider that I was wrong. I wish no criticism of the individual British soldiers who have been there and I'm perfectly aware that they have behaved honourably and bravely and done their best. I have no complaints against the soldiers – they're the lions. My complaints are against the donkeys who send them on what is an ill-conceived operation at best, a potential disaster at worst, in a country which has been a graveyard for foreign interventionists for centuries.

I don't recognize the new Afghanistan that you describe. We have succeeded in removing one gang of fundamentalist cut-throats, whom we played a very significant part in installing in Kabul, and replacing them with a patchwork quilt, a balkanized country controlled by dozens of gangs of fundamentalist cut-throats. The warlords are back in power in Afghanistan, that much is clear. The puppet [Hamid] Karzai controls the centre of Kabul and a few blocks, and he requires the protection of international soldiers even to do that. His own vice president was gunned down just a week ago, and he wasn't the first minister to suffer that fate. The drugs trade, which was actually always

17

far more associated with the Northern Alliance than with the Taliban, is up and running again. The women, who we were told were now wearing lipstick and high heels and buying *Playboy* off the newsagent shelves, are back in the kind of servitude which is a hallmark of the pre-Taliban and Taliban period. The international community is fast losing interest in Afghanistan and you will start to see, as we opponents of the war predicted, a disengagement, first by the Americans and ultimately by most others.

Whether bin Laden will be back in Afghanistan is immaterial. Afghanistan was always a side-show, so far as the phenomenon of 'bin Ladenism' is concerned. Bin Ladenism does not require Afghanistan, it existed separately from the Taliban regime, and will continue to exist even if the Taliban never came back in Afghanistan. My prediction is that they will be back very soon, in different forms in different parts of the country, and the warlords will make the same alliances with them that they made before. But whether or not they come back is immaterial. The men who flew the aeroplanes into the Twin Towers were not ragged-arsed, turbaned, mud-hut dwelling Afghans. They were PhDs, university graduates, clean-cut middle-class Islamists from everywhere except Afghanistan.

PM: *Would you advocate removing Western support from the House of Saud?*

GG: I regard the Crown Prince of Saudi Arabia as a very big step forward from what went before. I think that he is a person of some dignity, but I also believe that other members of his family are corrupt and are slaves of the West. The big struggle, the big question in Saudi Arabia is whether Crown Prince Abdullah will be able to establish full control of the country. If he does, I think you'll see a different policy from Saudi Arabia towards the Iraq issue, the Palestine issue, the question of whether the oil wealth of the Arabs is for the Arabs or the West.

The question may be answered for us, however. There are people in these buildings around here [Westminster] who have never heard the word Hejaz or Najd, who never knew anything about the struggle to unify Saudi Arabia by the Saud family, who are now openly discussing the dismemberment of Saudi Arabia, openly discussing its partition – a new Sykes-Picot in Saudi Arabia. Members of Parliament, ministers and ex-ministers have all spoken to me in the last few months. Their argument is: we are interested only in one small part of Saudi Arabia – the eastern province where the oil is. If the Islamists don't like us being in Saudi Arabia, then let's have two Saudi Arabias. Let the Muslims keep

Mecca and Medina. We're not interested in controlling their holy places; all we want to control is their oil. There is a neat demographic division between the eastern province and the others, allowing the potential for division : 25 per cent of the population in the eastern province are Shi'ite, for example. Saudi Arabia has so far refused to join the war plan against Iraq. The Americans may make them pay a high price for that.

The ambition of the Bush administration does not stretch only to the removal from power of Saddam Hussein. It recognizes that Bin Ladenism is looming as a threat to their interests in the region for a generation to come. They are looking at all sorts of ways to try and stymie it. One way would be the partition, the division of Saudi Arabia. They have other possibilities. They can, when King Fahd passes away and the Crown Prince becomes king, make sure that the Crown Prince appoints one of their men. Or perhaps we'll find the situation where Prince Abdullah doesn't make it to the throne at all. They are rightly very worried about the stability of Saudi Arabia. If the Saudis were to use their land for the 250,000-strong crusader army to invade Iraq, then the chances of survival for the House of Saud would be very, very slim. The Jordanian and Egyptian regimes would also be gravely imperilled by their complicity in that attack.

PM: *You have almost a messianic impulse in what you say. Do you have conversations with Geoff Hoon about this sort of thing?*

GG: Yes I have perfectly civilized relations with my colleagues in the government. I've spoken with the Prime Minister about these subjects. I've spoken with successive foreign and defence secretaries. Of course, I then speak to my friends who are ex-ministers in the Ministry of Defence and the Foreign Office, and I discover that actually they have a lot more sympathy with what I'm saying than they did at the time. If you look at people like Kilfoyle, Henderson (ex-Defence Ministers), Battle, Lloyd (ex-Foreign Office Ministers), it's clear that they recognize the force of my arguments.

PM: *Is it a moral thing? Is it a religious impulse, or has pacifism got more to do with it?*

GG: Certainly not pacifism. I'm willing to go eight rounds with more or less anybody. I'm a former boxer, I'm the vice-president of the Parliamentary Boxing Club Association. I'm a former boy soldier with the Army Cadets. So it's not pacifism, but it is moral and partly religious and above all ideological – I am an anti-imperialist. I don't believe that there is any God-given right for white, northern, Western people to rule the globe.

PM: *Do you see it as a self-fulfilling clash of civilizations? Or do you think Huntington's thesis is rather off the mark?*
GG: There is a clash of civilization going on. It doesn't matter how long we protest that we're not at war with Islam, if most of the bombs are falling on Muslims, and most of the people dropping the bombs are not Muslims, from the victim's point of view it's going to look like a clash of civilizations whatever your motives are.

I know that you don't have to be a Muslim to be hated by George Bush. The Cubans are on the 'Axis of Evil'. America is invading Colombia. The North Koreans are on the 'Axis of Evil', and there are not many Muslims in any of these three countries. And I know that you can be a Muslim and get on fine with George W. Bush, as long as you're a slave Muslim. But the 1.3 billion Muslims in the world do represent the biggest part of that swamp I talked about earlier: the swamp of indignation, rage, hatred and bitterness against us. Out of that swamp flew the mosquitoes that struck the Twin Towers on 11 September. If the crusader army invades Iraq and occupies it, then the 10,000 bin Ladens I had predicted would be created by an attack on Afghanistan would spawn 100,000 bin Ladens and the earth would shake for a generation to come.

The Father of the House – Tam Dalyell MP, Father of the House of Commons, has been a long-term critic of British military adventures. He spoke to Paul Moorcraft in the summer of 2002.

PM: *Presumably you oppose the current preparations for war against Iraq?*
TD: Totally . . . I went to Iraq with George Galloway in 1994. Our first meeting was with the British-Iraqi Friendship Group in Baghdad. There were seventeen people there. Half-way through the meeting George turned around and said: 'I am the only one here who hasn't got a degree from a British university.' Perhaps that reflected the extent to which, for many Iraqis, Britain is their second home.
PM: *It seems we are now close to war against Iraq.*
TD: I agree with you. But bombing and bullets are not the way to fight terrorism. And I believe there was no connection between al-Qaeda and the regime in Baghdad. I don't doubt that the regime has been very cruel in many ways . . .
PM: *Do you believe the cabinet will split if we go to war?*

TD: My view of the cabinet is totally cynical. It's not like the old days when cabinet ministers had their own power bases in the party. Blair can do what he likes in the cabinet and if they step out of line they will lose their jobs . . . I think Clare Short should have resigned long ago. But she will be hovering until the bombs start dropping and then she will find some reason to support the government . . . I see no one who is likely to stand down.

PM: *You criticised the war in Afghanistan and Kosovo. Do you have any regrets about that now?*

TD: Absolutely not. My criticisms have been more than justified. Look at what's happened in Afghanistan. The warlords have taken control again. The acreage of poppy fields has gone up fourteen times. [President Hamid] Karzai hangs on by the skin of his teeth. His colleagues are assassinated. And the situation is likely to get worse and worse.

There was great sympathy for the United States in unexpected quarters around the world until the bombs started raining down on Kabul. I believe it would have been much better, as I said at the time, to have done it through intelligence and particularly bribery. They might have been able to apprehend Osama bin Laden, and some of his colleagues, because at the time Libya, the Palestinians and even the Taliban on 12 September were sympathetic to the US. And I'm sure that the Iraqis didn't want this kind of terrorism.

As for Kosovo, I regret nothing. I am extremely angry about how Blair says Kosovo was a success . . .

PM: *May we return to your point about the failure to use intelligence and bribery in Afghanistan? It seems to me that is what is being applied in Iraq. Sure, there may well be the aerial blitzkrieg, but a great deal of effort is also going into using intelligence and bribery to support the Kurds, Shia dissidents etc. in order to promote an internal coup within the Ba'athist leadership.*

TD: It depends on collateral damage. If they can avoid that they will have achieved something which has not been done so far. In 1994 it might well have been possible to manage some kind of coup . . . In 1998 I went to Iraq with Albert Reynolds, the former *Taoiseach*, the Prime Minister of Ireland. I talked to people out of earshot of anybody and they said, 'Look, we didn't like the Ba'ath party. We didn't like Saddam. But after all these sanctions and this bombing, we are right behind him.' And I believe that they meant it.

PM: *So you think that Saddam is genuinely popular? That the Iraqi people won't dance in the streets when US troops enter Baghdad?*

TD: I don't think they will dance in the streets when the Americans enter Baghdad. And I'm sure they won't be dancing in the streets after American troops have been there for three months. This idea of a General Douglas MacArthur ruling Iraq!

I must tell you that I am not anti-American . . . I have a lot of American friends, and I was on the executive of the British-American parliamentary group.

PM: *If there is a little collateral damage, the rest of the Arab world is likely to greet the downfall of Saddam with quiet, if unofficial, satisfaction.*

TD: I've just come back from holiday in Jordan – paid for by myself . . . and I talked to a lot of people. There was a genuine sympathy with the Iraqi people. There was also a feeling that Saddam – for all his enormities – was sticking up for the Arabs. And, among people who spoke very good English, there was a certain admiration for Saddam not as a person but for what he symbolized.

Now it may be that he is killed [and his sons] and somebody will replace them. Albert Reynolds and I sat in the house of Tariq Aziz. He said to us: 'You might think that Saddam and I are extremists. We are as nothing to what will follow if the bombing and sanctions don't end.' I think we have created a generation that is growing up hating us. I got the same impression in 1994 when I was down in the marsh area of southern Iraq, at the confluence of the Tigris and the Euphrates.

PM: *If there is a swift, clean US victory in Iraq, there could be rapid changes in the Middle East. The first to fall would be the House of Saud and then the beginnings of democracy in other Arab autocracies . . .*

TD: It may be the Saudis who produced a lot of the al-Qaeda . . . In Baghdad in 1998 a number of people said to me separately: 'It wasn't in this city that a princess was taken to the market square to be beheaded publicly. Your friends in Saudi Arabia did this.' Take the position of women. The women in the Iraqi parliament are almost European women. This is very different from Saudi Arabia. I think it is very likely that the House of Saud would fall. The perception in Jordan was very strongly that the Americans were doing this because they were after the Iraqi oil reserves. I am coming around to that view. If it had simply been a question of weapons of mass destruction they would have been far keener to put in the weapons inspectors. All this reluctance to back the weapons inspectors going in just gives away that it's about oil.

PM: *There has been a fierce debate about whether 'a settlement' of Palestine should follow, rather than precede, a resolution of the Iraq 'problem'. What's your view?*

TD: I think they [the Americans] would do well to try to resolve the Palestinian issue before getting involved in Iraq. But I am so reluctant to get involved in Iraq, I would say that, wouldn't I?

PM: *Do you feel despondent that despite your best efforts it looks as if we are going to war?*

TD: I feel extremely alarmed but my efforts will go on and on. [*TD talked about his own experiences of war when he served in the army.*] Many of the people sitting on the green benches of the House of Commons have no clear idea of what war involves. . . . I fervently believe that a country is not entitled to ask young servicemen and women to risk their lives unless it is the overwhelming conviction of the country that the cause is legitimate, just and sensible.

A Liberal Dose of Realpolitik – Sir Menzies Campbell MP, the Liberal Democrat shadow Foreign Secretary, offered a personal *tour d'horizon* to Paul Moorcraft in the summer of 2002.

PM: *George Galloway MP has described sanctions on Iraq as 'criminal'. What is your opinion?*

MC: Sanctions are justified by UN resolutions. . . . What is criminal is that Saddam Hussein has exploited sanctions to produce the abuse, subjugation and degradation of his own people. . . .

PM: *You suggested, in a recent statement, that there is insufficient evidence of the production of weapons of mass destruction in Iraq . . .*

MC: I believe it to be an entirely reasonable assumption that he has biological and chemical weapons. I don't buy the Scott Ritter line that there is no evidence. I don't think you're going to get the kind of evidence that David Blunkett was talking about [in the House of Commons on 17 July], unless you're very lucky and have outstanding Humint [human intelligence] or get a break on Sigint [signal intelligence]. Because of what he was doing before the Gulf War, because of what he did between the Gulf War and December 1998, it is a perfectly reasonable assumption that he has chemical and biological weapons. I'm told that he does not have a nuclear capability, because the Gulf War and subsequent inspection dislocated or destroyed the process. I'm also told that, had it not been for the Gulf War, he might well have had a nuclear capability right now. So the reasonable assumption is that he has chemical and biological, and is working towards nuclear capability. But there is no evidence of that, and that's important if we are going to persuade the

British people that there is justification for military action. People say that with intelligence: we can't tell you precisely what the intelligence is, otherwise we'll compromise the source. As a general principle, who could object to that? But if we're about to ask the people of the United Kingdom to endorse a major military operation, with all the risks that involves, the government has a duty to explain precisely why that is necessary. And perhaps on this occasion to be more forthcoming with the intelligence than might normally be the case. We're told there is a dossier which, like the Grand Old Duke of York, has been marched up to the hill and marched down again. If the government does have publishable information, it ought to be in the public domain.

PM: *Saddam may have the capability and he has shown hostile intent.*

MC: The whole question of intent raises a very acute question as to Article 51 action. It's been represented to me very strongly by senior American diplomats that there is a 'clear and present danger', in the words of the American Constitution. But where is the evidence of that? The acquisition of weapons of mass destruction may be in breach of the ceasefire resolutions, but where is the evidence that there is an intent to use them? If there was evidence of an intent to supply them to dissident terrorist groups, then that might go some way towards a justification for a pre-emptive strike based on the imminence of a terrorist strike. So far, there is no clear evidence of that.

What would the legal basis be for military action? The Prime Minister said it would be in accordance with international law. So far as military action to enforce the ceasefire resolutions is concerned, which require the destruction of weapons of mass destruction, the offering of facilities for full inspection, if Saddam Hussein fails to implement his obligations under these resolutions, or obstructs those who are trying to implement them, that justifies military action of the kind seen in December 1998.

PM: *Why now? He's been ducking his inspection obligations for a long time [since December 1998]?*

MC: That was the only possible justification for December 1998. We took military action then which I thought was entirely sensible. Saddam Hussein was barring the admission of inspectors to facilities. The clear inference was that there was illegitimate activity taking place there. Since then, we've had a policy of containment and deterrence. If you're going to move away from that policy, you need to have some justification for doing so. Such a justification would have to be some enhanced threat, something which suggested that Saddam was doing more than simply building up stocks. So far, we have no clear evidence of that. We then

24

move on to the legal justifications, under international law, by which action may be legitimately taken. If it's not [UN Resolution] 687, or the sixty-five resolutions [concerning Iraq], we have to find it somewhere else. The only place where it seems we can find it is in Article 51. But we have to have evidence of a 'clear and present danger'. The mere holding of weapons of mass destruction cannot result in action under Article 51. There would have to be some indication, overt or covert, of an intention to use (or threaten to use) weapons of mass destruction. We don't have that yet.

PM: *American policy may not have a legal justification. It's a policy of regime change, whether it's in Iraq or with Yasser Arafat. And there are good arguments to say that the intervention in Kosovo was also illegal.*

MC: Blair was very good in his Chicago speech about intervention: where there is a systematic denial of human rights and a threat to the stability of the region, intervention is justified. Interestingly, no one has tried to make that particular case with Iraq. Human rights in Iraq are not high up the agenda; Saddam's continued presence in the region is by no means a stabilizing one. But he has not crossed the line yet to become a Milosevic. The thing to remember is that he's a very clever man.

PM: *I don't think he's mad.*

MC: No, he's not mad at all. Saddam works from the assumption that self-preservation is everything. Everything he does is logical according to that basis. This whole area is one which – if the government is to persuade a sceptical public that military action is justified – must involve the presentation of clearer, better defined evidence.

PM: *Let's assume the UN inspectors are either refused or not given un-fettered access. Let's assume that there is a legal justification for war . . .*

MC: These are pretty substantial assumptions. You also have to assume that there was published evidence, and that Mr Blair not only has a debate in the House of Commons but also puts down a substantive motion.

PM: *Politically, can the Lib Dems risk being anti-war?*

MC: We were anti-Suez in October 1956. But we supported action in the Falklands. We supported the Tory government over the Gulf from the very beginning, when the official policy of the Labour party was still behind economic sanctions. We supported military action and deployments in Bosnia, Kosovo and Sierra Leone. We have nothing to hide or be ashamed of. We haven't been peaceniks. We're not 'peace at any price'. We don't line up with Alice Mahon [MP], whose sincerity is beyond all question but whose conclusions I do not share.

PM: *But 161 MPs have signed it [her anti-war motion].*

MC: I am not against war but I am not persuaded in this case and I suspect that in that I reflect the views of the majority of MPs and people in the country as a whole. Can I just add that a number of senior Conservatives have expressed reservations about military action against Iraq on the floor of the House of Commons, including Douglas Hogg, John Gummer (both former cabinet ministers). So the assumption that these are monolithic positions is not borne out by what people have said in the past five or six months.

PM: *George Galloway also said that if we go to war with Iraq, it will divide the country in a way we haven't seen since Suez.*

MC: He said pretty much the same thing about Kosovo and about the Gulf. I don't doubt his sincerity for a moment. On these matters he has taken a clear and (he would argue) principled stand. But his judgements are not always justified. If you take a relationship between the Middle East in general and Iraq, during the Gulf War Bush senior's and Douglas Hurd's line was that there was no linkage between the two. They said: be part of our alliance, help us deal with this man, help us to restore stability to the region, and we will put a much greater effort into securing peace [between Arabs and Israelis]. And we did – we had Madrid and then Oslo. Now the whole thing has fallen apart. For a while the policy of the United States seemed to push for some kind of settlement or at least start a process. Today the policy has shifted to an insistence on the departure of Arafat. It's not going to happen. Nor would the idea of kicking him upstairs, as floated by [Secretary of State] Powell. The US policy is not based on a clear understanding of how Arafat works or how the Palestinians regard him.

PM: *No matter how much they may detest him, Palestinians will vote for Arafat simply to give the Americans two fingers.*

MC: Exactly. The more the Americans try to undermine him, the more Arafat emerges as a kind of totem. There must be people in the state department who are way ahead of all of this. I believe the Americans are not now interested in solving the Middle East problem ahead of Iraq. Some even believe that they should 'do Iraq first', to show that they really mean business. Their argument is that from the subsequent position of strength (if successful), the Americans will be in a much stronger position to persuade the Arab states bordering on Israel to come in behind them.

PM: *The Iraq problem has come to be seen as a pre-condition for resolving the Arab-Israeli issue. This has been proved, as far as the*

26

Americans are concerned, by Iraqi funds for suicide bombers' families.
MC: This is a reversal of the previous policy of Middle East first, Iraq next.

PM: *Can we move on to Afghanistan? There does seem to be a big difference between the British emphasis on nation-building and the American emphasis on resolving the al-Qaeda issue.*

MC: Condoleezza Rice says the Americans 'don't do nation-building'. This will have long-term implications, some of which play back into NATO. You might have a NATO in which the Americans do the high-tech big bang and the Europeans do the low-tech nation-building and peacekeeping. I'm against that, and that's why I support the increase in UK defence spending. So in a way what happens in Afghanistan is an illustration of how, if the Europeans don't maintain their capability, we'll get a two-tier NATO. That would have the effect of reducing the alliance's cohesion, and reducing the political influence the Europeans have with Washington.

PM: *I take your point, but I think we're so far behind the Americans that we've lost that race.*

MC: We are still their ally of first choice. The Americans would rather have the Brits with them in a war situation than any other ally.

PM: *Our intelligence relationship . . .*

MC: And, of course, we have got Trident and Cruise, elements that no one else possesses or has access to.

PM: *Although on the ground in Afghanistan it was felt that the American Special Forces did not do very well.*

MC: When I went with Jack Straw to Kabul, the first thing Karzai said to us was: 'Why can't we have a bigger, better ISAF in four or five cities apart from Kabul?' There's a report in *The Guardian* in which three American senators call for a greater US role within ISAF. They said there's a risk that all these achievements would simply drift away, and that Afghanistan would revert to a state of considerable instability. What you spend in advance is always much less than what you'd have to spend later. In view of this I wrote a letter to Jack Straw asking if he'd approached the State Department on the issue. We can't get a bigger ISAF unless the Americans are willing to participate. We have this quite delicate problem of the Turks in command, with a Turkish government in virtual dissolution. One of the ways to end this uncertainty would be if there was some indication from the Americans that they would be willing to take some part in an extended ISAF.

PM: *Despite what you said [about the need for US involvement in ISAF], the opposing argument runs that it's a good idea to get out of Afghanistan.*

MC: History [with the Soviet and British experiences] has a habit of coming back to bite you! I understand there's now a bit of a blockage. A lot of people who'd promised money at Tokyo are putting down conditions. Only when the projects and the supervision have been established, along with guarantees that money will not be siphoned off into the pockets of local warlords, will the money be released.

PM: *I understand the need for money and the need to extend ISAF, but fundamentally the Afghans are ungovernable.*

MC: It is a tribal society where loyalty is not national, like Scotland 800 years ago with the clans. I now owe more loyalty to Her Majesty than to the Duke of Argyll but it was not always so!

PM: *There has been a Whitehall rumour that if there were a settlement between the Arabs and the Israelis, and the Americans were looking for some Brits, some could be sent out as peacekeepers/monitors.*

MC: I'm wholly committed to the Transatlantic Alliance. I was partly educated in the United States and I take a strong interest in American politics. I have a great admiration for the United States. I think we are living through a period, which really began with Clinton, in which the United States is recognizing the effect of its influence as the world's only superpower. We in Europe have yet to come to terms with that. Our assumptions date from the Cold War period. That philosophy has changed.

I heard Richard Perle say at the *Wehrkunde* in Munich that the rest of the world has to accept that America will pursue the security interests of its citizens, if necessary, at the expense of its alliances. That's the substantial change that has taken place, related to the Americans' realization that they are the only military superpower.

PM: *Even in military terms, there is the assumption that the Americans can't do everything. They used nearly all their smart munitions in Afghanistan; they had one of their two Global Hawks shot down along with most of their Predators. They've got some problems . . .*

MC: And they went into [Operation] Anaconda, and found it much more difficult than they expected.

PM: *George Galloway has said that some politicians are talking about dismembering Saudi Arabia, with the fundamentalists taking the holy places with the West owning the oil.*

MC: One of the interesting features of the Russian-American accommodation is that it is as much to do with oil as the efforts of Putin to drag Russia forwards. The US gets only 8 per cent of its oil from Saudi Arabia now. In the United States there is continuing support for Saudi Arabia, but also a determination not to be dependent on the kingdom to the previous extent. It raises the very interesting question as to what would have happened if Saddam had waited twelve years and struck Kuwait now instead of 1990.

PM: *The majority of the hijackers were Saudis. Not a single Iraqi was on those planes.*

MC: And they weren't desperate about the plight of the Palestinians, nor those whose lives had been blighted by deprivation. They were middle-class and university educated.

PM: *Do you subscribe to the Huntington theory of the clash of civilizations? Is it self-fulfilling, particularly if we go to war against Iraq?*

MC: We're at risk of making it self-fulfilling. There is a domestic argument here in the UK about the extent to which the followers of Islam want to stand aside from the mainstream of British life. This leads to questions about integration, and whether you can be a devout Muslim and a loyal subject. My belief is you can be, but there are some radical Muslims who argue the opposite.

War, Church and State – The new Archbishop of Canterbury, **Dr Rowan Williams,** on Iraq, war and morality. Interview with Paul Moorcraft in Oxford in autumn 2002. The Archbishop's media handlers had insisted that there would be no interviews in the run-up to his investiture. When pressed, they said Dr Williams would give an interview only in his native tongue – Welsh. The interviewer accepted the challenge, brushed up on his second language and got the elusive interview, which was almost entirely in English.

PM: *You have described an attack on Iraq and a future war there as 'immoral and illegal'. Is this based on your views generally of a 'just war', or is this your specific interpretation of a war on Iraq?*

RW: I want to come at this from first principles, if possible. One of the first principles that we sacrifice at our enormous cost is that a pre-emptive strike is not a desirable tactic. The 'just war' theory assumes that the aggressor is somebody else. Although you can define aggression very broadly, the pre-emptive strike is something which is very problematic within that [just war] tradition. The phrase 'immoral and illegal' was not my phrase exactly, but that of the *Pax Christi* circular letter to which I appended my signature.

I would add a number of pragmatic points about the precarious situation in Iraq and the wider Middle East. If there is any sense in which Saddam Hussein can be represented in the Muslim world as the beleaguered champion of Muslim identity (which he certainly isn't), that could give some reinforcement to Islamic anti-government elements in some of those neighbouring countries. I worry about a possible 'chain-reaction' effect of instability an attack on Iraq might bring. And for Christian communities in the Middle East the consequences could be very, very serious.

PM: *A backlash specifically against Christians?*

RW: Specifically against Christians. We have already seen in Pakistan how Christian communities can be the targets of Islamist extremism in the wake of actions perceived to be anti-Islamic. I think that could happen fairly easily in some of those areas [in the Middle East].

Also, looking at the longer term pattern of regional security, there is Israel. If, as in the earlier Gulf War, attacks on Israel become a useful distraction for the Iraqi regime, in the present very explosive situation that could prompt Israel into taking stronger action against their immediate neighbours. I just can't see anything constructive emerging from that [Arab-Israeli conflict] in the next fifteen to twenty years. If I could add as a footnote: the United States has talked about the desirability of regime change in Iraq (and I don't think anybody could disagree with them about that), but to effect a democratization of Iraq within a finite time-span requires an investment of personnel and resources the United States is not in a position to make.

PM: *You could interpret the fact that the 'greater evil' argument expounded during the Second World War is as valid when applied to Saddam – that his removal would be worth sacrificing a small number of lives.*

RW: The question is twofold. It's not just a question of sacrificing lives, but also of the possible effect on neighbouring countries. Secondly, what's the cost of yielding the principle of pre-emptive violence? What message could that give to tense situations elsewhere, such as India-Pakistan? I think the India-Pakistan conflict is controlled in the same way that the Cold War was in the 1950s: the two sides have invented a position of mutually assured destruction, MAD, a balance of terror. But opening the floodgates on pre-emptive action holds serious consequences.

The problem is, of course, finding alternative courses of action. Heaven knows, I'm not a strategist, but three things come to mind that might enter the equation. One, in what ways can other regimes in the region be constructively assisted in such a way that they become stronger – how do you strengthen Syria, Jordan, even Iran as allies? Secondly, I'd like to pick up on something Michael Quinlan wrote in *The Tablet*: what is achievable by a continuation of the surgical strikes that have been used against Iraq? Quinlan believes that they can do quite a lot in terms of containment. The third, much wider, question concerns the supply of military hardware. *The New Statesman* contained a rather gloomy article about the arms fair in Jordan recently, and the very public presence of Iraqi representatives there.

PM: *So you take both a pragmatic and moral line. Would you be prepared to lead any kind of moral campaign against the war?*

RW: I would be prepared to register the unease I have expressed already, and to go on pleading for alternatives.

PM: *You did oppose the bombing of Afghanistan. It could be argued that the bombing was for the greater good, as schools and hospitals have now re-opened etc. I've spent time there and been on patrol with the troops. There is a notion at least of nation-building, and there have been improvements in Kabul, even if things haven't changed much in the countryside. Might you not admit you were wrong in opposing the campaign to oust the Taliban?*

RW: I may have been wrong. I expected the conflict to be more protracted in Afghanistan. And the fact that it ended relatively speedily and with fewer civilian casualties than many of us had feared obviously made me think I have to look at that very carefully. My inner jury, so to speak, is still out on regime-building and nation-building. But what might have been achieved if, early on, the bluff had been called about submitting Osama bin Laden to some sort of Muslim jurisdiction? Because that was something which the [Taliban] regime offered; whether that was a cosmetic offer, a bluff – who knows? But if there had been a way of securing a trial in Islamic jurisdiction outside Afghanistan that would have raised some very interesting questions, and might have produced a more robust Islamic critique of what had been going on. Because one of the things that one longs to see more of is a sophisticated Islamic response to the Islamically illiterate terrorist philosophy that is presented as Islam.

PM: *Do you think that [Professor Samuel] Huntington's thesis of a clash of civilizations is becoming self-fulfillingly true?*

RW: 'Self-fulfillingly true' is a very important phrase here. What Huntington leaves out is the degree to which there is a common history, which different Christianities share with Islam. All the successor states to the Roman Empire – which is where it all starts – have historically moved at different rates. You could say that in the Middle Ages the Muslim world was more advanced in certain respects – political sophistication, for example. The Ottoman period has a lot to answer for there, but that's a long complicated story.

So a self-fulfilling prophecy it needn't be. I've found that in discussions with Muslims, more locally, in this country and indeed in South Wales, the sense of hanging onto some shreds of common language and common history is a basis on which Christians and Muslims are well able to talk. I had to share a platform early this year with a distinguished Shi'ite cleric from London who was speaking about human rights in the *Koran*. There is still a great deal of common ground there. I would be loath to say there's a complete collision. Where the collision comes is in the different attitudes in historically Christian and historically Muslim societies to political authority and the unity of society. Islam is more than simply a religious ideal. It is about authority and society. And therefore the questions raised about how you deal with pluralism or dissent are rather different from those that arise on the basis of a Christian history, which has learned to be more comfortable with dissent.

The Road to Baghdad – Paul Moorcraft went to Iraq in September 2002. He had challenged George Galloway to take him along on the MP's next visit to Baghdad in the hope of an audience with Saddam Hussein. The Iraqi President was not available, but Tariq Aziz did provide an interview (see following section).

The journey through the desert from the Jordanian capital takes about twelve to sixteen hours, depending upon the mood of the men with moustaches at the border control. Nearly every adult Iraqi male sports the Saddam bristle. They are almost as ubiquitous as long beards were for the Taliban. The border post is also festooned with pictures and statues of the 'Great Leader'. Iraq is in the grip of a leadership cult as intrusive as those of North Korea, Stalinist Russia or Nazi Germany.

It is another four or five hours from the border to Baghdad. The greatest danger is the madcap motoring – so many graduates of the 'martyrs' school of driving'. There is very little sign of military activity, although the well-maintained motorways can double in places as airstrips. On the outskirts of Baghdad, one rather slack group of troops man a roadblock; nearby is an old-fashioned anti-aircraft gun.

Accommodation is the famous Al-Rashid hotel, long a watering hole for foreign correspondents – if they are lucky enough to get a visa. I have joined a small delegation headed by George Galloway, a Labour MP so aggressively against war with Iraq that his Westminster nickname is the 'MP from Baghdad South'. The hotel entrance is adorned with the infamous floor mosaic of George Bush Sr., with broken teeth and fixed grin. The inlaid caption announces: 'Bush is criminal.' A British journalist dances a jig on the face of the former president. An Arab delegation, wearing traditional dress, stands bemused in the foyer, but soon starts to laugh and cheer.

The hotel is hosting two consecutive conferences: one advocating peace, and then one to boost tourism. Both seem unlikely prospects. A massive poster of Saddam posing jauntily in an historical site quotes one of his great sayings: 'Tourism is a river of gold.' Daily newspapers, besides being full of his doings, also carry headline panels of the leader's words. Even in Arabic, his musings seem trite or plain confusing.

Yet President Saddam Hussein is a genius at survival. He has led his turbulent and talented nation for over twenty-three years. His methods are ruthless. He doesn't need tanks on the streets: his secret police has the country wrapped up. My room is bugged, but in a cack-handed way: the bathroom light trips the phone bug. The regime's PR style is equally ham-fisted. The minders from the Ministry of Information are trying to keep George Galloway's guests happy. Their aim, presumably, is to boost anti-war opinion in the UK.

Tariq Aziz, a Christian who acts as the external face of the regime, tells the peace conference that journalists can visit any alleged site of weapons of mass destruction (WMD) they choose. We do choose and there is a lot of foot-dragging. Despite its best efforts, this looks like a regime with a lot to hide.

Ordinary Iraqis are very hospitable, however. Western journalists can slip their minders sometimes. I roam around the alleyways of the souks, in search of information and, if truth be told, of Saddam paraphernalia: watches, clocks, plates, radios and lighters as souvenirs. Many of the shopkeepers are professional men – graduate salaries can be as low as £10–15 a month – and they are keen to talk English. But it is difficult, even when you are alone, to get them to talk freely. Often they parrot the official line. '11 September was a Mossad [Israeli secret service] and CIA plot,' one teacher tells me. 'Look at those 3,000 Jews who called in sick to avoid going into their offices in the World Trade Center.' Many dictatorships internalize their own international propaganda.

Others insist that the UN weapons inspectors are spies. 'Why should we let them in? They will only tell the Americans exactly where they should target their bombs,' said another shopkeeper. This is a more valid point.

The markets bustle with life. Conditions have improved in the last year or so in Baghdad, despite sanctions. The restaurants are full and the food abundant, if dull. Smart shops sell smuggled or fake Western designer clothes. Life is good for some, especially the elite, who have benefited from an economy which survives on contraband. But making a living is hard in the poorer districts, such as Saddam City, and in the countryside, where malnutrition lurks, especially among the young.

Government spokesmen play down the imminence of war, but there is evidence of stockpiling of food by ordinary citizens and hospitals. The general mood displays both a truculent determination to resist 'American imperialism and Zionist aggression' and a general passivity and war-weariness. As in most modern wars, more civilians than soldiers are likely to be killed.

The Amiriya bunker is evidence of this. On 14 February 1991 two American bombs killed 408 civilians, mainly women and children. I visit the bunker and talk to a survivor. I spend a long time looking at the photographs of those killed. Whole families were burnt or blasted to death. Long lines of haunting portraits of children. Oddly, it reminds me of similar photographs in the holocaust museum in Israel.

Baghdad's imposing 'Mother of All Battles' mosque was begun in 1998, and is still not complete. The towers are modelled on Scud missiles and their launchers, future targets perhaps for an American general with a sense of irony. The *Imam* is in full flow. From the tone of the blaring external loudspeakers, he sounds as if he's launching a *jihad*. Inside, as I listen to his 'sermon', in fact he is preaching about good relations within marriage.

A small group of Western journalists finally get access to Tariq Aziz, the deputy Prime Minister. We wait around all day and then get taken in a fleet of Mercedes to a palatial building owned by the ruling Ba'ath party. I ask Saddam's deputy about Israel – Iraqis call it 'the Zionist entity'. 'Would Iraq hit Israel if war comes?'

'We will fight only in our homeland,' he says. He explains that, just before the Gulf War, US Secretary of State James Baker had warned Aziz that America would reduce Iraq to a pre-industrial power and it would get rid of its leadership. 'Baker asked me if I would attack Israel. I said: "Absolutely, yes." '

'And this time?' I ask.

'That's a meaningless question. Now we don't have long-range missiles.'

Actually, it's a vital question, because Israeli generals have told me in stark terms that if Iraq hits them with weapons of mass destruction, they will retaliate in kind . . . even if there is not a single Israeli casualty. Nuclear war in the Middle East could spell a latter-day Armageddon.

Mr Aziz appeals to Britain to restore normal relations. 'We had a dispute in 1972, but this was settled peacefully . . . . I personally met Mrs Thatcher in the 1980s. Why should Mr Blair want war with Iraq?' He insists that his country can pose no conceivable threat to a country so far away.

What is the state of mind of Saddam Hussein?

'Calm and serene . . . very strong and very stable.'

The last phrase strikes an odd note. Nobody has dared suggest that the Iraqi strongman is unstable.

Mr Aziz also supports George Galloway's suggestion that an 'eminent persons' group' – made up of former presidents such as Nelson Mandela – could police the work of the weapons' inspectors. 'We don't have anything to hide . . . The inspectors, when they are back, will prove we are honest in what we are saying . . . We are sure that we don't have weapons of mass destruction. The Americans know that. They are only using this as a pretext.'

But Britain and America are about to go to war because of WMD. Does Saddam have the capability and the intention to use these terrible weapons? Tony Blair's dossier and many in the Pentagon say he does.

I ask one of the British delegates to the peace conference: 'How would you feel if the Iraqis are revealed to have lied about these weapons?'

'Betrayed,' he replies.

That is the tragic paradox: as in 1991, only during or after this coming war can the real truth be discovered.

In the Bunker –Tariq Aziz, then Iraq's deputy Prime Minister, was interviewed by Paul Moorcraft in Baghdad on 21 September 2002. He joined a small group of senior British journalists who were treated to a wide-ranging defence of Saddam Hussein's policies.

Q: *What is your view on President Bush's commitment to regime change?*

TA: Regime change is an American slogan, an American plan. We are not scared by that; because they did not bring us to power, they could not remove us from power. We came to power by our own patriotic national means, and we have been running Iraq for thirty-five years. Our people support us strongly, so no foreign power can change the government and leadership in Iraq.

Q: *UK policy may differ from Washington on this issue. What would you like to say to the British people?*

TA: In the past, in the 1990s, when the Americans under Clinton were repeating this intention, we heard from a number of British diplomats that it's not really on their agenda – the British agenda is the implementation of UN resolutions, coloured with a hostile attitude towards Iraq. If Mr Blair has now embraced this American objective, that's his decision, but it's not going to add anything. He's going to fail, as Bush will, in his effort to change the leadership of Iraq.

Q: *If there is a conflict with the US and UK, would Iraq retaliate against Britain?*

TA: Britain is so far from Iraq that we can't reach it. We will fight within our homeland against foreign aggression. That is both our intention and our capability. I hope that the British government will not participate in this aggression. My personal analysis is that we have no conflict with the UK, so why should the government wage war against Iraq? As you might know, this endeavour is not fully supported by British public opinion.

We don't have a conflict with the British people or even with the British government. We had a dispute in 1972 with the British government about the nationalization of the oil companies. That was solved peacefully. The then Prime Minister, Sir Edward Heath, did not take a hostile attitude towards Iraq at that time (now he speaks against the current threat of war). So from our side there is no enmity between Britain and us. We had normal, economic relations in the 1970s and 1980s. We used to go there – I personally met Mrs Thatcher and her foreign ministers, other Iraqi ministers visited London, and we received a number of visitors in Iraq. So why should Mr Blair wage a war against Iraq?

Q: *Can you give an insight into the mood of Saddam Hussein?*

TA: Saddam Hussein is a very strong person, very stable. He deals with the dangers in a peaceful and balanced manner.

Q: *There is concern in Iraq that inspectors could be used as a pretext for war. George Galloway MP has suggested that the UN could set up an 'eminent persons' group' to act as an intermediary.*

TA: I would welcome that. I would welcome any transparency, whether arising from the UN decisions or voluntarily provided by us. We have nothing to hide. We are sure that we don't have weapons of mass destruction. We have said many times that the Americans are using this matter as a pretext, because they know themselves there are no weapons of mass destruction in Iraq.

Their inspectors stayed for seven and a half years. They destroyed all the equipment and facilities that worked on these programmes in the past. They destroyed the weapons themselves, and in 1998 both Britain and America attacked all the facilities they suspected of being used for that in the future. Those facilities attacked in 1998 were under a monitoring system – there were cameras and sensors in each and every facility. Each facility was inspected hundreds if not thousands of times before the December 1998 attacks.

Therefore, when they accuse us of rebuilding those sites, of course we have, but at the time of the attacks they were working for civilian purposes. They were under strict monitoring. If we have a facility that produces helpful agricultural and industrial materials, and it is bombed, of course we will rebuild it. We have done that in each and every case. We are trying to rebuild our country.

Q: *How can Iraq ensure that some of the weapons inspectors won't again be spies for the US?*

TA: We hope that they will not. We have no assurances, but we have statements made by Mr Blix. We hope he will keep his word and prevent these inspectors exceeding their remit. And we hope that the Security Council and the Secretary-General will monitor the weapons inspectors' activities.

Q: *Is the Iraqi government actively preparing its people for war?*

TA: As I said, we are taking the American threat very seriously. If you ask any Iraqi what he knows, he will answer that he listens to the radio and follows the news. The Iraqi people are politicized people and they know what they might be facing. We don't know if UN resolutions can prevent a US attack, because they have imperialistic objectives.

The implementation of the UN resolution is not going to provide them with their imperialistic objectives; on the contrary, it is going to put them in the corner. They then have to comply themselves; they don't want to comply, they want to achieve their own objectives. But we have to be careful and, anyhow, we have done what we were asked to do by the international community and the Security Council.

The Americans are going to violate the Security Council resolution, to violate international law and to commit an unjustifiable aggression on

Iraq. It is their own decision and they will have to face the consequences.

Q: *Won't allowing unfettered inspection of the presidential palaces alleviate some of the pressure on Iraq?*

TA: In 1998, Mr Clinton and Mr Blair made a very vicious campaign against Iraq by telling the public in Britain, the United States and the world that those [presidential] palaces were full of chemical and biological weapons, that they contained equipment to produce these weapons. Then the inspectors entered those palaces, the eight presidential sites. They inspected each and every corner and finally they didn't find anything. Mr Blair and Mr Clinton did not apologize.

They told big lies about this. Mr Blair himself said in the House of Commons that one of those palaces is as large as Paris. Paris is 1,400 square kilometres. The whole of eight sites were surveyed by the UN and the eight of them were only thirty-two square kilometres. He misinformed the British parliament about the realities and, when the reality appears clearly, he did not apologize. Therefore, from that experience, we could judge he is misinforming public opinion, misinforming the parliament and its representatives.

Q: *You said that if the Americans commit aggression they must face the consequences. What does that mean exactly?*

TA: We will fight. We will fight that aggression.

Q: *Will you take that fight abroad?*

TA: No, I persist in saying that we will fight within our own homeland. And we are capable of doing that.

We went through a war in 1991. This is not going to be a surprise to us. We know what kind of weapons they are going to use. In 1991 they attacked us for more than forty-two days with thousands of aircraft and missiles and bombs . . . and we survived. So if they are going to repeat that, they are going to face a strong nation, completely ready to defend its independence, sovereignty and national interest.

And the Americans will fail. Their first objective is to create destruction. Yes, they can do that. Secondly, they want to change the leadership. They will fail in that objective. Even in the first objective they will fail in the long term.

I will remind you of 1991 when I met [US Secretary of State] Mr James Baker in Geneva. He told me two things, which are now the same objectives of George W. Bush: 'We will take you back to the pre-industrial age and another leadership is going to decide the future of Iraq.' So he missed both targets. We are not in the pre-industrial age. We recovered from the damage inflicted upon us within a few years, and we retain the leadership of Iraq. If George W. Bush is going to repeat what his father did in 1991, I think the consequences will be the same.

Q. You just said you would fight within your own homeland. Does that mean you will not extend the war to Israel?

TA: We don't have the means to attack Israel. We are very honest and frank. I was asked in Geneva, after the meeting with James Baker, whether we were going to attack Israel, if the aggression starts. I said: 'Absolutely, yes.' This was on the record. Why? Because we did have long-range missiles to attack Israel. So it is a meaningless statement to say that we might threaten Israel. We are going to fight within our homeland, within Iraqi territory. That's clear.

The 'official' line

The beginning of the war – Geoff Hoon MP, the UK Secretary of State for Defence, was interviewed by Paul Moorcraft just as the war against the Taliban in Afghanistan was beginning in late 2001. The interview took place in the Old War Office, Whitehall.

PM: *How does it feel to be a Secretary of State at war?*

GH: It has crystallized all the responsibilities I've had since I started, in that I've taken some of these decisions before. I've had to take a decision to send men and women into situations where they risk their lives. But I don't believe I've ever had to do so with the prospect of continuing actions of a very difficult and dangerous kind in the future. That in a sense is a definition of war. We've been engaged in individual operations in the past while I've been Secretary of State for Defence but, in a way, these last few weeks have pulled all of the experiences that I've had since I started, but in a very concentrated form.

PM: *Have the events of 11 September changed you?*

GH: We haven't really been at peace in the last two years, but the operations have been discreet operations, apart from the air crews flying over the no-fly zones. There's always been the prospect of a conclusion. There have been difficult decisions in committing people with a guarantee of an end date or at least working towards one, for example in Sierra Leone or, more recently, in Macedonia, whereas this current operation is open-ended, and much more difficult to foresee how it might turn out.

All the experiences I've had since coming into the job are all now coming together. One sees this particularly among military colleagues:

this is why they do the job; this is what they have been training and preparing for. I certainly see a sharpness here that perhaps was there before but was disguised by the range of other activities that they were engaged in.

PM: *Sitting in this office so full of military history, do you feel you are living history now?*

GH: It's far too soon to say. I certainly believe we are engaged in something quite different from what has gone on before. It will be a significant challenge for the government and Her Majesty's armed forces. It has already involved some – perhaps 'historic' is too strong a word – fundamental realignments of traditional thinking. For example, the week before last I went to Russia and talked to the Russian Defence Minister in a way perhaps inconceivable to previous holders of this office – at least since 1917.

PM: *As it's impossible to define terrorism concisely, can you define what we are fighting?*

GH: I accept that terrorism operates within the boundaries of a considerable number of states. What we are dealing with now is an organization that has no real interest in the concepts of the state and indeed uses some of the weaknesses that exist between states – the freedom to move, the increased ease of travel from one country to another; perhaps exploiting gaps in our exchange of information, security procedures – to further its appalling aims. This [bin Laden's] group is an organization which is not specifically concerned with change in one country – that's not to excuse terrorism in one country. This is a new phenomenon.

PM: *All the defence doctrine that has been taught at staff college – especially the importance of an exit strategy and clear military and political end states – seems to have been overturned.*

GH: That is what feels different from anything I have done before and that may be a modern definition of a war. From a different perspective, I remember as a child talking to my dad about his experiences of the war. The thing that got to me more than anything else was that he never knew when he was coming home. There are not many experiences that people have in the modern [Western] world where their existence is so uncertain. One of the hallmarks of civilization is to have that predictability in people's lives. Compare this with the First and Second World Wars, when people often had no idea where they were going to spend the next months and years, and perhaps no knowledge of when they would be returning home to their families.

PM: *But there was a clear goal for the UK in both world wars. Victory* *was a clear and definable aim. Now we are in for the long haul, with perhaps no end in sight.*

GH: I am not suggesting that this is an exact analogy [the comparison with the world wars], but we have got to bring Osama bin Laden to account, to shut down his organization and his ability to operate around the world. We've got to deny him a haven in Afghanistan or indeed in any other country that might choose to support him. We've got to look at the kind of organizations that might want to emulate his example.

PM: *If Afghanistan is Stage 1, what then is Stage 2?*

GH: I don't believe we should be thinking about Stage 2 until we have resolved Stage 1. In the resolution of Stage 1 we shall be sending a very powerful signal to any country that is tempted to follow Afghanistan's example. Therefore I hope that in Stage 2 the same military way should not prove necessary. But I don't shy away from the fact that if other countries are prepared to harbour terrorists of the same kind, of the same fanaticism, of the same international reach, then we might have to address that. Our primary preoccupation is with Afghanistan and sending a clear message to such states that this is what will happen if they allow their countries to be used in this way.

It may be that some of those countries where they are concerned about internal terrorism might well welcome military support to deal with that threat. So it won't be like Afghanistan in the way that, after a number of opportunities, we concluded that the Taliban were not ever likely to give up Osama bin Laden. It may well be that in some countries the government, because of its fragility and its difficulty in dealing with terrorists in its own borders, might say to the international community: 'We need your help. Here's a problem for us and it might also be a problem for you. Let's tackle it together.' So I don't think this [current operation] is a prescription.

PM: *I appreciate you can't talk in detail about what comes next, but it still goes against the grain of classic defence thinking – Clausewitz et al and the need to define a clear end state – but we can still talk only about the first stage of a war which may last five or ten years. What is the strategic thinking on a wider scale?*

GH: We clearly have to deal with the manifestations of international terrorism wherever they arise. Having started in Afghanistan, it's important that we finish there before we turn our attention elsewhere, if we need to. I would hope that what is happening in Afghanistan sends a pretty clear signal. But if it does happen in the future that we turn to another state and say: 'Look we know that you are harbouring this group or that group; it's time that you shut them down, handed them over' then they will realize that the international community means business.

PM: *I have doubts about the historical analogies [of previous British adventures in the country], but what happens if the allies actually lose in Afghanistan?*

GH: I don't think we're contemplating losing.

PM: *How will this conflict impact on US-Europe relations?*

GH: It was always inevitable that the first phase of the military operation would be the US's call. The overwhelming majority of people killed in the World Trade Center and the Pentagon were US citizens. And I don't think it realistic for anything other than a US-led operation. We were able to play our part because of our strong support for the United States and also because of the equipment capabilities we had available at the time which was largely a matter of good fortune because of Exercise Saif Sareea. We might not have had that capability so readily available. Equally, other countries are now playing a part and, as the military operation unfolds, I expect further countries to be playing a practical part in what happens. You could say they are already doing so because the AWACs [Airborne Warning and Control System] planes, for example, have crews drawn from across NATO, and they are already participating.

PM: *On the domestic front, will there be a UK equivalent of the US office of homeland security?*

GH: I don't think it will be as formal as that. At the party conference I suggested that we should look at a new chapter in the Strategic Defence Review dealing specifically with asymmetric threats. Without pre-empting that work, there may need to be some consideration of homeland defence, if that's what you want to call it. Certainly, we should look at whether our domestic security arrangements are sufficient to deal with the kind of threats we know are out there, and manifested themselves on 11 September.

PM: *And a response to the feeling that there is not enough being done to control domestic Islamic extremists?*

GH: Speaking as a lawyer, we have some of the toughest legislation against terrorism that any country has – certainly in western Europe – because of the appalling experiences we've had in relation to Northern Ireland in the past thirty-odd years. That is not to say, however, that all our legislation is necessarily right. There are some details of the existing laws that the Home Secretary has announced will be changed, subject to parliamentary approval.

PM: *Does 11 September mean a tougher approach to the IRA [Irish Republican Army] in the event of further terrorism in Northern Ireland?*
GH: It is important that we are consistent; we can't be seen to be taking action against one set of terrorists without recognizing that there are others who are more immediately threatening us. In the end the issue is about means. There is a strong peace process in Northern Ireland; it's got the support of the principal players, without saying we've got an agreement on the outcomes. What we have to do in Israel and the Palestinian Authority is to get back to the process. We are more advanced in Northern Ireland because of the difficulties experienced in recent years. I don't believe that a military solution is necessarily always the only way of reaching a satisfactory conclusion. We have to look at the best means of achieving our ends; one of those may well be those parts of what in the past have been terrorist organizations choosing to engage in a political process. I believe that is what is happening in Macedonia.

PM: *What is the current operation in Afghanistan costing?*
GH: It doesn't work like that I'm relieved to say. Nobody makes the assessment until afterwards. We know the costs of the bullets, missiles and the fuel; the cost of the salaries and the equipment is already paid for. The real issue is how often we use those people and that equipment.

PM: *But this war is bound to have an effect on the defence budget.*
GH: The extra costs – the bullets, missiles etc. I mentioned – are always provided; that is never an issue. The underlying issue is whether we have the right sort of equipment, enough people and whether they are properly trained to deal with the kind of threats we are now facing. That's partly why I judged it appropriate to look afresh at asymmetric issues. That in turn may lead to having to look at our budget in a different way.

PM: *So you are not constrained in the war cabinet by costs issues?*
GH: Cost is not a factor and that has been made quite clear. That doesn't mean that we suddenly go out and buy lots of new equipment that I suddenly decide is necessary. That's why it's important that we look at these implications as part of the continuation of the SDR, so that we do know what kind of people, equipment and future spending this might involve.

PM: *But there must be major implications for the size of the defence budget.*
GH: You are asking me to prejudge the outcome of the further work that is underway. It is logical to go from relatively static Cold War forces, lined up to face a monolithic threat from the Soviet Union, to the key change, which the SDR highlighted: the importance of having more

43

flexible, more manoeuvrable, rapidly deployable forces that could respond to a crisis quickly. Generally, this could be caused – and this was the foreign policy element of the SDR – by ethnic conflict, internal state conflict, probably in places like the Balkans. It's not a strategic leap to say you go from there to dealing with failed states. Some people might have argued that the former Republic of Yugoslavia was a failed state; certainly in that it failed to hold together its ethnic diversity, and ended up with huge internal conflicts. Afghanistan isn't entirely the same as that, but there are many of the similar elements: ethnic tensions and rivalries; a degree of fanaticism in the Taliban.

But I don't think that, strategically, there's going to be a huge difference between the conclusions of the SDR as far as the post-Cold War is concerned and where we're going to be in dealing with asymmetric threats. There will be some things that will be different and we touched on one – homeland defence – but, generally speaking, it's still going to be about getting our forces quickly into a conflict; it's going to be about forward bases and what kind of equipment you need in order to do that. It's going to be about what training individuals require as part of rapidly deployable forces to deal with those sorts of threats. It's not the same, but this is not a new SDR; this is a new chapter, a continuation of the work that has been done already.

PM: *There was a feeling among British forces that, even before 11 September, they were being asked to do too much with too few people.*

GH: There is an extra threat out there which they may be asked to deal with, and I accept that might lead to further pressures of the kind we saw previously; if you go back to November 1999, not long after I first came here [to the Ministry of Defence], I did talk specifically about over-stretch and recognized that, because of our deployments in Bosnia and Kosovo at the time, we were asking people to do more than was reasonable. I reduced numbers in Bosnia and in Kosovo in order to deal with that. But the reason for the overstretch is deploying people without knowing when the end of that operation is going to be. The real over-stretch arrives when you have to find the same number of people again to replace them and to allow them to have to have some well-deserved leave, further training or simply a respite from intrusive operations.

We're not into that in Afghanistan. The lesson of history in Afghanistan is that those who try to occupy ground are the ones who suffer most. Part of my strategic thinking about how the operations will work will be to try to avoid having people on the ground for any length of time because we only have to look at our own history and the Russian experience to illustrate that 'foreign invaders' are not particularly popular in that part of the world.

PM: *The Russians, though, deployed many unwilling conscripts . . .*

GH: I'm not saying that if the British forces did have to do that they wouldn't perform superbly because I am confident that they would. But I believe that the kind of pressures we are trying to bring to bear on Osama bin Laden, the al-Qaeda [network] and the Taliban regime are about keeping them guessing, about limiting their operations, about reducing the space in which they can manoeuvre freely, about closing down their opportunities; this can all be achieved without necessarily putting large numbers of people on the ground for any length of time. In that case the issue of overstretch may not arise in the way it has arisen in the more conventional operations in the Balkans.

British air power – Air Chief Marshal Sir Peter Squire, Chief of the Air Staff, Royal Air Force, discussed air power with Paul Moorcraft on the eve of coalition operations in Iraq.

PM: *Have the previous lessons of Kosovo and Sierra Leone, for example, been completely subsumed by the dramatic events following 11 September?*

PS: They haven't been overtaken. The lessons that emerged from Sierra Leone are the ones that would emerge from any operation of that nature which was principally a mixture of hostage rescue and peace support operations . . . except for the hostages, the environment was relatively benign; there were firefights and engagements of aircraft but it was benign in comparison with Kosovo and the Gulf War. One of the reminders, rather than lessons learned, because of the need to deploy support helicopters quickly – and doing it by self-ferrying, rather than taking them apart and putting them in the back of transport aeroplanes – was how useful in-flight refuelling would be for support helicopters. This is a capability that we intend to get with the Chinook Mark 3 and perhaps also with Merlin. Air-to-air refuelling (AAR) would have helped with deploying assets over that kind of distance. The deployments were successful and rapid, but it would have reduced the elapsed time if we had had AAR for the Chinooks as they went south.

The only way Sierra Leone might be related to the New Chapter [of the Strategic Defence Review] work , which has been done since 11 September 2001, is the conclusion that the geographical focus of the

1997–98 Defence Review was a little narrow. We decided then that the key areas of geographical interest were Europe, including the Balkans, the Gulf and the North African littoral. As long as we provided defence capability to cover those areas, then if we were required to do anything outside, we could use the forces we had for our key areas – and adjust as necessary. What has emerged from the New Chapter work is that this area is slightly too small. We perhaps need to look further east than the Gulf and further south into Africa. Reach has again become of greater importance.

The theatre of operations in Afghanistan was a relatively benign environment in terms of use of air power. There were some ground-based air defences, but they were relatively quickly dealt with. Thereafter, only hand-held SAMs and small arms posed a problem for air operations. Reach was clearly important and stealth wasn't quite so important. In an area such as the Gulf, or Kosovo in 1999, stealth took on a significant importance. I am delighted that we will get a stealth capability when we acquire JSF [Joint Strike Fighter] in due course.

At the operational level, we need to think about capabilities and effects far more than roles and missions. Roles and missions are OK for the tactical level, but at the strategic and operational levels effects and capability are more crucial. In simple terms, a B-52 – traditionally thought of as a strategic weapon system – is now frequently used in a very tactical way, doing close air support for small parties of land forces on the ground in Afghanistan – a B-52 orbiting for hours and dropping individual weapons as required. Equally, on other circumstances, an F-117, F-16 or GR4 Tornado using a precision weapon against a specific target could have a strategic effect. These were originally procured very much as tactical platforms.

PM: *Can we draw specific lessons from Afghanistan?*

PS: Yes, it reminded us of the huge advantages of ISTAR [Intelligence, Surveillance, Targeting and Reconnaissance], the ability to find, fix and attack very quickly before the target has moved. You get into what is now called network-centric capability. While currently the term means a lot of things to a lot of people, it is fundamentally the ability to find, fix and attack quickly using a systems approach.

PM: *Because the Americans are so technologically advanced, can the RAF – apart from supply or refuelling – really go into combat alongside the USAF? There is especially the technology gap regarding blue-on-blue dangers. Does this worry you?*

PS: Yes, it does. One of our key goals is to remain interoperable, as far as we can, with our American allies. We do think that, whether in a NATO or within a coalition-of-the-willing environment, if there's a serious job to be done then the Americans are more often than not likely to be there. They are likely to dictate the minimum entry standards for the weapons systems involved. Interoperability is absolutely crucial. That doesn't mean you have to buy exactly the same equipment and platforms. Interoperability is more about communications and data links. That's the important part. That's where the interoperability is derived, not because you're using Eurofighter/Typhoon and he's using F-22s or whatever; it's the ability of those two systems to be able to talk to each other. Both in the traditional sense and in the passive data link technology.

Regarding blue-on-blue incidents, of course any commander is worried about them. It's unrealistic to think that mistakes won't happen, when the pressure is so intense and technology has not entirely removed the fog of war. While blue-on-blue has become more of an issue in visibility terms, the casualties in combat – which are not blue-on-blue – have been reduced out of all proportion. When we were planning for the 1990–91 Gulf War, we were trying to predict daily casualty levels, which were significant. They didn't happen, and therefore the blue-on-blue incident received a much higher profile than it would have had if the expected combat casualties had actually occurred. I do worry about blue-on-blue but it is symptomatic of the fact that we have managed to reduce casualties hugely in every other way.

PM: *How has the experience of operating for a decade in the no-fly zones impacted on your current operational planning?*

PS: Kosovo and the no-fly zones have given us a depth and breadth of operational experience at the medium level of seniority – particularly wing commander, group captain and one-star – which the air force has not seen for sixty years. We have benefited from that. At the strategic level we have learned that containment works only so far. If the target of that containment is determined to circumvent you, eventually you have to go for the source of the problem. At the tactical and operational levels you come back to the clear need for interoperability. That is my priority: to get proper data links into all our aircraft. We tended in the past to think that data links were important only for air defence aeroplanes, but they are just as important for offensive aircraft. Clearly defensive aids are also important. These were lessons which emerged from Kosovo. We have progressed quite well since then; secure radio communications have been fitted to a lot of our platforms. The need for autonomously guided precision weapons came out of Kosovo. This is not so important in the Gulf where the weather tends to be pretty good. As a result of Kosovo we do have an autonomously guided precision weapon with a GPS facility which is being used in the no-fly zones at the moment. And it's working extremely effectively. That has been a swift improvement, and an even better one will follow in due course.

PM: *May I ask a tabloid question about the RAF's performance in the no-fly zones: is it because you are damned good or just plain lucky that no plane has been shot down?*

PS: It's probably an element of both. Saddam could get lucky. He's clearly concerned about radar because he knows they are likely to get hit. But he's being very cunning. He's forever developing new ways of operating his systems so we have to be on our guard the whole time. And our crews and the Americans are very professional in the way they go about their business . . .

PM: *There has been a lot of criticism of the projected withdrawal of the Sea Harrier; is this more of a naval matter?*

PS: It's not wholly a naval matter. The FA2 is part of Joint Force Harrier which comes under the operational commander of C.-in-C. Strike Command. I regret the withdrawal of the capability which the FA2 brings to bear, but it's getting long in the tooth. And in order to complete its service to its assumed out-of-service date, it was going to require a considerable amount of money to be spent on it . . . Therefore, in the context of limited resources, we came to the conclusion that the money should be invested in upgrading the GR7 to increase its capability to see it through to its out-of-service date, rather than putting money into the FA2.

PM: *That's the official line, but there is still a big capability gap. Could that gap become more apparent in a possible war with Iraq?*

PS: Yes, there is a capability gap. It means that we will have no embarked air defence capability. But in a serious war fighting situation we are almost certainly to be working alongside our American colleagues. Under these circumstances, they will provide the air defence of the maritime component. Although I am sad to see it go, I don't have huge concerns that we will be naked when we go into operations, wherever they may be.

PM: *Wherever – does that include Iraq? How do you rate the Iraqi air force?*

PS: We don't see a huge amount of them. It's a relatively small air force. If you set aside the ground-based air defence assets, the actual number of its manned platforms is small. However, they have some capable platforms – the MiG 25s, for example. They are quite clever in the way they use their air force. It's not a threat to be dismissed . . . they don't, perhaps, have access to the same level of technology, certainly as the Americans have. If those two air forces were pitted against each other you can draw your own conclusions as to what the outcome is likely to be.

Virtuous intervention – and good luck – The Rt. Hon. Lord Hurd of Westwell, former Conservative Foreign Secretary, on over-stretch and intervention. Paul Moorcraft interviewed him in January 2002.

Douglas Hurd had attacked new Labour spin-doctors for claiming that so-called 'virtuous intervention' – along with all new thinking – began in May 1997. It started long before, he said. Lord Hurd also pointed out that the coalition to free Kuwait in 1991 had much in common with the war on terrorism which began in 2001. For the moment, meddling in other countries' affairs – once called neo-colonialism – was justified to heal failed states and to drain the swamps of terrorism. He argued that there could be a strong reaction, led by leaders who demand economic and political independence, not religious war.

PM: *You said in a recent* Spectator *article that we have 'no substantial strategic interest in Bosnia'. But many would argue that stability in the Balkans is vital to NATO security.*
DH: I never thought that the Bosnian war or, before that, the fighting in Croatia and, after that, Kosovo had the makings of a major Balkan war. Although people did use that argument, I don't think it had partic-ular strength in either the decisions we took about Bosnia or the present government took about Kosovo. The overwhelming impulse was that something should be done to prevent the killing, not on a wide strategic grounds, but because in itself it was unacceptable.

You will never find among the [FCO] papers a measured recommen-dation from the chiefs of staff that such intervention, whether in Bosnia or Kosovo, was required to safeguard the general stability of the Balkans as a basic British interest. That was not the way the decision was taken.
PM: *Wasn't the implicit reason, for example in Kosovo, to prevent a general breakdown which might have sucked in Greece and Turkey and pulled NATO apart? Perhaps such implicit reasons didn't need to be stated.*

DH: No. They had a certain validity. But they were not as a matter of historical fact the moving force in either of those interventions.

PM: *You used the term 'virtuous intervention' in your recent* Spectator *article. Take Sierra Leone. I know the official line, but I've never been given a persuasive explanation of why the Brits are in that country and not, for example, in Sudan.*

DH: Because it was felt that Sierra Leone was 'do-able', Sudan is not. It's difficult for ministers to give that answer because it implies a certain 'ad-hocery' which of course is true. There is not a single doctrine which is applied in all circumstances. The doctrine of 'virtuous intervention' is applied by this government – but also by all governments – when they think they can do something useful. But the Sudan war, which is awful beyond belief, has gone on for nineteen years with one break; and years continuously before that.

That's one of the difficulties of having a general moralistic approach. If you are openly ad hoc you can do something useful where you can.

PM. *You have said regarding the overstretch issue that we [the British] have had a lot of luck. Sometimes senior officers say we need a debacle to prove the point that more money and better kit are required.*

DH: We *have* had a lot of luck. With overstretch you need to build in a bit of a reserve against the day when the luck runs out.

I gave various scenarios [in the *Spectator* article]. I am not saying they will happen but they are the sorts of things that do happen in life. As Shakespeare said, bad luck comes not in single spies but in battalions. I am cautious by instinct so we do need to keep something in hand.

I was particularly alarmed by Geoff Hoon . . . declaring a deadline [in Afghanistan] and, after that absolute deadline, we will pull the troops out. It's a gamble . . . We're now at the end of January . . . The Karzai administration is asking for peacekeeping troops to be extended beyond Kabul . . . We have said: 'We'll train your army.' But that's not the point. The crisis is now. Are we going to pull out? The Turks will take our place? The Germans? The situation is not clear; the lack of clarity is normal in these kinds of situations. That's precisely why we shouldn't make these very definite statements [about withdrawal]. We were lucky in Macedonia, where it worked. We were able to pull out in time. It didn't work in Kosovo – that's why we're still there. Who would have said in 1995 at Dayton that British and American troops would still be in Bosnia in 2002? It would have been very bizarre.

PM: *What would the Conservatives do if they were back in government?*

DH: Where we can usefully intervene with others or alone – as we did in Sierra Leone – we should do so. But we are now near or at the point where, if something new comes up, we should have to say: 'Sorry, our commitments are such that we can't do anymore.' There is a strong case for expanding the defence budget so that we could do more. As far as I can judge from outside, we're at or near the point where we're fully committed and relying on a certain amount of luck to see us through the existing commitments. There's no single commitment that I'm against. But we're in a state of full stretch or verging on overstretch, and somebody should tell the Prime Minister!

PM: *Both in government and official opposition circles there appears to be a reluctance to advocate an increase in defence spending.*

DH: Either you increase the defence budget substantially or you acknowledge that you've reached the state of overstretch. We should be encouraging the Japanese and certainly the Germans to change further – they are changing the structure of their defence budgets.

PM: *Where do you think the US war on terror will go next in the so-called 'second stage'? Sudan, Somalia? Or should the target be Iraq?*

DH: Obviously there is a second stage. The Americans are doing things in the Philippines that fit into that; they're scouting around in Somalia, although there isn't much to hang on to there. The danger is that you simply side with Ethiopia, and that probably is not a recipe for success. The Yemen is doing what Sudan is trying to do . . . They backed the wrong side in the Gulf war. This time they are trying to back the right side. The Americans might use the official Yemeni apparatus to root out people who they think might be connected to al-Qaeda.

Iraq is on the agenda; it was on the agenda before 11 September. It's unfinished business and very unsatisfactory. Iraq poses a real danger as the [US] State of the Union message indicated. I'm a bit of hawk on Iraq, not that it's sensible to bomb Iraq now, more than they are [being bombed now]. It is sensible to go back to the Security Council and get good support. The council should say to Iraq, 'You must agree to inspection on reasonable terms.' If, after a period, it refuses that, then there's a case for action. It has to be done that way.

PM: *Do you envisage the Kurds and the Iraqi National Congress being a parallel to the Northern Alliance in Afghanistan?*

DH: No, I don't see the Kurds providing such a solution in Baghdad as the Alliance did in Kabul. That's always been the difficulty. There hasn't up to now been a valid opposition. Even if you could get rid of Saddam Hussein there was no guarantee of a successor regime which was adequate. It needs time. But I do accept the American argument that Iraq is on the agenda. The biological threat poses the greatest problem.

PM: *Do you regret not finishing the job in the Gulf War? Saddam was on his knees – intelligence now suggests he held only one of the country's nineteen provinces.*

DH: We couldn't have done that. We would have broken the alliance, broken unity in this country, which was touch and go . . . The war aim at that time was to liberate Kuwait. So he survived . . . and he's dangerous - even more so since 11 September.

PM: *Do you think the clash of civilizations is becoming a self-fulfilling prophecy?*

DH: Let's take Pakistan. President Musharraf has got away with it. He has engineered what we would call a moderate reaction. Or Mrs Megawati in Indonesia, a very difficult country to govern, has reacted in the same way. One doesn't have a sense of an extreme form of Islam sweeping through these countries, despite the American action. This could have happened. But it's early days yet. I think the argument inside Islam goes the other way.

The danger is not a religious but a nationalist one. Ho Chi Minh was a nationalist hero, but his appeal didn't really extend beyond Vietnam. Nasser did appeal beyond his own country. Castro tried and failed. There is no obvious [pan-Islamic] nationalist at the moment but there could be.

PM: *What of current criticisms of American unilateralism?*

DH: The US does act on its own, and I can quite see why – from Bosnia and Kosovo – they're not very keen on sharing command. But we've reached a situation in Afghanistan and to an extent in Iraq in the context of stopping Saddam where they can't do it on their own; the aim is not achievable without help and cooperation . . . They need financial, political and military support. In Afghanistan a big international force is an important component of America's plans, although they don't want to take part themselves.

PM: *But America is so technologically advanced that even close allies such as the British cannot keep up.*

DH: That's true of sophisticated weapons but it's not when it comes to patrolling the streets of Kabul. This is low-tech stuff which requires things which the Americans are not trained to do or do not need to do. Holding governments together – re-building bridges, in both senses – these are not high-tech. But obviously Bush's announcements about more defence spending will increase that technology gap.

Pearls of Wisdom – Richard Perle, former US Assistant Secretary of Defense for International Security Policy, is a leading US hawk. He discussed the current crisis in the Middle East with Paul Moorcraft in London in autumn 2002. Perle was called the Prince of Darkness in Washington, but he had far more influence than his namesake in the UK, Peter Mandelson. Above all, Perle's hard-line views on Iraq had the regular ear of the US president.

PM: *Do you consider an escalation of the air war over the no-fly zones – especially if an aircraft is shot down – a suitable* casus belli? *The so-called trigger?*

RP: What I understand President Bush to have said is that our policy would be zero tolerance, which implies that any violation of the UN resolution would at the very least constitute, by definition, a material breach. There is no inclination to say that this is a small violation and that is a large violation. Or three violations are OK but four are not. The President has tried to set an absolute standard; that doesn't mean – and I hazard a guess here – that a violation will immediately mean war. But if there is one violation there is likely to be more than one. If they fire on aircraft they are likely to do it on more than one occasion. A pattern is likely to develop and develop fairly quickly. This President is serious. He believes that the international community has allowed its own resolution to subside into meaningless rhetoric without any insistence on compliance or determination to compel compliance. He's had enough of that. No one should be shocked if there is a very tough response to violation.

PM: *What happens on 8 December [2002] if Saddam Hussein says he has no WMD? Bearing in mind the allegations, intelligence and dossiers proffered by Washington and London, would that constitute a material breach?*

RP: I believe it would constitute a material breach if he were to make a false declaration. And to say he has nothing would be false. We have evidence contradicting that: it's important to remember here that judgements about a material breach will reflect all of the evidence available, not only the evidence that can be collected by inspectors on the ground in Iraq. There may be some evidence that can't be collected by the inspectors but can be gathered by means not available to the inspectors, for example, the firing on aircraft. The inspectors have no way of determining that aircraft have been fired on. We do. The inspectors may not have the capability to judge the technical characteristics of a weapon to determine whether it fits within the limitations. We do.

PM: *What happens if Iraq declares some dual-use facilities and even admits that they have 'found' some new weapons, and then they offer to help the inspectors in the country's disarmament?*

RP: There are a lot of tactical manoeuvres to which Saddam could resort in an effort to give an appearance of cooperation by turning over something of no consequence. Most people won't be taken in by that. We certainly won't be. Suppose he says, for example, 'In our search preparedness declaration we found a canister of mustard gas which was mixed in with something else. It was unauthorized.' For us to accept that he has made a truthful declaration simply because he has turned over something of no consequence . . . we would not be taken in by that, although we can't preclude that he will attempt that sort of manipulation. We know something about what he's got. We may not know the precise locations because in the four years when there were no inspectors and, indeed, when there were inspectors, he had the capacity to move things around . . . and things have been relocated. We know of mobile chemical weapons laboratories on heavy lorries. Our inability to locate the precise coordinates of things he's not entitled to doesn't mean that he doesn't have them.

PM: *Even if Saddam does come clean, the high levels of fear and cumbersome bureaucracy in the country might create breaches . . . even with the best will in the world.*

RP: I'll be astonished if we see any sign of goodwill. Saddam Hussein is not a man of goodwill. Already the signs are there. Tariq Aziz gave an interview to Jonathan Dimbleby the other day in which you could see his planting the seeds of future obstruction, referring to the dignity of the Iraqi people.

'Of course,' he said, 'we will allow the inspectors in but they must respect the dignity of the Iraqi people.' What is that supposed to mean? What I think it means is that they will insist, as he said, in 'working out modalities' – that are in fact the details of the conditions under which inspection will go forward. So they're unconditional except for the modalities – which are conditions. He's giving every indication of the Saddam that we've always known.

PM: *Let's assume that a breach leads to war; how do you see it panning out?*

RP: He's likely to commit a material breach, because he will lie on this [8 December] declaration. He will conceal weapons of mass destruction.

He will prevent some of the rights of the inspectors from being exercised. For example, the right to remove people from Iraq for their safety, so that they can speak without fear of reprisal. We know of people who talked to inspectors and were killed, even those who didn't volunteer to be interviewed. These people have to be protected. This issue came up in the interview with Tariq Aziz as well. He said these people have to agree to be taken from Iraq. You can already see them applying the pressure on these people: 'If you agree, we will get you and your family.'

PM: *The level of trepidation in Iraq is very high. You can almost squeeze fear out of the atmosphere in Baghdad.*

RP: It's very difficult to judge what people are thinking in those circumstances. No one considers that expressing oneself is worth the risks, so people don't. Capitalizing on that fear, Iraqi officials will try to frustrate the ability of inspectors to interrogate people. There are already reports – I don't know if they are true – that people with knowledge have been sent abroad so that they are unavailable to the inspectors. That's a risky game because it may be easier to defect, but their families are still in Iraq.

If I had to guess, I would guess that there will be breaches that any sensible person would recognize. At some point, a decision will be made that Saddam has not decided to relinquish weapons of mass destruction. And there will be a war. I'm not sure of that, and it's certainly not my decision.

PM: *What if the regime has shifted equipment and weapons to Syria and Libya?*

RP: He's done that before. He's sent aircraft to Iran. He never got them back. If he shifted it all out of the country that would amount to an unconventional form of disarmament. If he ships stuff out of the country and we find it, I should think that would constitute a breach. Because he's obliged to turn it over, not export it.

PM: *After the air war, will the ground war probably last just a few days?*

RP: I think so. Very few Iraqis will fight for Saddam and many would happily join in bringing him down. This is not well understood in the West. It's so intuitively obvious when you consider the way Saddam rules that you make a great many enemies, the majority of the population. And, the moment the fear that grips that nation is broken, you have a completely different situation, more or less instantaneously. A bit like [Nicolae] Ceausescu.

PM: *It's been said that many Iraqis will dance in the street when the Americans arrive.*

RP: I agree with that. That conviction is one of the reasons why President Bush has taken such a strong position. He's confident that, despite the predictions of 'the Middle East going up in flames', the US getting bogged down in a war and suffering terrible losses etc., the war will be short and we will be regarded as liberators. That has important implications not only for the well-being of the people of Iraq but for the whole region.

PM: *But what happens if Saddam uses his chemical and biological weapons?*

RP: Chemical weapons first: they are not easy to use effectively on the battlefield and we are not without protection against chemical weapons. We may turn out to be rather better protected against them than the troops called upon to use them. So, if we're talking about a battlefield use, that won't constitute a major problem for American or British forces but we have to be ready if it does happen. Someone has to give the orders too. Someone has to commit a war crime and we will have made it very clear that those Iraqi troops who choose not to defend Saddam will be treated in a different category from those who carry out orders, particularly those who commit crimes against humanity. While there may be some fanatics, you'd have to have the coincidence of fanatics trained in the administration of chemical weapons, in possession of them at the right place and at the right time. It's going to be more difficult than some people imagine.

Biological weapons are another matter. If you have fanatics of the al-Qaeda sort it's enough for them to infect themselves and mingle. There's no protection as a practical matter against that. But Saddam's supporters back him because they benefit from his dictatorship. By and large they are not the sort of people who commit suicide in order to inflict damage.

There's also the issue of use of chemical and biological weapons against a civilian population, which he's done before. And it's feared he might be prepared to do it again – this time against the Israelis. He has some Scud missiles that could reach Israeli targets from the Western desert, but he has very few of them. This time we have a fighting chance of finding those missiles before they can be used, and a very good chance of finding them after the trajectory has been exhibited. They might get one or two through but they don't have very many. And they've got to move them into position – we will be paying very close attention to the positions where they can reach targets outside Iraq.

The possibility certainly exists that he will do something terrible of that nature. It is not a certainty, nor are we defenceless.

PM: *Israeli generals have warned that if Saddam uses CBW against Israel – even if the CBW missiles land harmlessly in the sea – they will retaliate with unconventional weapons.*

RP: I would take that extreme formulation with a grain of salt. If a missile goes into the Mediterranean, would it make sense for Israel to use nuclear weapons, and against what? Baghdad? I don't believe the Israelis would use chemical weapons. Clearly, they want the most intimidating possible deterrent. So you will get statements of that sort. You don't need to overstate the case to sober Saddam up. I am sure he understands that if he were successful in delivering a weapon of mass destruction, the Israelis would be furious and their reprisal would be equally furious.

PM: *Tariq Aziz told me in a recent interview in Baghdad that he would not use WMD against Israel because they didn't have long-range missiles, and so they would fight only in their homeland.*

RP: He is in a bit of dilemma. He can't threaten to use weapons he claims he doesn't have. Admission of his possession would constitute a material breach. So he's in a difficult situation. By the way, the use of any weapon against Israel, which has not committed any aggressive act with respect to Iraq, is such an obvious violation of international law that it sometimes amazes me that people discuss scenarios in which Saddam attacks civilians in Israel. And then go on talking about the overall situation as though we are not dealing with a particularly monstrous threat (which of course we are). It is unprecedented to say that if I find myself in a conflict I will destroy an innocent bystander. That's what is in fact suggested by the idea that he might attack Israel.

PM: *Let's assume that, after a brief period of interregnum chaos, and just before US forces reach Baghdad, Saddam goes into exile or is shot.*

RP: I hope Saddam is captured and put on trial. It would do the world a lot of good to see the likes of Saddam Hussein tried and either packed off to jail for the rest of their lives or, depending on the jurisdiction under which they are tried, to be given the death sentence. It is of course impossible to predict what happens in the chaos of a military action.

PM: *What happens in Baghdad post-Saddam? Who is your Karzai Mark 2?*

RP: There is an Iraqi opposition. It's been around for a long time. Until 1996 it was pretty active in the north of the country. There is some experience in democratic outlooks if not democratic institutions, and the Iraqi National Congress which is weak because it's been largely without support and because it's been largely in exile since 1996. It's an inchoate democratic institution. There will be a strong desire to end this awful brutal dictatorship by nurturing the emergence of a benign administration; ideally, one with enough of a democratic orientation to evolve into a full-blown democracy. One of our tasks, alongside the rest of the international community, will be to provide the security environment in which a political process leading to democratic institutions can take place.

PM: *The opposition is very disorganized and fractious; there's no clear alternative leader.*

RP: Leaders emerge in situations like this. There's enough of a political process outside Iraq gathering momentum. Whatever leadership begins to emerge will have to be broadly representative of the country as a whole. It will be a terrible mistake to impose a leader, in particular a leader who is not committed to a pluralist democracy. I have been impressed by some of the Iraqi opposition. They are going to have a conference quite soon; I hope the press pays some attention to it.

They are not as fractious as you are suggesting. There are different points of view, to be sure. And there are vigorous debates, perhaps more impassioned than what we are accustomed to, as laid-back Englishmen and Americans. The nature of those debates are well within the traditions of discourse we respect . . . .There's work going on, on what an Iraqi constitution will look like . . . I find all this very encouraging.

PM: *But there will be allied military occupation – MacArthur style – for three, six, nine months?*

RP: The historical analogies are not helpful. There will have to be some security presence. It may be limited to the training of the Iraqi military police and superintending their organization. It depends on what we find on the ground. If we find that British and American forces are welcomed as liberators, that's a very different situation from one in which their presence is bitterly resented, where they have to hunker down and operate from cantonments.

PM: *The defeat of Saddam might lead to the collapse of other nasty dictatorships such as Saudi Arabia.*

RP: The Saudis have some hard work ahead of them. The population has grown very rapidly. It's now of the order of 28 million; per capita income has declined precipitously. While the figures don't reflect the full situation, per capita income has gone from $20,000 to $5,000, which is very difficult for a society to absorb. Some people in Saudi Arabia live in an ostentatious way, in such extreme luxury, that it has to be a source of instability. And they have been funding organizations which have

58

been perpetrating extremist views and become the collection point for recruits to terrorism.

So that's about to change. I think the jury's out on whether the Saudis will be capable of internal reform and controlling the most troublesome aspects of their policy, which would involve, from an outsider's point of view, the subvention of institutions which are involved in terrorism. I hope they will.

PM: *After victory over Saddam, will an extra-confident US be prepared to knock heads together over the Arab-Israeli conflict and establish a Palestinian state?*

RP: I would not describe the establishment of the Palestinian state as knocking heads together. That sounds to me as though that means the knocking of Israeli heads. The problem, in my view, between Israelis and Palestinians, is to do with the readiness of Palestinians to accept a Jewish state. They had a very promising opportunity at Camp David and rejected it. I don't believe you will ever get peace with [Yasser] Arafat. So, if that's one of the heads to be knocked, I would be very doubtful. On the other hand, if Iraq goes from the column of opponents of the peace process, encourager of suicide bombings, into the other camp where they encourage resolution, that could have important differences. It could brighten the prospects for the initiation of a new approach to peace. This idea that the US will come rolling in on the wings of victory and say to its democratic friend Israel: 'Now you have to accept something that you are not willing to accept.' That's quite wrong.

CBW genie out of the bottle? – Professor Richard Holmes is a media don, best-selling author and a former brigadier – the most senior Territorial Army officer. He is also co-director of the Security Studies Institute at Cranfield University. He was interviewed by Paul Moorcraft in November 2002.

PM: *Intelligence reports suggest that the Iraqi regime is very brittle, and that only 10,000 troops are prepared to fight. Is that over-optimistic?*

RH: One needs to look as hard as one can at human intelligence, assess how people are likely to behave, and avoid easy assumptions. Having been a military historian all my working life, with the occasional interlude of light soldiering, I believe passionately that people are the most important factor in war. If we believe that technology gives us easy answers, we miss one of the great truths. One doesn't necessarily need an awful lot of good men – on either side – to make a difference. Wars across history are won in the hearts and minds of men. The war with Iraq is going to be about traditional qualities of cohesion, belief and determination. And it's very hard to assess those qualities.

PM: *Compared with the last Gulf War or even Kosovo, this is going to be an extremely smart war – if we consider munitions – but you are talking about old-fashioned values.*

RH: It's important that we get a sensible relationship between the old and the new here. What I'm not suggesting is that you can 'de-technologize' war. You never could, least of all in the twenty-first century. You need to be clear that you can make use of tactical victory. We face a real problem in military thought: to make some sense of the paradigm that tactics – the art of winning battles and engagements – gears to operations and has a strategic result. In other words, you win a battle – tactical – that takes you on to operations, say a theatre campaign plan, and that contributes to a strategic result, which takes you to the political end state you identified before the conflict started. It's becoming more difficult to make sure that you can convert tactical victory into strategic result.

PM: *Was there a difficulty in defining the strategic end state in Afghanistan? So what is it in Iraq? Getting rid of the Taliban/Saddam is not enough.*

RH: There are two broad lines of argument. Officers trained in Western staff colleges will say: 'Please tell us what the end state is going to be. And then we can advance towards it.' And there's another view, which I've certainly encountered in the United States, which says: 'Hey, we didn't have an end state when we took on Germany in the First World War and Germany and Japan in the Second. There are times in history when you do what you need to in the short term, without being absolutely clear what the details of the long-term end state are.' My own position is to favour the former school of thought. It is essential to identify, in as much detail as you can, what the required end state is.

War is a philosopher's stone which transforms everything it touches. The minute you're doing it for real, with a magazine full of live rounds in your weapon, or with real missiles strapped on your aircraft, all the bets are off. The very act of fighting changes the combatants, and lots of external things as well.

War is a difficult-to-control medium, which is why we invent notions such as limited war. The more you can be clear about what you're trying to do, so that you are telling in particular your coalition partners (especially the uncommitted ones) what you are striving to achieve, the better.

There's a perfectly respectable counter-argument, but I happen not to agree with it.

PM: *Do you think the use of chemical and biological warfare is likely in Iraq or the terror war?*

RH: In the broad context, I don't think we are going to be able to keep the nuclear, chemical and biological genie in the bottle. Sadly, I think it's a case of not *if* but *when*. Whether the Iraqis have these weapons or whether they would use them, I simply don't know. In the last Gulf War, Saddam Hussein had a golden bridge, as it were, to retire. He was unlikely to be pressed to the last extremity. I don't know how he will react if he's facing at least deposition, probably followed shortly after by death, then he has no room for manoeuvre, before there is an appreciable chance that if he has such weapons he will use them. On what scale and against whom is idle speculation.

Events such as the Cuban missile crisis were more dangerous. We had the ability to blow up practically the whole world in a dreadful way. It will require careful and deliberate management if we are to avoid weapons of mass destruction being used over the next ten years. I think they will be used; I just hope this [the Iraq war] is not the time. A lot of the constraints and taboos are being removed.

PM: *May we talk about homeland security? Presumably you think it was a mistake to cut back on the Territorial Army a few years ago?*

RH: Our armed forces across the board are too small. Perhaps surprisingly, given that I've spent thirty-six years as a Territorial, I think it's increasingly unhelpful to try to differentiate between regulars and reserves. We need to integrate them as well as we can. But they are all too small. Sharp, goodness me, yes; the British army is better now than it's ever been. Very sharp indeed, but not perhaps with the long-term tensile strength I would like. And that's a question of numbers . . .

PM: *What of the TA's new role in counter-terrorism?*

RH: This will, I suspect, not be popular with my old friends in the TA. I would not want to re-invent the TA as what it started out as, which was a homeland defence force. We go back to R. B. Haldane, Secretary of State for War, who brought the TA together from a disparate number of volunteer armed forces in the early twentieth century. It was called 'territorial' not because it was organized territorially, that is regionally, but because it was 'territorial' not 'expeditionary'. It wasn't liable for foreign service; you had to volunteer to go abroad at the start of the First World War. By and large they did volunteer and fought extremely well.

61

While part-time servicemen living locally have particular abilities which regular servicemen not living locally might not have, I would still like to see the TA in the context of one army. What we don't want to do is to suddenly say, 'We have this apparently new strategic requirement and we have an organization which feels unloved and which is after roles. Let's put the two together.' It's not that simple. There are going to be bits of homeland defence for which the TA is particularly suited, but there are roles for which it may not be suited.

At the risk of sounding too messianic I was a Territorial all my adult life. I joined as a private soldier at the age of eighteen and ended up as a brigadier, because it mattered enormously to me. The TA, whatever else it does, is part of the velcro sticking the armed forces to society. That is extraordinarily important. We are a society which is quite properly demilitarized and if you were to ask the man on the Clapham omnibus how large the armed forces are, what percentage of the GDP they consume, the difference between a bombardier and a brigadier, or a commander and commodore, he probably wouldn't know. The last thing I would want is to go back to national service days, but we do need a better understanding between armed forces and society. In that respect reserve forces are a crucial part of the mix. That's why I was very proud of every job I did in the TA.

Last Chance Saloon – Peter Rodman, US Assistant Secretary of Defense for International Security Affairs, on rogue states. He was interviewed by Gwyn Winfield in September 2002.

The showdown may not be here just yet, but the signature tune is building. The US is playing a tough game of poker with some of the best bluffers in the world – Iraq, Iran and North Korea. Since they are keeping their hands very close to their chest it is difficult to see what cards the 'bad guys' may have, but it looks like the US may hold all the aces.

Peter Rodman is one of those people who have glimpsed the hand and has a good idea of how the cards will fall. He advises the Secretary of Defense and the Under Secretary of Defense for policy on 'formulating international security and political-military policy for Africa, Asia-Pacific, Near East and South Asia and the Western hemisphere' – a big job. It could hardly be a busier time. Along with Iran and Iraq, Mr Rodman has to keep a watch on Israel, Syria and Saudi Arabia in the Middle East, Libya and Sudan in Africa, Cuba and Colombia in the

Western Hemisphere and North Korea in Asia-Pacific (to name a few). When it comes to 'Axis of Evil' countries there are very few secrets he does not need to know.

The phrase 'Axis of Evil', generated by the President's State of the Union address, might even be seen as the *axes* of evil, as some think that the original three, Iran, Iraq and North Korea, should be joined by countries such as Cuba, Libya and Syria. But what is the difference between the two categories?

Mr Rodman offers a precise definition: 'The three that were mentioned are particularly dangerous – North Korea, Iraq and Iran. Certainly Iraq and North Korea require no explanation. Iran is going through an interesting internal revolution, but its sponsorship of terrorism makes it the premier state sponsor of terrorism, and its weapons of mass destruction [WMD] programme is the most advanced of its kind in that area . . . You see in a lot of our public statements about Iraq, Iran and North Korea that they all have, or are eager to have, WMD. That is why the President has singled out those three: these are hostile states that are extremely dangerous because of their regional ambitions and involvement in a variety of misdeeds, including terrorism and, most importantly of all, their weapons of mass destruction.

'Libya, for example, wasn't on the axis, it didn't make the cut, it didn't make the first division. With Libya we might see a settlement of the Lockerbie business, which would be . . . interesting. But since it has been liberated from sanctions, Libya has been more active in the WMD field,' said the Assistant Secretary. [Since this interview, Libya has renounced its WMD programme.]

Terrorism and WMD are a continuous theme throughout Peter Rodman's discussion; this is no surprise in the run up to the anniversary of 11 September. While the US may have been caught napping a year ago, there is a determination that they won't be victims again of terrorism or terrorist nations. The difficulty of trying to change terrorist regimes, however, is that successor governments may revert to the same old policy. Iraq, for example, could still want weapons of mass destruction; aspiring to be the pre-eminent Arab state in the region is a long-term Iraqi policy, which predates Saddam.

'That is unlikely, frankly,' said Mr Rodman. 'A different Iraq would have a different set of priorities and be more reachable by international partners. There are basic remedies against these WMD – ballistic missile defence, for example. Ballistic missiles are the weapon of choice for all three of these countries. One of the purposes of ballistic missile defence is to devalue ballistic missiles, to make them less attractive to resort to (and proliferate) ballistic missiles as a means of intimidation . . . '

The trouble with this approach is, of course, that – as soon as an effective ballistic missile defence is deployed – the interest will be in cruise missiles that would be able to evade this costly defence.

The Assistant Secretary agreed that this is an issue: 'That's right, there could be problems with cruise missiles. But all these countries pose a variety of threats and anything that we have some means to counter we should counter. Right now people are proliferating ballistic missiles, partly because there is no defence against them and partly because they have political prestige.'

The axis is not fixed in stone, however; countries can join the table for bad behaviour as much as leave it for good. Take the current speculation about the status of Saudi Arabia. How long can the West turn a blind eye to the autocracy of the House of Saud?

Peter Rodman strongly denied that there has been any policy shift towards Saudi Arabia but admitted that the situation is not as clement as it was. 'The previous several months have been difficult for our relationship with Saudi Arabia. The Afghan war has put the relationship under some strain, and Wahabbism is a disturbing phenomenon in the region. But the policy of the US, without a doubt, is that the relationship with Saudi Arabia is strong and very important. This famous briefing at the Pentagon [the 10 July 2002 briefing by the Rand Corporation in which the Saudis were accused of supporting terrorism] did not reflect US policy in this department, or the government. We value the partnership we have with Saudi Arabia, and whatever stress it is under we do not want to do damage to it. We will not be the ones to abandon or change a relationship that serves mutual interest in this area: every relationship has its difficulties.'

The sort of suggestions that George Galloway has made [regarding partition of Saudi Arabia] is roundly squelched and Peter Rodman asserted that, while the Saudis have internal issues, it is for them to sort out, not the US. Yet none of these problems can be looked at in isolation. Nations in the Middle East, more than in other parts of the world, have complex relationship dynamics. What happens in one country can have massive repercussions in another. Iran and Iraq have been trapped in posturing, and hot or cold sabre-rattling, against each other for twenty years. It would not be inconceivable that a regime change in Iraq may see a cooling of antagonism in Iran and calm the whole region (or, conversely, may increase antagonism in Iran).

Peter Rodman suggested that the whole area is too complex to make hypotheses: 'It is hard to predict. Since the fall of the Shah you have had an Iraq problem and an Iran problem and neither has been a fit partner for us against the other . . . ' Apart from during the Iran-Iraq war when the US gave Saddam a great deal of support!

Mr Rodman agreed: 'We did support Iraq – that's true – because we didn't want to see Iran defeat Iraq. This is all hypothetical; but if there were a change in Iraq it would have interesting reverberations within the region. Iran is going through an internal crisis because of its own dynamics; a revolution that is decaying, a regime that has lost its legitimacy. It would be hard to predict what effect external events would have on it. US policy has, at least at the beginning of the year, been very forthright about Iran. There is disillusionment with the (so-called) reform forces, which seem to have failed. The regime seems to be discredited in the eyes of the Iranian people. We are identifying ourselves with the people, who seem ready to throw out the whole lot – not ready yet perhaps, but there is considerable ferment.'

One country that might have made the shortlist if it hadn't been defeated in short order was Afghanistan. The Assistant Secretary saw this as a positive template for the war against terrorism – an enemy that was soundly routed and a basic governmental structure and stability achieved by, and for, the Afghans.

Even better, this has been done without a massive deployment of troops and the expectation of a lengthy stay. 'We are managing this with a modest US presence, and an even smaller international presence, and we are managing it with a light touch precisely because we don't want to be "occupiers". The Afghans have to learn their own political processes and it is difficult, but they may be doing better than people give them credit for,' commented Mr Rodman.

The fear of being 'occupiers' seemed to worry Mr Rodman when it comes to military operations. The model would appear to be short surgical operations that don't involve nation building. The Balkans, where the West has been welcomed as anything but occupiers, seems to be the opposite of what US policy would want to be.

'The Balkans are a success from one point of view, but on the other hand how many decades must we keep military forces there? Is it really a success if the region is permanently dependent on some outside force? This is what we ask ourselves. We don't want to destroy something that has been achieved, and we take our alliance obligations seriously, but there is an issue that if places are stable only with our presence, then in how many places can we do this? The US and Secretary Rumsfeld feel strongly about this. It is only going to feed isolationism in this country if, every time we do something internationally, we are stuck in that place forever. Take the example of the tiny forces in Sinai: the mission has been accomplished, there is stability there, but there is a dependency on an American presence at a certain level. We want to continue the US presence there, but at a lower level. It cannot be that any time we do something we cannot extract ourselves. It is much healthier for the American people to know that when we engage somewhere there is a mission that can be accomplished and doesn't become a permanent burden on us. That is part of our reluctance. We are still a global power and we are engaging ourselves in lots of new and interesting places, but it cannot be that every time we touch something we are locked in at a high level for perpetuity.'

Conduct of the War – Overwhelming Iraq

An overview of the land, sea and air operations – John Chisholm

It is tempting to see the Second Gulf War (Operation Telic/Operation Iraqi Freedom [OIF]) purely in the light of the First Gulf War (Operation Desert Storm) some twelve years before. Certainly, being the last high-intensity conflict, in the same place against the same enemy, led many commentators before the war to expect a re-run of Desert Storm with added technology and with the objective of removing Saddam Hussein's regime instead of liberating Kuwait – an objective that some thought should have been adopted the first time around.

The legacy of Desert Storm is clearly apparent in many of the following pieces. General Claude Christianson, for example, uses it as a yardstick to measure much of what the US Army logistics chain managed to achieve; the same can be said of Brigadier Graham Binns's comments on the agility of British deployments. Nevertheless there were key differences that weighed on the minds of planners and commanders resulting in a number of significant departures from Desert Storm and these too emerge from the essays.

In the first place, there was a significantly different objective. In 1991 the liberation of Kuwait was a clear and tangible aim that had brought together a broad coalition. Although the breadth of nations involved provided planning difficulties, the strategic solution to liberation was startlingly simple: a massive air campaign lasting over a month, a 'wave of the matador's cape' by amphibious forces against Kuwaiti beaches that tied down Iraqi forces and a massive deep hook that sliced through the demoralized Iraqi conscripts, forcing Saddam's forces to retreat from Kuwait or be totally encircled. Nonetheless, this plan brought the coalition command structure close to collapse, friendly fire incidents and real-time media put pressure on military organizations unused to being responsive to the press and a series of operational and logistic failures were confronted and muddled through.

In many ways OIF was not a fair test of coalition capabilities. Arguably this was the most benign situation an army has faced for a very long time. Saddam's forces were considerably weaker in 2003 than they were in 1991, both in terms of *matériel* and numbers. His air defences had been debilitated to almost nothing by the aircraft policing the no-fly zones and naval patrols were allowed to move into Iraqi waters to enforce the anti-oil-smuggling legislation. The coalition had been preparing for war with Iraq since 1991; certainly for the US he was 'likely enemy number one' and they had the advantage of a grateful Kuwait and friendly Gulf states from which to conduct their campaign – the refusal of Turkey and Saudi Arabia to play ball was an annoyance rather than an obstacle to overall success. The 1991 war had driven forward the revolution in military affairs (RMA) underway in the US, with its emphasis on networks, precision munitions and other forms of hi-tech warfare and Iraq was always seen as the most likely place for the next high-intensity conflict to take place.

In contrast, Saddam Hussein's forces had been filleted in 1991; much heavy equipment had been lost and the Soviet-inspired mass armour concepts from which the Iraqis drew their doctrine were fatally undermined. It was clear that Iraq could never hope to compete with the coalition on anything approaching even terms. That left the asymmetric threat – a concern that runs like a red thread through many of the articles on the war itself. For maritime forces the swarm-attack threat by suicide boats in the confines of the northern Gulf or around the Straits of Hormuz was real enough. Both Admiral Snelson and Captain Robinson-Brown both mention suicide boats found by coalition forces. Not all the volunteers 'melted away', as Snelson puts it. As the First Sea Lord points out, an attempt was made to bring some suicide boats down the Shatt al-Arab where the Iranians shot some up and the rest failed to make contact. Other efforts were foiled by accurate reconnaissance and helicopter attacks. The other threats posed to maritime forces, missiles and mines, proved less serious than in 1991. The elderly Silkworm missiles were used to bombard only Kuwait City rather than the coalition's ships. By operating far up in the northern Gulf, coalition ships and aircraft kept the Iraqi minelayers bottled up, constraining their ability to lay mines to the extent they had in 1991.

Land

For ground forces in particular the key asymmetric threat they identified was that of chemical and biological weaponry that Saddam Hussein was alleged to have possessed and which formed the key legal plank in the justification for the war. Responses to this varied. Detectors and other new technologies were deployed, but either seem not to have been fully trusted or there were not enough of them to go around. The Royal Marines are rumoured to have taken the 'Mk1 Canary' into the field with them on a purely unofficial basis. The US, more publicly, deployed chickens to detect potential attacks (nomenclature PCCD: Poultry Chemical Confirmation Device). In one of the war's more comic moments the chickens were released in response to a possible threat and several hours later started to keel over. Panic ensued as suits were donned and detection devices were deployed. Eventually a bright spark pointed out that the chickens had been out in the desert for several hours in the heat of the day and were keeling over with heatstroke. Such incidents underline the nervousness that the CBRN threat created. Plans for a potential attack were mixed. General James Mattis of the 1st MEF [Marine Expeditionary Force] declared that he was ready to fight his way through a CBRN attack if it came his way. More sober, and some might say realistic, assessments expected that an attack would slow coalition tempo but would probably cause more damage to Iraqi forces and would be devastating to civilians. The political damage would likely be far higher than the military.

All these factors, and many more, had to be incorporated into the overall plan. One initially surprising feature was the absence of a drawn-out air campaign. Certainly this seems to have been discussed. General Jim Dutton, for one, alludes to it, but was superseded by the 'shock and awe' concept: a short sharp blitz designed to undermine Iraqi morale and chop the head off the regime. This would also allow the element of surprise to be retained. This was vital for operations such as Dutton's assault. As Dutton points out: 'For a long time it was perceived that there was going to be a protracted air campaign that preceded the land campaign. We, as the land community, didn't really want that to happen. We knew that if we were going to seize the oil infrastructure intact then it depended on a large element of surprise. If we had an air campaign that lasted only a week it would still have given them plenty of time to make preparations and blow things up.'

Amphibious assault

Indeed the amphibious assault, well documented here, is a good case study of how planning develops. The coalition began with the idea that during the war significant refugee movements would take place and that the Kuwaitis were unlikely to accept them over the border (indeed they refused to accept Iraqi civilian wounded for the first few days of the conflict). This meant that the port of Umm Qasr had to be taken early and intact so that humanitarian aid could be delivered in quantity to southern Iraq. The next step was the clearing of the Khor Abd Allah; this would have to be undertaken to prevent ships being mined on the way to Umm Qasr. To protect the mine countermeasure effort (MCM) the west bank of the channel had to be secured to prevent Iraqi forces taking pot-shots at MCM assets. The solution was to land a single Commando unit to protect them. Consequently, as both Dutton and Snelson explain, the plan grew to incorporate the securing of oil fields to prevent an economic and environmental catastrophe, until what started as a small operation became a fairly significant and complex amphibious assault. For the Royal Navy and Royal Marines, this proved their evolving concept of operations and made clear the expeditionary capability being invested in was valuable and useful.

Air

Another weakness thrown up was the issue of close air support on the first day. With air support weathered in – despite claims of all-weather capabilities this is still a major factor in any aviation operations – the coalition was denied a significant force multiplier. The fact that Admiral West can say 'Our planners said that we would take a bit of naval fire support along just in case. The Americans said: "You won't need it." But our guys said: "Well, we'll just put it in there." What happened on the day? Weather was not very nice. There was no air' illustrates how overconfident airpower enthusiasts can be and underlines the scepticism that their claims can generate in other people.

The air power aspect to OIF, the weather notwithstanding, was almost entirely tactical. After the first night's 'shock and awe' effort to decapitate the regime and undermine the will to resist by a massive show of force, air operations concentrated on the tactical support of troops on the ground using, among other things, the B-52 and B-1B bombers originally designed with the ultimate strategic role in mind.

Command and control

Although it is unclear how well the command and control of the operation held up, it seems clear there was not the danger of imminent collapse that there was in 1991. For the British, though, rumours of problems surrounding the performance of UK 1 Division continue to circulate. Perhaps the most damning is the accusation that the three Brigade commanders got together to produce their own plan of attack because they were dissatisfied with the performance of the divisional staff. It is alleged that this led to a stand-up row between the Divisional Chief of Staff and the three brigadiers, during which they were accused of undermining the divisional staff's authority. Things do not seem to have improved as the campaign went on. Another rumour that refuses to die is that the orders to take Basra were hurriedly written by 1 Division staff after the city had fallen, rather than allowing it to go on record that Binns and Dutton had acted on their own initiative. In response to these and similar allegations the MOD offers: 'As you would expect in the run-up to any major operation, there was much discussion at the strategic and tactical levels of command in the planning to take Basra. We wouldn't discuss the details of military planning, but the outcome was a significant military success which speaks for itself.' In other words 'no matter how it happened it all turned out all right in the end'. Hardly a satisfactory assessment of how the UK can manage to put together an effective divisional staff.

Lessons

The degree to which the odds were stacked in the coalition's favour calls into question how many lessons that could be valuable in the future can actually be learned from this conflict. Certainly General Christianson, with his logistic challenges, was facing the twin enemies of time and distance – much of his experience is transferable to almost any conflict. On the other hand at no point did the Iraqi regular army seem to stretch the coalition forces militarily. There was no repeat of the symmetric tank battles of 1991, no effort to fight even when the terrain offered itself for defence, as Brigadier Binns makes clear. Instead the weight of attack, or rather credible resistance, seemed to fall on the shoulders of irregular forces. It is here that the coalition needs to take and absorb lessons, and it is here that these lessons could be conveniently skated over in the flush of military victory and post-war occupation.

General Christianson makes the point that: 'When you have a battle-field that looks like our battlefield, with its non-contiguous nature, you have operations here and there and I have to bring sustainment to them across an area that was secure yesterday but may not be secure tonight, how do you do that?' Successful hit-and-fade tactics on rear echelon units have several effects that are detrimental to the attacking forces. Firstly, they reduce security of supply by making it hard to define secure routes to front-line units (a term that is increasingly irrelevant in modern warfare). Secondly, they provide easy targets and cheap victories for guerrilla forces. This in turn brings popular and experienced leaders to the fore who can become future insurgent leaders in an occupation environment. Thirdly, they allow the enemy to inflict the one thing that Western countries have traditionally wished to avoid: casualties, or in some cases hostages. It is here that lessons need to be learned in terms of doctrine and procurement. The battlefield is a more fluid place, the enemy indistinguishable from the civilians, often quasi-independent units with loyalty to their immediate leader and an ideology rather than an effective chain of command. This is something frequently seen in post-war environments; in OIF it was seen during the short military campaign itself. There is, however, the danger that future procurement and training will focus on the sharp end without realizing that in modern warfare every end is a sharp end.

Desert Rat – Brigadier Graham Binns, Commanding Officer 7 Armoured Brigade, described the taking of Basra to John Chisholm in October 2003. The campaign displayed a great deal of necessary impro-visation at the brigade level.

JC: *As an infantryman by background, how did you feel having to handle all those unruly cavalrymen in 7 Armoured Brigade?*
GB: All army officers are skilled in the business of combined arms from a very early age. The fact that you have an infantry officer commanding an armoured brigade, with 116 Challengers in it, poses no problems. I did have more infantrymen than Royal Armoured Corps in my brigade and my experience with combined arms over a number of years helped me out.
JC: *How far down the food chain was your brigade HQ when it came*

to operational planning? When you were originally tasked with the job, was Basra already part of the plan or were you working on the Turkish option?

GB: Our planning started formally in September of last year [2002], so we were brought into the operational planning at a very early stage.The planning in September last year was focussed on the practicalities and the force required for an attack through Turkey into northern Iraq in concert with 4th US Infantry Division. That planning round took us through until before Christmas and generated an outline concept of operations and the ideal force structure. Then we went on Christmas leave.

Then we came back in the New Year and discovered that Turkey was looking less likely and the whole business of an attack from the north as a supporting attack to the main effort from the south was questionable. We came late into the game in planning with the US for an attack from the south and we were involved with planning alongside the US Marine Corps, mindful that they were much further down range than we were. So we were blistered on to their plan and we were offering discrete capability in areas where they were carrying risk with their plan. That was particularly the case in southern Iraq because the US Marines had come to the conclusion that they would have difficulty doing what was asked of them with the force structure that they had there, and they welcomed the UK involvement with ground troops in southern Iraq. We were always facing a challenge getting there in time for the likely start of operations, so our ability to contribute was constrained by our ability to deploy and to be ready for operations on their predicted start date. There was always doubt as to whether or not we would be ready, particularly if 7 Armoured Brigade would be ready.

That constrained what we could do, because – until we got there – there wasn't absolute confidence that we would be there in time for the start of likely operations. So our planning, and the planning for 7 Armoured Brigade, was constrained to such an extent that we were never likely to be in the first echelon of the attack in the planning stage. Instead we were given a task to conduct a relief-in-place in southern Iraq and the task of protecting the right flank of the US Marines in order to enable them to move towards Baghdad. So the tactical tasks that we were given were all related to enabling the US Marines to move across the Euphrates towards Baghdad. They were not particularly focussed on the holding of ground or the entry into urban areas. In fact the only urban area we needed to take was Umm Qasr, to secure the port. We did not, at an early stage, anticipate moving into Basra. Our task was to confront the Iraqi army coming out of Basra, which was threatening to interfere with the US Marines.

JC: *So you were not tasked to take and secure Basra?*

GB: The tactical tasks that I was given included securing Basra international airport, to block the Shatt al-Basra on the outskirts, to take over the security of the oil infrastructure, and we anticipated having to find, track and disrupt the elements of the Iraqi army that were deployed as far as the Shatt al-Arab north of Basra. In pure military terms, therefore, in order to achieve those tasks, there was no requirement at an early stage to enter Basra. Implicit in that, at a later stage, was a requirement to secure Basra. I always articulated the need to do that with the minimum of conflict. I certainly didn't expect to have to fight for Basra. There is a spectrum of conflict that we anticipated for Basra. At one end was a glorious entry supported by a possible uprising and we would be welcomed in – what I described as the Pristina option. At the other end of the spectrum was Stalingrad or Berlin. There was no way were we going to fight for Basra because that would defeat the purpose – we would have to destroy large parts of it – so my preference was to create the conditions which would allow an entry under relatively benign circumstances.

JC: *A siege has certain rules and characteristics, but how do you go about conducting a twenty-first century siege in the full glare of the world media?*

GB: I defined the effects that I wanted to achieve and then, as the situation unfolded on the ground, developed a concept of operations for delivering those effects. The effects I wanted to achieve were to isolate Basra: that is not to lay siege to it, but to isolate it, and to prevent people coming out of Basra and interfering with the US Marines. I also wanted to isolate it from Baghdad to prevent the regime maintaining its influence. I was focussed on removing the regime from Basra.

JC: *How did you hope to achieve that?*

GB: Incrementally. Basra was not the first problem. Al-Zubayr was the first problem: a town of 100,000 people. So we tested this concept on al-Zubayr. We decided that we would stand off, we would establish a series of checkpoints where we knew we were secure on the outskirts of the town and we would attract people to us. We were fighting a war amongst people and there were not hordes of refugees as expected. The tomato farmers were still bringing their crop in and normal life was continuing.

73

JC: *But that is a very eighteenth-century scene: warfare continuing alongside civilian life.*

GB: The taxi services were still working, telephones were still working, TV was working, radio was working and people were coming out of Basra to pay the doctors, nurses and teachers in al-Zubayr and so life was still going on. Our job was to separate the regime from normal life, and the regime as it manifested itself in al-Zubayr was militia and elements of the Ba'ath party. It was all about building up a level of intelligence to enable us to attack the regime precisely. We built up intelligence in a number of ways: firstly through contact with people, secondly through aerial surveillance and thirdly through the conduct of raids. Now all that combined to give us a good idea in al-Zubayr as to where the militia strongholds were and then we attacked them. In al-Zubayr it was easier than I thought it would be, and it happened a whole lot more quickly than I thought it would. So we transferred that principle to Basra, and Basra was slightly different. The militia fought a lot harder, they had access to armour and it was a far bigger problem in terms of scale. It was a progression of that concept of operations that allowed us to create the effects, but judging *when* we had achieved the effects was the difficult part.

JC: *There was the impression at the time that the fate of the city was uncertain: first there was an uprising, then there wasn't, maybe it was going to fall, maybe it wasn't . . . it was a nasty affair.*

GB: We found it difficult to get a picture of what was going on across the whole city. We had a reasonable understanding of what was happening on the outskirts and in the suburbs that we could see, but we really didn't have a clear picture of what was happening in the depths of the city. It took us a while to build up that picture, and I was concerned about being dragged into Basra before we were ready. I was conscious that if there was a humanitarian disaster then we would be pressured into going into Basra before the conditions were right. I also didn't really know how hard they were going to fight. Every time we went into Basra, on a raid, they fought. We were very well protected so we were not suffering casualties on the raids but they were fighting to such an extent that it was not safe to stay and hold ground. What we had to do was create the conditions where we could go in and hold ground, and secure lodgement. That took the time: it took time for us to build up the confidence in our ability to do that and to try to build up a picture of what was actually happening in the hinterland of Basra.

JC: *What was the tipping-point for Basra?*

GB: Early on in April we were targeting the regime. We got good intelligence that Chemical Ali and his henchmen were meeting in a particular house. So we attacked that house using air power, and I thought then that we may have missed him, but the intelligence subsequently confirmed that he had been in the house and that he had been killed, injured or escaped. What was apparent was that he had been removed: either he had been killed, injured or he had left and we started to get reports that the situation had changed as a result of that attack. The police were no longer on the junctions, many of the Ba'ath party officials had either gone home or they had left the city. People were on the streets and some looting had started.

That was the weekend 6–7 April. That led me to the conclusion that perhaps the conditions were right – as an aside, Monty's Pass won the Grand National, maybe fate was trying to tell us something – so on the Sunday morning two of the battle groups had planned coordinated raids and I said to the COs, 'If the conditions are right, stay, and if you judge the conditions are such that you can stay and then start exploiting, keep going.' The Scots Dragoon Guards attacked across one of the bridges, secured a lodgement, and then encountered some quite brutal fighting in the area of an Islamic college. We took casualties there and we had some difficulty, but in the centre the Black Watch attacked, met some resistance on the outskirts of the town, broke through that and then the CO decided that here was an opportunity. Exploiting that opportunity, he just kept driving. Before we knew it he was two or three kilometres in towards the centre of town. So we stood up the Fusiliers, who were in the north at that stage in the area of the airport, on forty-eight hours' notice to move. They attacked to secure some of the infrastructure in the north of the city. Again, there was some fighting, they took casualties, but they secured their objectives.

So by about early afternoon we were in and we were going to stay. What I had to do then was link up the various parts, because here is a city of 1.3 million people; we had three battle groups in there but it was not well coordinated and we really had three probes into the city. So we brought a battle group out of al-Zubayr and passed them through the Black Watch and sent them down to secure the heart of the city and the main government buildings and then to make sure that this regime had really gone. They did, they went into town quickly, secured themselves and so by early evening on that Sunday we had four battle groups relatively secure, most of the fighting was over, people were out on the streets welcoming us. I felt that we had done it then.

75

JC: *Can we rewind a little and look at the sorties the Iraqis made out of Basra – what did your intelligence indicate to you? What do you think they were trying to achieve?*

GB: The first question is, why was there no real defence? The terrain lent itself to defence. One point of view is that they were expecting a larger gap between the start of the air campaign and the use of ground forces. Therefore they had not deployed to their battle positions nor had they prepared a positional defence, because to do so would have required them to expose themselves to air. So that is one point of view. Another point of view is that their intention was to delay, to control and to cause attrition, knowing that we had overwhelming force and that they couldn't hold ground anyway. There is some evidence of an intention to delay, there were some makeshift efforts to prepare some demolitions on the bridges, but they were not particularly professional. 51st Division, who were in the south, withdrew and dissolved into Basra, taking some of their armour with them.

What we think happened was that those elements of the Iraqi army fell back into Basra and then hard-line elements of the regime turned them round and ordered them to go back out. They coerced them into fighting and they coerced them in a number of ways: threats of physical violence, holding their families hostage, that kind of thing. Coercion resulted in one or two foolhardy attempts to retake bridges and to possibly retake the airport. So it was a culmination of all of those things that resulted in one or two armoured columns coming out of Basra, but in so doing they played to our strengths because we were able to sit back on the bridges and kill them at longer range and we could fight much better than they could at night. They were also moving across this diffi-cult terrain. So the one or two armoured columns coming out were dealt with very quickly indeed. There were also a number of dismounted probes and in fairness they were quite professional; these were people crawling a kilometre and a half on their bellies in an attempt to close up with us and cause us casualties. Because we were aggressively patrolling forward between the Shatt al-Basra and Basra we picked up on them. It was an interesting few days: it was almost siege warfare. People did criticize us, saying that the reason we were raiding and patrolling was in order to maintain the offensive spirit until we could find something better to do, and there was a bit of that. But in maintaining that offen-sive spirit we gathered intelligence and I got greater clarity about what we had to do in order to achieve what I wanted.

JC: *How did you fare as a customer of logistic support? As you said, the planning was a little bit rushed because you had to switch quickly from Turkey to the south.*

GB: You never get everything you need, and it was a rush, and there are a number of lessons that come out of our ability to sustain people. The headline is that we moved the same number of people and a similar amount of equipment, not quite as much ammunition. In broad order terms we deployed the same amount this time as we deployed to the Gulf last time and we did it in half the time. So in terms of our agility in getting the force there it was pretty impressive. But that masks the fact that there were problems. Our principal problem was our inability to know where things were in theatre. That is because we do not have a robust system for tracking our logistic *matériel* and all our equipment. We were being told, and we knew, that things had been delivered into theatre but it was not that easy to find them. Once we had found them it was not that easy to deliver them to a point where we could get to them. So I felt that we were carrying a lot of logistic risk. That didn't constrain my thinking but it was always there in the background. We were carrying risk with personnel equipment, we were carrying risk with NBC protection and we were carrying risk with spare parts.

JC: *Humanitarian relief operations are increasingly happening along-side war fighting. At the brigade level you are fighting the enemy, policing rear areas and providing basic humanitarian relief. What sort of strain does this put on a BHQ having to perform all of these disparate tasks?*

GB: I am not sure we did all of them that effectively. I am not sure that we were structured for anything other than the war fighting bit. We had done some planning in the so-called post-war, post-conflict, but we were expecting a humanitarian crisis, which didn't occur. We were expecting that our main effort in phase IV would be sustaining life through the delivery of food. That wasn't required. There are apocryphal stories that we were out and about delivering humanitarian daily rations in al-Zubayr and people turning round and offering us fruit because they thought that that is what we ate – the humanitarian daily rations. We'd done some planning but we had done the wrong kind of planning, and we had to switch very quickly to what people actually required and what people really wanted: the immediate benefits of liberation, to live their lives to a better standard than under the regime. What we had to do was turn the water back on, turn the electricity back on and get fuel supplies running. That's not something that an armoured brigade has the im-mediate ability to do. So although we could think it through in the concept stage we had difficulties when it came to getting to grips with the practical realities of running a city of 1.3 million people. That was a major challenge

JC: *Former Ambassador Timothy Carney, who was a member of Jay Garner's team, says the lack of intelligence about who was a member of the Ba'ath party was remarkable. The upshot being that the people who knew where everything was and how it worked were, in many cases, the people you least wanted to deal with – that caused some problems early on.*

GB: Indeed. We couldn't deal with the Ba'ath party, we were worried about the tribes; we tried to target the middle-class professionals, and with limited success. I had early meetings with the head of the chamber of commerce; he wouldn't have been head of the chamber of commerce and not had links with the Ba'ath party, but at least he was someone who had a business mentality and (probably) had a personal interest in moving things forward. So we had to deal with people we were not comfortable dealing with in the first few days and weeks in order to give us an 'in', and in so doing we got the reaction of others. We watched those reactions and allowed them to shape our views. That eventually turned us towards people we could deal with in the longer term. I was always conscious that we were entering a whole new period, and I think we got away with it for the first couple of months. But then, examine our failure to deliver real improvement, because that started to cause trouble. In the euphoria of liberation in those early days expectations were high but the damage to the infrastructure, not caused by the war but by a lack of investment in the infrastructure over the years, proved incredibly difficult to put right. I'm not aware that people died because of our failure, but it was difficult to sustain, and there were water shortages and there were queues for fuel. There weren't food shortages because it was summer, it was harvest, and people were bringing in food supplies from the rural areas – plus they had food supplies from the World Food Organization – and that prevented starvation. They were heady days really, there was a sense of euphoria, we were conscious that we were in a honeymoon period and we tried our best to embark upon the process of rebuilding. We created a rather ad-hoc police force and within the first week or so we got the police back on the streets and we opened up the police stations. We'd sustained part of Basra and we had embarked on dialogue with the locals and started to put in place the foundations for a structure, but we got some of it wrong.

JC: *During the operation if you had to choose one moment that had the greatest impact on you, what would that be?*
GB: First casualty. It was an adventure to go into the desert, it was an adventure to take this huge armoured brigade overseas, it was wonderful fun training this armoured brigade, and it was fantastic getting it ready for war. There was a real sense of buzz about it at the beginning. But I had never been to war – I'd been in a war – but I'd never been to war, and the reports of the first casualties changed everything. And suddenly one realized the seriousness; it is no longer a Boy's Own adventure, suddenly it becomes very real. So reports of the first casualties, and then knowing that we had had soldiers killed, that was the thing.

Allied amphibious assault – Major General Jim Dutton,
Commandant General, Royal Marines, on planning for the al-Faw amphibious assault. Interview with John Chisholm in January 2004. Dutton was responsible for the biggest British amphibious operation since the Falklands.

The war in Iraq brought the Royal Marines' amphibious capability to the fore yet again. Unlike the British land forces, the Royal Marine amphibious force was always intended to go to the south of the country, but during the initial planning it became clear that there was going to be some form of amphibious operation. Major General Jim Dutton was then Brigadier commanding 3 Commando Brigade, and his formation was clearly going to be involved in the early stages, but when did planning actually start for him?

'It started from our point of view in late August early September 2002. That is when we first got wind of any involvement. At that point participation was going to be at a fairly low level with a single Commando unit on amphibious shipping with the necessary support shipping. This was for the specific task of protecting the northern flank of the Khor Abd Allah waterway (KAA) leading up to Umm Qasr and we allocated 45 Commando to the task. We did a proper estimate, along with Commodore Amphibious Task Group (COMATG), about what was involved and what the actual requirement was.

'It became increasingly clear that there was the need for a larger force. There were a number of reasons why this happened. First, we did the estimate and realized that the ratios had changed, because there was an enemy armoured division in and around Basra (the 51st) that had previous experience of dealing with forces on the Al-Faw peninsula, notably against the Iranians in the Iran-Iraq war, so consequently they knew the country. They were obviously a potential threat to any amphibious forces deployed on the al-Faw. Secondly, there was the recognition that the Iraqis could blow the oil terminals, pouring crude oil under pressure into the northern Arabian Gulf, causing a huge environmental catastrophe. This was coupled with a concern for the economic future of Iraq because the engine for the reconstruction of post-war Iraq was always going to be oil.

'Tied into that was the seizure of Umm Qasr because there was, for quite a long period, a feeling that the al-Faw operation might be separate and some time earlier – before the main attack. Umm Qasr was on the boundary (between the amphibious forces and land forces) and there are always problems on the boundary between zones of command.'

In early, surely not?

The whole idea of going in well before the major land offensive would initially seem like a risky business – after all, there was little in the way of a beach, and on-shore sustainment would have to be by way of helicopter support until Umm Qasr could be opened up – which certainly did not happen quickly in the real event. Was this a realistic option?

'That is a difficult question to answer. There were so many variables. For a long time it was perceived that there was going to be a protracted air campaign that preceded the land campaign. We, as the land community, didn't really want that to happen. We knew that if we were going to seize the oil infrastructure intact then it depended on a large element of surprise. If we had an air campaign that lasted only a week it would still have given them plenty of time to make preparations and blow things up.

'This, as a precursor operation, though, was rather separate to that argument. It was seen as something that we could do and *then* the main event could take place. Remember, the Americans, initially, were not sure – and even at the last minute were not 100 per cent sure – that we were going to take part for political reasons. In light of that they always had to have a plan in the back of their minds that allowed them to go without allies.

'All these reasons led to a bigger involvement alongside a genuine UK desire to be seen to do more. Of course the UK main effort had been assigned to the north [the Turkey option] so the amphibious element was always going to be a small part of the overall UK effort. As the autumn

80

wore on it was becoming more and more apparent that, whatever else happened in the north, it wasn't going to include British ground forces. The decision was then taken to switch the main effort to the south, but that was not finally taken until later and I was not made aware of it until 6 January.'

From north to south

In fact the shift from north to south was a major factor in UK planning, and meant that some rather hurried decisions had to be taken. Brigadier Graham Binns of 7 Armoured Brigade claimed that he was not tasked to start on the southern option until after Christmas. How did the sudden arrival of a divisional HQ and two further British brigades impact on the planning by the marines?

'I first went to Kuwait with the chief of staff just before Christmas,' General Dutton said. 'While we were there we set up a planning meeting for a large staff group, around fifteen officers, to go to San Diego on 2–6 January. In fact it was while we were there that I got the news and got a message from Major General Brims (GOC 1st Armoured Division) to the effect that he was going to hold a planning meeting the following weekend, in Germany, to which all UK brigade commanders were invited. That was quite late in the day.

'Of course the involvement of 3 Commando Brigade was always as a brigade-minus not as a full brigade,' General Dutton said. '45 Commando had originally been allocated to the mission, later they were unallocated – by me – and 40 Commando was allocated instead. We had to produce a company for the firefighters' dispute and the only sensible way of doing it, without going into detail, was to take it from 45. We were also tasked to provide two large companies to do Special Forces work. The deal from the Americans was that if the UK produced a brigade headquarters, two commando units and all the combat support that came with it, then they would attach 15th Marine Expeditionary Unit (MEU) to the brigade in order to be able to do a coordinated Umm Qasr/al-Faw operation – which made sense.'

The trouble with beaches

To do a beach landing you need a beach, and there wasn't one that really deserved the name in southern Iraq, although the grandiloquently named 'Red Beach' was identified as the most likely place to bring anything ashore other than by helicopter. Like all amphibious assaults, there were both foreseen and unforeseen problems.

'The critical thing that was planned from the very beginning was the landing,' General Dutton explained. 'We started studying maps and charts in September last year and it was immediately apparent that there was no such thing as a beach. We knew this from historical data taken ten years ago but then, of course, the situation was slightly easier for amphibious operations because they were potentially going to land in Kuwait. That was enemy held territory but there are beaches that could have taken conventional landing craft.

'The fact that there was no beach was a huge constraining factor from the outset. This was essentially an operation from the air with a possibility of using American hovercraft and our own small hovercraft. As planning developed I became more and more concerned about the weather – the possibility of not being able to do helicopter operations but at the same time still having to do the operation anyway.

'Relatively late on we had a plan for going up the Shatt al-Arab in small assault craft all the way into Umm Qasr itself. Now nobody really wanted to do that.'

It is hardly surprising nobody did, with UK forces not really equipped for riverine operations, a potential mine threat, and if the weather was poor, then no air cover. It would have been enough to make the most hardened marine blanch. There was also another plan, put forward by a Kuwaiti officer with contacts in the shipping trade, to slip troops up the river in dhows under the noses of Saddam's forces.

Thankfully none of these more interesting planning variants had to be adopted. As General Dutton explained: 'We never really got political clearance for the use of the Shatt al-Arab, but I was always very conscious of the fact that we were a small, although a very important, part of this vast plan by General Franks. Not wanting to be apocalyptic, but when General Eisenhower spotted the gap in the weather for the 6 June and said 'go' he didn't mean 'go if the weather in the channel looks all right to brigadier so-and-so and commodore somebody else'. So when Franks said 'go' then we had to go, one way or the other. If that meant going without helicopters then that meant that we had to have a fallback position. Of course the ultimate, and very imperfect, fallback position would have been to take Umm Qasr and force a crossing from there to the other side, put troops ashore using LCD ferry, and then advance down from there. But was that going to achieve the aim of seizing the oil infrastructure intact? Certainly not, because we would have lost surprise.

'So we had a base plan, using helicopters, which is the one we essentially used in the end but we had about fourteen contingency plans for the various "what ifs?" The weather was significantly worse in the first few days of March than historical data suggested it should have been. I think we were told that there would be three days in the month of March when we would not be able to fly helicopters. By the end of the first week we'd had five of them.'

Dealing with the opposition

Apart from obstacles that Mother Nature might have put in the way, there were also the Iraqis to worry about. A series of potential threats to an amphibious operation had to be considered. Given the very risky nature of amphibious assaults these were carefully considered.

'We were very conscious of their air defence capability,' General Dutton said. 'Manpads and heavy machine guns can be particularly devastating against unprotected helicopters. We had a very comprehensive Istar package and we tried to produce the most detailed Istar picture we could on the al-Faw peninsula and the southern end of Basra. The actual assault itself, which was led by the US Navy Seals, was preceded by a ten-minute intense bombardment. This principally consisted of JDAMS dropped from aircraft on to the known positions. There were also two AC-130 gunships.

'Nevertheless, we reckoned that we had it covered. If they opened fire with their air defence weapons then they would only fire once – then we would be able to take them out. Of course we had to accept the damage that they might do in that interval. We did our utmost to determine where the threat might be. The plan was, having inserted 40 Commando behind the Seals, to concentrate on the task of capturing the oil fields. I wanted to put in 42 Commando to act as a buffer, as north flank protection, so that if there were any interference from Basra or the northern end of the peninsula then there would be a Commando unit there to take that on. Their landing, preceded by a ninety-minute artillery bombardment from guns positioned on Bubiyan Island and naval gunfire support, was largely undirected, unobserved fire. We hit known enemy positions. It also was directed against poor Iraqi morale. So if, as we believed, there were a lot of deserters and conscripts who were not loyal to the regime, then it would encourage them to give up more quickly.'

Best laid plans

As usual, and to nobody's surprise, things went wrong. What was more surprising for General Dutton was that, apart from the lack of air support due to the weather, far less went wrong and casualties were far lighter than he had anticipated.

'The only thing that went wrong was that some US Navy Seal desert patrol vehicles got bogged in. They landed on fairly soft mud and that caused a problem because we couldn't get the helicopter off. I was watching all this on a monitor back at headquarters. The aircraft sat on the ground for what seemed like an inordinate amount of time and then we got a message in the chat room to say that they had got bogged in and they were having difficulty getting the vehicle off the ramp. The only other thing that went wrong was that on one of the 40 Commando designated landing sites, one we had selected from aerial photographs, was a road. This was not apparent from the photography. This road had lampposts and we had to wait until they were blown up by the assault engineers so the helicopters could land. In terms of timing, by my recollection, it was almost perfect.'

There was also the helicopter crash which created problems but, given the scale of the operation and the risks undertaken, the Royal Marines were very aware that they had got off lightly.

Working with the Leathernecks

The British are well-used to working under US overall command, but it is unusual to have such large formations as a US Marine MEU under a British brigade HQ. This was something of a novelty. How did the Americans fit in to the overall British command structure and culture?

'The press has made a lot of this,' General Dutton admitted, 'harking back to the Second World War and so on. We have been practising procedures with the USMC, certainly for as long as I have been in the Royal Marines and indeed longer. There is no doubt about it: we are structured differently and we have different communications systems. Having said that, we understand how each other is structured and we are able to communicate between ourselves quite well. I met the C/O of 15 MEU on 4 January while they were still in San Diego and we did a lot of cross-training when they arrived in the Gulf. I gave them orders in the same way as I gave orders to the rest of the brigade units. They went away and did their own estimates and then briefed back along with joint war-gaming and planning.

'I could not utilize them as I utilized 40 and 42 Commando: apart from anything else they were 2,000 strong. They were a huge organization that was used to operating together. That was fine because the scenario for this particular operation lent itself to that: we had Umm

Qasr and the area up to the north as far as the al Zubayr naval base and port was a separate discrete task with a fairly well-defined waterway between it and the al-Faw peninsula. That fitted quite nicely with the structure we had. We also didn't break up their orbat very much. We took the guns, the M198 155 mm, because of their extra range so we could cover more of the al Faw, but in exchange we gave them an AS90 battery which they were delighted with. The AS90 had slightly less range but it had far greater mobility and a much higher rate of fire so they were very happy.

'The brigade reserve for the al-Faw operation was the battalion landing group from 15 MEU, available to fly in, in their helicopters, at call. So it worked extremely well. They, of course, have got Siprnet and we haven't. The war was fought on Siprnet and we had access to it at various levels; controlled access with the Americans, quite rightly, controlling it. We made all that work. If you ask me: would it have worked more easily if we had a fully compatible IT system? – then the answer is yes. Then again we don't have a compatible IT system across our own forces anyway.'

No CAS

One critical element that was missing was the close air support (CAS), seen as vital in most staff planning to support an amphibious landing. Although assured by the US that it would all be there when needed, the Royal Navy still insisted on some ships available for shore bombardment. This was a helpful addition when the planes couldn't fly and reliance was placed on good old-fashioned artillery bombardments and frigates forming line-ahead and bombarding targets inland. Still, it created other problems too, and the issue of CAS was a bit of a running sore with the brigade HQ.

'Yes. The weather had the greatest impact on 42's insertion when it was aborted,' General Dutton explained. 'The difficult and annoying thing was that the weather over the target was quite reasonable, but the weather in Kuwait was appalling, with very high winds and smoke from the oil fires and dust storms. I never in any way felt, despite claims in some parts of the media that we were short of the necessary fire support.

'The Americans have a very good system for the provision of air support and it is completely centrally controlled. It is then allocated according to the area of greatest need. That can be incredibly frustrating if you have some good targets and you want assistance from the air but you are not considered the area of greatest need so you don't get the close air support. But it does mean that it is controlled at the highest level and it is allocated to the tasks as necessary. When we really needed close air support we got it. The most frustrating element of this was we had planned the insertion of 42 at dawn on 21 March using UK helicopters but we wanted to send US Cobras in first to sanitize the landing site. We had fired on the area with artillery some eight hours previously so we really needed to clear them again. We requested them several times and each time they were re-directed elsewhere. On the sixth time, I think, they arrived. It was frustrating, but in operations of this kind issues like this are bound to arise,' General Dutton concluded.

Over the horizon?

The Royal Marines clearly undertook a risky opposed assault in less than ideal conditions and successfully carried it off. Things will likely improve, with the entry into service of HMS *Albion* and HMS *Bulwark* followed by the Bay class, providing greater capability for UK amphibious forces. The Iraqis were, though, not particularly adventurous in their use of forces and their command and control system was already in a parlous state before the war began. It is hard to counter any offensive if you have no way to direct your forces above the company level. The Iraq planning, and the criticisms levelled at UK 1 Division's HQ in particular, should provide us with plenty of lessons to learn, but if the UK is going to continue undertaking opposed assaults every twenty years or so then this is a capability that must be kept sharp.

Holding the Red Card – Rear Admiral David Snelson,
Commander Royal Navy contingent, Operation Telic, talked to John Chisholm about operations in the Arabian Gulf.

JC: *Before Operation Telic was announced there was an awful lot of shadow boxing taking place. Did this uncertainty in any way hamper the actual deployment?*
DS: I was out in the Middle East from August last year as the deputy coalition commander for Operation Enduring Freedom, so I was acting in that role at the 5th Fleet Headquarters anyway, and the Operation Telic requirement came in on top of that. Although the naval task group (NTG) '03 forces had prominence, they were by no means all of the forces. There were quite a lot of maritime forces already in the region: the mine countermeasures forces were already there before the

amphibious task group even sailed from the UK and the normal frigate and destroyer forces doing the Iraqi oil-smuggling patrol were already there. NTG '03, led by *Ark Royal*, was beefed up in terms of its capability – it had an amphibious bit bolted on to the side – as it sailed in that direction it could be diverted into the Gulf to add to the forces that were already there. The forces that we needed were characterized by four capabilities: Tomahawk precision strike capability, the mine counter-measures (MCM) capability, the amphibious capability and the escort capability. Actually, Tomahawk, MCM and some of the escorts were already in place.

Now, the preparation in terms of people; those that were out in theatre already knew that there was a possibility of war against Iraq and those that were sailing in the amphibious task force were well aware that was possible. The difficult thing, from the commander's point of view, was making the necessary logistic preparations in a period when the government was not able to give complete clearance and sanction to talk to contractors and others outside the immediate defence community, because the government, politically, didn't want to declare its hand at that moment. That's one of the dichotomies of modern warfare, where we contractualize our support, whether or not you can bring the contractors in on what you are doing actually makes it quite difficult preparing. Now, that wasn't a problem that I personally faced directly, that was a problem for the people in Fleet Headquarters and Defence Logistics Headquarters. Preparing the people was not difficult. People in the armed forces know that they might have to go into conflict.

JC: *The staff itself had a great deal of experience with Saif Sareea, and then in operations in support of activities in Afghanistan, so it must have been a fairly smooth shift into a part of the world with which they were very familiar.*

DS: Yes, it was a smooth shift, and that was one of the benefits of having moved a small headquarters ashore into the 5th Fleet Headquarters soon after 9/11 – that was post Exercise Saif Sareea but before the Afghanistan operation. Testament to that is the decision that has subsequently been taken, and in fact has just been enacted as we speak, to have a permanent commodore in Bahrain. It gives us a presence in the CentCom command structure. Of course, it brought us into a slightly different era of command and control. Traditionally, we have envisaged the maritime component being based at sea in a command platform.

JC: *I spoke to Commodore Richard Leaman earlier this year and he said that you had got it all working fine at sea but you still had to test the ability to take it ashore.*

DS: Technology in the last two years has moved on a lot, as has C2 at the component level. It is now done by three or four fundamental devices; I have just exercised it in this way in Exercise Northern Light. The first of these devices is the use of web pages, the second is email, the third is chat rooms and the fourth is telephone connections. Fifth, in many ways, is traditional signal messaging, although the volume of signals is still high, but even that is still handled inside the emails and web-based broadcasts. And all of those things now arrive at your location multiplexed over a high bandwidth satellite or landline connection. So from my perspective I can do much the same thing afloat in *Invincible* as I have just done in Northern Light, as I can do ashore in Bahrain. You give me a bare room, a satellite dish outside the door – which is what we had in Bahrain – flood-wire the room with fibre optics and plug in our deployable laptops and our telephones, and you have yourself an MCC [maritime component command] headquarters. A bit of a sweeping generalization.

JC: *I'm sure it can't be that simple . . .*

DS: It isn't quite that simple but that, fundamentally, is it. You don't have to be at sea to be a maritime component commander.

JC: *Are there any advantages to being at sea compared to being on land?*

DS: It depends on command relationships and the scenario. A very important factor for me as to where I go is my connectivity with the joint force commander and the other component commanders. In Iraqi Freedom, or Op Telic, being co-located with the American maritime component commander and having the benefit of his very good American communications, video telecomms and so on, gave me an influence on the plan and a presence within the organization which allowed the UK maritime component command's presence to be felt. On the other hand, if you are into war-fighting at sea and a complex rules of engagement scenario, which I was to an extent in Exercise Northern Lights, you may wish to be much closer to the action at sea. You may wish to have much closer control over minute-by-minute events, particularly rules of engagement (ROE) constraints which put you right at the edge of political sensitivity and you want to have very close control over what your maritime commanders are doing. If they overstepped the mark, then the UN's case, say, could be totally undermined by some intemperate action. Then you might feel that you are better placed at sea in closer contact with your subordinate commanders. It is horses for courses. What technology has given us are options, and that's great.

JC: *Despite the overwhelming preponderance of the US Navy in the operation, Britain was still able to pull off a few showstoppers, notably the amphibious landing on the al-Faw peninsula. How was this amphibious operation developed in the overall plan and how nerve-racking was it?*

DS: The amphibious operation was part of the planning right from the outset, but it was actually in support of mine countermeasures. One of the specified tasks, which were identified very early on, was to open the port of Umm Qasr for humanitarian aid. If we were to open the port we were almost certainly going to have to do minehunting in the Khawr Abd Allah waterway, because it was very likely that the Iraqis were going to lay mines – they had done it before, they had mine stocks, and indeed they did it. When we looked at that task, the left bank of the Khawr Abd Allah waterway was Kuwaiti territory almost up to Umm Qasr, but the right bank of course, the al-Faw peninsula, is Iraqi territory. So as we looked at it we said, well, we can't do mine countermeasures operations early on and we had to open the port of Umm Qasr quickly, because at that point it was envisaged that humanitarian aid would be a key consideration, we thought there might be a significant refugee problem. In the end that proved not to be the case but we had a plan for it.

It was quite clear that you could not put mine countermeasures vessels in the waterway if you had not occupied the ground on the right flank of the waterway. That is where the plan for an amphibious operation came from. In talking to the US Army and the US Marine Corps, were they going to occupy the al-Faw? No, their main effort was straight towards Baghdad. I discussed the options with Admiral Keating and looked at the options with what we were going to do with *Ark Royal* and *Ocean* – should we take *Ark Royal* as a fixed-wing carrier, should we take her as an LPH [landing platform helicopter]? We identified this particular task of guarding the flank of the MCMs as tailor-made for UK amphibious forces. So we decided to maximize our amphibious effort into those two ships and protect the flank of the MCM. That is where it started. The objective of the al-Faw operation subsequently became, firstly, to secure the oil infrastructure, and, secondly, to protect the flank of the MCM. As we did more detailed planning and came to study the al-Faw, it became obvious that there were some key oil pipelines there as well.

JC: *Hadn't we been here before in 1916?*

DS: I carried an article from a magazine with me around in my briefcase for a few months called 'Britain's bastard river war' – a rather curious title but it was all about paddle steamers and ships that had gone up the same waterway in the First World War when towns well up the Euphrates were captured from the Turks by a lieutenant and two stewards. Of course, subsequently, we got beaten back but, yes, we had been there before. But that was the origin of the amphibious operation. The second part of your question: were risks involved and was it high risk and had we considered risks? The answer is yes. However the risks of not doing it, that the oil infrastructure would be blown up and the northern Gulf would be polluted, would be disastrous from an environmental perspective, and also from a maritime operations' perspective. So we had to capture that piece of key territory in order to stop there being a disaster and protect the MCM operations. The question was: had we got the right forces to do it and what were the risks we were taking? That's probably the thing that would keep me awake at night: thinking about the risks to an airborne assault on a defended position. But we had an awful lot of combat power to counteract that and the fact that 3 Commando Brigade was coming under the tactical command of the US Marine Corps with its very sophisticated air-land cooperation – calling in close air support and so on – gave us confidence that we could deal with threats on the ground. Actually, close air support didn't play much of a part on the day because the weather was bad and traditional naval fire support and artillery were used more than anything else.

JC: *So we're back in 1916 again . . .*

DS: Except we are a lot more accurate! We could put the shells exactly where we needed them and they were very effective both against the shore and further inland.

JC: *What sort of defensive operations did the Iraqis try to adopt, if any?*

DS: My perception was that, while individual Iraqi units down at platoon strength or lower put up a good defence and had to be countered, there was no joined-up defence. The heavy armour the Iraqis had in Basra could, in the conventional sense, have posed a very significant threat and pushed us back off the al-Faw if it had been manoeuvrist in any way. But they weren't manoeuvrist. A combination of the Airborne Early Warning (AEW) Sea Kings with their new radar, which is incredibly effective against ground targets, and the rather old, but still very effective, Lynx Tow, gave the Royal Marines the ability, supported from the seas, to counter Iraqi armour moving south out of Basra. We could detect it with the AEW Sea King, an extraordinary role for them and never envisaged, and you could counter it with the Lynx Tow. So this screen of airborne interdiction protected the light forces on the al-Faw.

It did, for me, highlight the fact that there are key bits of hardware we didn't have in this operation – notably *Albion* and *Bulwark* – that ideally we needed. Although we had all the combat power we needed for ship-to-objective manoeuvre of getting the troops on the ground to take objectives on the al-Faw, what we lacked – without the help of the US Navy – was the heavy lift landing craft to follow up with heavy combat power on the ground. We were fortunate in that the enemy was not manoeuvrist, so we could do without it on this occasion.

JC: *You are on record as saying one of your major concerns was the asymmetric threat. This doesn't seem to have manifested itself in the way that some thought, so was this taken too seriously?*

DS: There is a known asymmetric threat in the region, as we have seen, because asymmetric attacks have occurred on the USS *Cole* and the *Limberg*, a French tanker, only a matter of months before. That was very much in my mind in terms of planning. Intelligence we had, much of which is still not in the public domain, about al-Qaeda's intentions to attack maritime targets, indicated to me very strongly that an attack at sea, through the choke points, was very, very possible and there were good indications. It didn't manifest itself because we took huge steps to make sure that al-Qaeda couldn't get close to us so that the deterrence effect of overt escort of all the merchant ships coming through had an effect. I know that our posture was recognized. The Royal Marines found suicide boats already rigged when we took position up the banks of the Shatt-al-Arab waterway. Now I suspect that this was a plan and people had been detailed off to do it – these were Iraqis not al-Qaeda – but the plan had not come to fruition and people just melted away and went home.

JC: *Did all the equipment hold up, or were there issues shaken out by the operation?*

DS: On the equipment front the navy was in pretty good shape. It had much of what it needed. We had rapidly to augment mine counter-measures (MCM) capability because of the shallow water operations, but that was fine, because we were doing something for which the MCM were not designed; we had identified the sort of thing we might want, and we were able to procure it just in time and it worked extremely well. Some areas of procurement which we had identified in the run-up to the operation we had not been able to afford but were able to procure. Things like night vision goggles and so on, done under urgent operational requirement [UOR] action. Purely from the perspective of an operational commander, I would have wished that we had that capability to start with and had trained with it for longer.

Some of the biggest advances we made were in connectivity, and I referred earlier to emails and web-browsers and so-on; of course that's all good, but in a coalition with three key nations who were doing most of the heavy lifting (the US, the Australians and us) you actually needed to be on a common system to be able to use chat rooms and emails in a seamless way. The development by the Americans of the coordinated wide-area network, sometimes called the coalition wide-area network, which is just a system that looks like any other modern IT system, was rolled out rapidly to all three coalition partners at sea to enable us to have seamless communications. That was an absolutely key thing and one of the things that I decided early on was to place my units under the tactical command of the American task force commanders so that we were operating in a joined-up way. One of the big issues in coalition operations is how we do this sort of thing and it worked well, although not without a lot of forethought and hard work.

Previously, we used to have to design our own software and that was very expensive; these days we can go to a commercial supplier and say, 'We need another set of Outlook Express, another server and put it in this encrypted compartment' and you've got yourselves the heart of a command and control system.

JC: *Clearly you were under US overall command; was there any friction on the maritime side or was it all totally smooth? Were there any incidents such as the 1991 disagreement over MCM deployment?*

DS: Integration was extremely good, and there was no friction in Bahrain, certainly not within the staff organization. We were embedded in their planning right from late August [2002]. On several occasions I took the daily morning NavCent briefing in Admiral Keating's place and the briefings were given to me as his deputy. I sat with him in every video teleconference with General Franks and the CentCom organization, so we were completely seamless in that respect. That was then reflected in the planning and the way we worked together. I had, of course, a national 'red card', if I didn't like what was being done with our forces, but I never had to use it. All we had to do was say, 'Well, we would do it this way' or 'Wouldn't it be better to do it that way?' and 'We are better at this' – it was those sorts of discussions. There was a lot of toing and froing to make sure that we didn't have fratricide or blue-on-blue, but modern email communications allow you to overcome those difficulties, in a way which would not have been possible ten or fifteen years ago.

JC: *The RN had an excellent opportunity in this operation to demonstrate its MCM skills, and in these circumstances – with the media crawling all over – a great deal of trust is placed in fairly junior officers.*

DS: There is absolutely no point in long screwdrivering what somebody is doing right at the tactical level and in the front line. You have to trust that the training is good, the equipment is good and that the mission command – that is the key thing – works. I had enormous confidence in the COs of the units, and in their training and preparation. Never did I feel that I needed a close control over what was happening.

JC: *HMS* Roebuck *had an equally interesting time and ran quite a few risks.*

DS: She had an important job to do. The northern waters of the Gulf had not been charted for a long time, somewhat to my surprise I had to admit; the American navy had no capability to do that and did not plan that capability in their force package. We had the capability and realized how vital it was. Actually, our interest was greater because our amphibious units were landing close in to the coast. *Roebuck's* survey boats were inside Iraqi territorial waters prior to the start of the operation, legitimately dealing with Iraqi oil smuggling under UN Security Council Resolution 661. Surveying inside Iraqi territorial waters was part of the international force mission, because it gave us greater operating freedom with the frigates. Nevertheless there was quite a lot of risk taking, but we had forces around, lots of helicopters and surface escorts.

JC: *Finally, if you had to pick a moment in the operation that most affected you, what would it be?*

DS: I think it would be the opening night of the campaign when the assault on the al-Faw happened. It had been my own idea to start with, something I had conceptualized myself, and I had been involved with the planning. My concerns were whether it was going to go smoothly or whether we were going to lose life on the initial assault. We did, but in a helicopter accident and not as a result of enemy action. It was an extraordinary experience, sitting in the NavCent command HQ and watching reports coming back in various chat rooms from different tactical commanders, all the while seeing our helicopters land in the dark and the troops running out of the back of them, and I could see all this live from an overhead feed.

Engaging the enemy more closely – Lieutenant Commander Mike Leaney RN, Lieutenant Commander Andy Swain RN and **Captain Roger Robinson-Brown RFA** on being on the front line.

The media coverage of Operation Telic, and particularly the naval aspect, focussed heavily on the big ships: the carriers and destroyers and the nuclear submarines and their land-attack capability. But, down at the coal face, individual ships, officers and ratings were making their contribution to the overall success of the operation.

HMS Roebuck

In theatre, long before the war began, the lightly armed survey vessel HMS *Roebuck* under the command of Lieutenant Commander Andy Swain, was sailing in the northern Gulf. *Roebuck*'s job was vital to the success of the mission, as the Commander pointed out: 'The mission profile was to provide the user with information about the battlespace so that they could see exactly what was available to them. There was very shallow water at the northern end of the Gulf but, as we surveyed it, we found that it was a lot deeper than was charted. This meant that people could get a lot more manoeuvrability for the larger ships and the MCMVs could get a lot closer.'

The northern part of the Gulf had been an area of operations for Western navies, but it had not been surveyed for a long time, much to everyone's surprise. 'The main channel had not been surveyed for forty years,' Lieutenant Commander Swain said. 'To the left of the channel (looking at it facing north) the water had not been surveyed for sixty years. There were a considerable number of wrecks, not only from the Gulf War of 1991 but also the Iran-Iraq war. These wrecks were quite large and were not fully charted and not necessarily in position where they had been marked on the chart.'

Roebuck and her captain were not averse to taking risks in order to get the vital data. Initially, *Roebuck* was operating under UN resolutions designed to prevent Iraqi oil smuggling. This didn't necessarily provide a great deal of comfort or protection when *Roebuck* and her survey boats were almost down the throats of the Iraqis. 'There was considerable risk,' Lieutenant Commander Swain admitted, 'and the first risk was actually navigational. Ships that had used this area previously – and we are talking about some very large tankers – had used the marked channel. Outside the channel there was little guide and we were probably the first ship in many years to go east-west across the channel rather than north-south. We needed to do that to provide more room for the force that was expected to operate in that area.'

There were also potential Iraqi threats. *Roebuck* was operating in well-known fishing areas. As the Commander said, 'Any dhow could have been loaded with explosives and used to ram the ship. When we first arrived I decided that two miles was the safe distance I would keep from any of them. Within the first two days we had hardly achieved any work because we were continually dodging fishing boats. We reduced it to a mile, and then to 500 yards and in the end we were as close as 200 yards.'

Defensive measures had to be taken by *Roebuck* herself. 'We started out by having to build a citadel,' Lieutenant Commander Swain said. 'We blocked off passageways, sealed doors with plasticine and everything else. There were wooden bungs in certain areas to provide three decks' worth of NBC protection: the bridge, the officers' flat and the NCOs' flat and galley. This was totally secure and could be used as an NBC haven or sanctuary in case of attack. We couldn't use it to fight the ship, but we could use it as a place to gather everyone together and then the ship could transit through a hostile NBC environment to safe water without the people being contaminated. Of course most of the ship would have been contaminated.'

Roebuck's heroics have brought their own reward. Lieutenant Commander Swain said: '*Roebuck* was actually expected to pay off in April, but due to our exploits in the Gulf the ship has now been extended to 2014 and they are already talking about what should replace *Roebuck* rather than just paying her off.'

Swims

Whilst *Roebuck* was busy laying the ground up in the northern Gulf, the Royal Navy was looking at the provision of humanitarian aid by sea in order to cope with the expected crisis. This would have to go through the port of Umm Qasr, and the Iraqis were expected to use naval mines against coalition naval forces.

Brought in to deal with one such mine challenge was Lieutenant Commander Mike Leaney. 'There are three aspects that you need to consider for this,' he explained. 'The first is the actual mine threats that would be used against us, and we had a pretty good idea of that from the previous Gulf War. The second thing is the environment that they were going to be used in. From fairly early on it was decided that we would use Umm Qasr for the delivery of humanitarian aid so it needed to be cleared. The weapons systems we currently had, that would cope against those types of mines in the Umm Qasr type environment, have limited effect. The second consideration was very poor visibility. Using our remote controlled mine disposal system [RCMDS] and our divers is difficult in poor visibility because we use video cameras and divers' eyeballs to identify the mines. The third thing is the tidal streams, because in much more than one and a half knots of tidal stream divers start struggling, and the same is true for the remote operated vehicle [ROV] system really. So the problem suddenly became much more difficult than it would have been in a coastal environment.

'So we came up with a shallow-water sweeping system and developed a remote control system for the boat. Given the mine threat we were against, and looking at the Umm Qasr waterway, that seemed like the best way to go.'

The system chosen, Swims, was an Australian design. Lieutenant Commander Leaney said: 'We did a review of all the in-service systems and all the off-the-shelf systems and, given the narrow dredged channel and the depth, we wanted a small system. That reduced the range of equipment available at a stroke, so there wasn't a great deal to choose from.

'At QinetiQ we did two things: we got hold of one of the Australian Defence Industry [ADI] mini-Dyad systems, and we made some noise-makers very close in specification to the Australian ones and carried out a series of trial exercises. They showed that sweep performance was what we were looking for in something like the Khawr Abd Allah waterway [KAA]. QinetiQ had already been working on a remote control system for small boats and it was a logical step to get that part of QinetiQ to look at the combat support boat, fit it and trial it. It all worked very well,' he said.

Unfortunately Swims is no longer with us. It is not going to be kept in service, as the Commander explained: 'It was procured under an urgent operational requirement and, as such, it is only supported for a year. One of the interesting factors was that we were embarked on HMS *Brocklesby*, the first minehunter up the KAA. From here we were sweeping ahead whilst she was hunting simultaneously. That is a capability that the Royal Navy hasn't achieved before. So with this very quick bolt-on system we could both sweep and hunt for mines at the same time, representing a step-change in MCM Ops. I am hoping that, in demonstrating that this sort of system is viable in estuarine-type operations, the

MOD will be looking at a new minesweeping system, not for 2016 but significantly closer.'

RFA Sir Galahad

Catapulted into the news for her humanitarian efforts, RFA *Sir Galahad* was the first ship into the port of Umm Qasr with humanitarian supplies. Captain Roger Robinson-Brown puts the choice of his ship to lead this effort down to luck.

'It was being in the right place at the right time,' Captain Robinson-Brown said. 'We had been in Kuwait a week previously and we had offloaded all of our combat stores for 3 Commando Brigade and the ship was empty and available. From my perspective I got the best job of the war.'

Although the approaches to Umm Qasr had been swept several times for mines, the approach was still tense. Captain Robinson-Brown said, 'We had two days' delay at the mouth of the river. The first day was due to weather: we had 45–60 knots that night. The next day, the two MCM craft ahead of me found two mines the night before we were due to transit. That delayed us an extra day while they made doubly sure that nothing else had been laid in our way. I had high confidence that anything that would have been in our way was found.'

The asymmetric threat was the key cause of concern for everyone and Captain Robinson-Brown was no exception. 'It certainly wore on the mind,' he said. 'The night before we entered the KAA, four suicide boats were located in the Shatt Al Arab waterway and they were pursued by aircraft. That certainly focussed the mind and with us already having been in the world's press by that time I wondered whether they had actually targeted us deliberately. Fortunately our intelligence was second to none and the capability to find them, track them and stop them all came together. They never got within twenty miles or so of us.'

Navigating down the KAA was an incredibly tortuous process, but Captain Robinson-Brown was able to weave his way through. 'We are blessed now with an outstanding satellite system that is clearly the best way for us to navigate. In a mine countermeasures lead through, with HMS *Sandown* in front of us, all I had to do was follow over her ground. Certainly the waterway itself is very, very indistinct for proper navigation marks. The main marks in the channel are the wrecks, and quite often the position of those can vary.

'The thing that brought it home to me that we were not playing games was the night before we were due to enter, finding those two mines, one of which was in the perfect position – if you had one mine that is where you would have put it to catch us. It had an effect upon the ship. Whilst I fully expected them to be 100 per cent professional it certainly upped the ante with my people.'

Interviews by John Chisholm in late 2003.

Showdown in the sun – Chief Warrant Officer Stacy Jeambert talked to Gwyn Winfield about biological and chemical warfare planning for the 1st Marine Division in Iraq. Jeambert was interviewed in August 2004.

During the first Gulf War there was the expectation of Saddam using his chemical and biological arsenal against allied troops. The destruction of his forces and the truly international aspect of the coalition against him frustrated any military or political pretensions he might have had. It was assumed by many pundits that now, with his back against the wall, he had nothing to lose from using them and everything to gain. It was not just the idle armchair speculators that had this thought; many military planners expected the use of what remained of his arsenal against their forces.

One of those planners was CWO Stacy Jeambert. He had been pulled from his previous unit, the 1st light Armoured Reconnaissance Battalion, and was placed on General James Mattis's staff to handle the NBC [nuclear, biological and chemical] decontamination and logistic plans. From the outside General Mattis, Commanding General of 1st Marine Division, was an interesting individual to watch: he had stated before the war that if his men were attacked by chemical or biological weapons he would fight straight through them. This was contrary to established Cold War NBC mores, where convention said you either sat tight and waited for the event to pass, or you went around the affected area. Attacking through a chemical, or biological, attack had always been warned against, and exercises that had been done that had a blue force attacking through a chemical attack had always resulted in high casualties. Politically the US is often seen as risk-adverse with their soldiers' lives, so to make the statement that any chemical/biological event was going to be fought through meant that the statement was cavalier, a major change in political policy, or part of an evolution in a new strategy of NBC defence.

Unsurprisingly it was the last, and one of the persons in charge of this new strategy was Chief Warrant Officer Jeambert. The major change that allowed this new strategy was a reappraisal of NBC weapons and the way they could be used in this conflict. 'This caused absolutely no problems when it came to planning,' said CWO Jeambert. 'For years I have known that while chemical weapons used in the right conditions, and in large enough quantities on the battlefield, could have devastating affects, I also believed that Saddam Hussein's army and any other army, with the exception of the former Soviet Union and the Republic of North Korea, did not have the ability, nor the capability, to launch such an attack. I felt that even if the Iraqi army did use chemical weapons against us, the amount of contaminated personnel and equipment would be minimal at best (one company out of a battalion was the worst-case scenario and I believed this would only happen once) and it would not slow us down. To this end, we ensured all units had an organic capability to conduct decontamination and we also had two additional decontamination teams that we could quickly manoeuvre to assist and speed the process; thereby getting the units back into the fight much faster. One team was an ad hoc platoon organized and established within 3rd Amphibious Assault Battalion (3rd AABn) and augmented by the 1st Marine Division NBC Defense Platoon.

'Why 3rd AABn?' he asked. 'Because they had the function of managing the roadways and movement of units throughout the AO, they controlled the priority of movement. So if a unit was contaminated and needed assistance, theoretically, 3rd AABn could stop all movement on the crowded roadways and push the decon team ahead to the contaminated unit. We also received a platoon, along with a support section, from the 101st Chemical Company. This platoon was very robust and could operate two decontamination sites at the same time and was capable of split operations, so both decon sites did not need to be in the same location. Additionally, during "Opening Gambit" of OIF we integrated six British NBC reconnaissance vehicles and six decon sections from the JNBC regiment of the British army. We worked with Lieutenant Colonel Patrick Kidd and his staff quite extensively to ensure his units were integrated with our units and were familiar with the division's scheme of manoeuvre.'

While there was much political speculation about what might be in Iraq's arsenal, this had to be seen in a military light: Saddam had to have a complementary delivery system for each agent. Without an effective dispersal method the threat to military forces was low. So while the US Marine Corps was expecting chemical weapons, mainly those used in the Iran/Iraq war – Sarin, mustard and VX – the biological threat was downplayed.

The chemical weapon threat was a real one, however, and to be the most effective would have been likely to be used at choke points or at large–scale gatherings – such as jump-off points or logistics dumps. One of the most likely choke-points to be hit was the river crossings, of which the Euphrates and the Tigris rivers are among the most daunting. 'I believed he would have used them to stop or slow advancing front line troops,' said CWO Jeambert. 'We thought he would employ them on four occasions: when we crossed the line of departure, when we crossed the Euphrates, when we crossed the Tigris, and when we closed in around Baghdad. Looking at it from Kuwait we thought that when we crossed the rivers that would be when he hit us, but when we got to Baghdad that he was definitely going to hit us then. I know for a fact, however, that our artillery took him out pretty rapidly and he didn't have a chance to get that much indirect fire on top of us.'

The worst chemical weapons fear would have been thickened, persistent agents over the few navigable bridges. This, combined with traditional attacks, would cause the US to slow their advance and force the attackers into physiologically draining IPE. CWO Jeambert admitted that this was the expected scenario: 'That was what we thought, if he was going to hit us that was where he was going to do it, and we had plans in place to conduct decontamination. When we crossed the border, in Opening Gambit, we worked with Lieutenant Colonel Kidd quite a bit and he came up with good strong decontamination plans. Part of Lieutenant Colonel Kidd's involvement was doing that Opening Gambit for us, because they were going to take over that area they had a vital interest in making sure that they assisted, or took over, in the decontamination.'

The pinnacle of river crossings would probably have been the Diyala River, that needed to be crossed to get into Baghdad. If there had to be a lengthy decontamination once the river had been crossed, the force would have become a sitting target for hostiles emanating from Baghdad. Conversely if troops had just motored through the contaminated area they risked rushing into urban warfare at too fast a tempo. As far as Baghdad was concerned, this problem didn't arise: 'Once we got into Baghdad, quite honestly we didn't have a care in the world. We had defeated the enemy, it was done. I remember the day that we sent a unit north to take Tikrit; General Mattis came to me and said, "Look, we have got to get out and intermingle with the people and I want a less menacing posture. I want to drop the flak jackets and the field protective mask. How do you feel about the field protective mask?" I was like, "Sir, I believe that is fine". He had checked with intel folks and they believed the same thing too and we took the mask off at that point, put everyone in camo and sent them out into town to do their job. His thing was he didn't want the Iraqi people thinking that we were going to use something against them and that was the reason why we had our mask on, so that is why we took them off. I didn't think it was much of a threat once we got into Baghdad city limits, it was over and everyone was just glad to see us. So I didn't see it as an issue from that point.'

While this was fine with hindsight it still had to be planned for, and river crossings near towns would be defeated by the same speed that they would use to defeat the Iraqis throughout Iraq: use superior speed to get within the enemy's decision cycle while disrupting communications and troop concentrations. If the coalition forces had to take stock every time they were hit by a chemical or biological agent then this blitzkrieg would rumble to a halt and a style of fighting more suited to the Iraqis emerge.

CWO Jeambert explained further, 'Our process in the 1st Marine Expeditionary force was that if we got hit it would be a small group of people. You are talking a couple of hundred out of a group of 17,000: we were all spread out. I know for a fact that if we had got hit that we would have left those people with a small security force while we went forward. It would have been one unit out of many that would have needed to be decontaminated and then put back into the fight. They wouldn't have been that far behind.'

It seems that in the non-Cold War paradigm speed is the key protection against NBC, in the same way that manoeuvre was for NATO forces during the Soviet era. 'The key to it is speed,' said CWO Jeambert. 'If we took the time to find the limit of contamination and manoeuvred around it, this would have eaten precious time. Again, we believed that the Iraqi army did not have the means to employ the amount of chemical weapons necessary to cause enough transfer contamination that would have made this a risky move. So, yes, we would have rolled through the contamination and worried about the decontamination later. The thing to remember is USMC battalions are trained and prepared to conduct operational decon if any unit within the battalion becomes contaminated. If a unit was contaminated, the NBC officer would have reported this up the chain of command along with his plan, based on his battalion's mission, of when and where he wanted to decon those personnel and equipment that were contaminated. Once I received his plan and assessed the situation in regards to the number of personnel and equipment that were reported as contaminated, I could have directed additional decon assets (personnel and equipment) to the site the battalion NBC officer identified in order to support his efforts in expediting the decontamination process if required.'

Decontamination is not a zero-sum game, however, and to fully decontaminate the vehicles and troops to a 'fourth-stage' level would have required far longer than the war lasted. Instead the 1st Marine Division was focussing on operational decon and a swift recycling of troops. 'Thorough decontamination is a laborious, logistically challenging task that the 1st Marine Division was not willing to perform. Our units in the 1st Marine Division were going to conduct a notched-up version of hasty/operational decontamination. What this means is that we would have conducted the standard MOPP [Mission Oriented Protective Posture] gear exchange, moved to a clean location, conducted unmasking procedures and continued the mission. This process would take approximately one hour to do 200 personnel whereas doctrinal-thorough decontamination could/would take up to several hours to complete the same task. For vehicles and equipment we were going to wash them down with five per cent solution of HTH and water. The thought process was speed – "speed is the dynamic", as General Mattis often stated. Risks? Negligible. With new studies conducted by the USAF on agent fate we (NBC defence officers) felt confident in this course of action.'

The major problem with this as a strategy is biological weapons. Biological detection and identification take time, and if it isn't detected this means that the force might be incubating a potentially contagious agent. CWO Jeambert felt that they could carry the risk because intelligence indicated that the Iraqi military would be unable to effectively employ a biological agent. He admits that the speed, which aided them against the enemy, created problems for biological detection. 'To be honest we were moving too fast to conduct bio sampling. Our plan was to watch for symptoms in the aid stations.'

One biological attack scenario that had been mooted was the possibility of willing Fedayeen infecting themselves with smallpox or other virulent agents and using themselves as vector transmission agents. This would avoid most of the detectors, and by posing as normal civilians or refugees, they could get close enough to US troops. CWO Jeambert admitted that human vector transmission had not been seriously considered, 'It is a unique approach to use people as vectors. I don't think I had considered that people may be willing to die. As far as the biological threat, it was a major concern of General Mattis and it was one of his critical information requirements. If you saw mass sickness in a particular area you were to report that immediately. It was left up to the medical personnel to report that and there were a couple of cases reported, but it was mostly people who had stomach flu and things like that. We were pretty much monitoring the aid stations, people going in to get treated, that sort of thing. It was a concern, but smallpox and anthrax weren't that much of a concern; it was other things that could bring down the force. The amount of people that got sick from stomach flu, that'll bring down a force quicker than anything. It was a detect-to-treat method, not a detect-to-warn; we really didn't have the time to do that testing. I know that we had preventative medicine folks take an air sample for their own benefit – but I know for a fact that some of the environments that we passed through were not conducive to biological sampling.'

A great degree of biological sampling is dependent on air sampling which, in a particle-rich environment like the desert, is not a good idea. The speed of the operation also made for problems with casualties from chemical or biological weapons. To stop the force being slowed down, the casualties would need to be separated from the force and medevaced to safety. This then poses problems of cross-contamination of medical and transport facilities (which was a major problem during the Sarin attack in Tokyo). 'Each unit was responsible to triage and decontaminate all contaminated casualties prior to evacuation to a proper medical facility,' said CWO Jeambert. 'We planned to ground medevac to a semi-clean area, conduct decontamination and move the patient to a nearby LZ and helo the patient out of the area.'

The final NBC burden for a force keen to use its speed is its logistics supply. Logistic supply is always a challenge for a blitzkrieg force and while a certain amount of risk can be carried on NBC, not having fresh suits and masks is not just a morale problem but also a safety one. In an NBC-rich environment the relevant supplies, and this includes medical countermeasures such as atropine, not just suits and masks, move far up the priority scale. If any part of the supply line breaks, water, food power, ammunition, and in this case NBC supplies, then the whole operation grinds to a halt. 'The supply line was huge and it was stretched out and it was definitely stretched to the maximum point during that war. I was told to expect a twenty-four hour delay on NBC logistics. This caused no great concern because each unit carried enough equipment to re-supply contaminated personnel and our regimental headquarters held a robust re-supply of NBC equipment,' said CWO Jeambert. As for atropine, 'Every marine and sailor in the 1st Marine Division carried three atropine kits and if you have an entire company that gets hit with a V agent, the chances of all of them going down with symptoms where they would have to administer first aid are not that great. So you would have a small percentage that would have to receive that first aid. I don't think that you would have seen a massive use of atropine across the battlefield. It would have been a few people but not that many. Of course if he [Saddam] had got round to doing what he wanted to do, or what he wanted to do in the first Gulf War, which is consistently bombard us with chemical agent, then we would have had an issue, but not at this scale.'

There have been a large amounts of lessons learnt from OIF by all nations and it is important to note that NBC lessons are only a small part of this. Any future scenarios that have NBC as a problem will have to be assessed afresh as many of the solutions thrown out of OIF would not work against more prepared red forces – combined minefield and chemical attacks, for example. It is also important to note that, thankfully, coalition plans were never tested and still await their baptism of fire (or gas). That said, lessons learnt on tempo, logistic supply, decontamination, biological testing and Colpro ('not worth the logistics' burden') are going to be of interest to a wide variety of nations.

Lessons learned

Ruler of the Queen's Navy – Admiral Sir Alan West, First Sea Lord, talked to John Chisholm about overstretch, operations and procurement priorities. The interview was held in January 2004.

JC: *Is the Royal Navy overstretched?*
AW: I won't answer that in a straightforward way, because you don't expect me to. There is no doubt that the navy is extremely busy. If we look back a year ago, when we had Operation Fresco to deal with the firemen's strike, we needed ships to fulfil our normal operational tasks – the two standing NATO forces, ships in the Gulf – what used to be the old Armilla patrol. Add all of that together, plus running a training package to bring ships up from scratch, then that over layered on Iraq, there is no doubt, if that had continued, the elastic band would have snapped. But, of course, Fresco came to a conclusion. We completed

what we would call the 'hot' war part of Iraq and, because we are explicitly designed for expeditionary operations, we were very good at recuperation. We have been quicker than the other services at being able to recuperate back into our normal mode of operations.

So the answer is we are very busy, people feel very busy. In the amphibious ships' area we probably have a few shortfalls but we could rapidly get that back together again. We are designed to be expeditionary, flexible and all these things. That is our classic mode of operations. If you sail from Portsmouth it makes little difference to us whether you are off Land's End or whether you are off Australia. For the other services this is huge because they have got to get out there and set up bases.

JC: *The classic littoral threats – mines, fast attack craft, conventional submarines, speedboats laden with explosives – all of these were not really being considered when we designed the platforms currently in service. We are reducing numbers of people on new ships, but the stress of manning machine guns and other add-ons is going to impose greater strains on crews. What can be done about this?*

AW: We are operating ships closer inshore than we ever would have considered. The classic for that is the recent Operation Telic where we had the escorts operating right up in the Khor Abd Allah (KAA) waterway in very shallow water. Certainly the US Navy were delighted that we were going to go up there because they have got deeper sonar domes and were not willing to go up there. What we found was quite interesting. When we interrogated Iraqi prisoners we discovered that by operating so far up we prevented them from laying the mines where they wanted. Nevertheless the asymmetric threat is far stronger than we ever thought it would be a few years ago. Quite rightly these ships were designed for the tasks faced then. The Type 23 frigate was thought of in the seventies. The original design was effectively going to be a tug with a towed array on it. Luckily we managed to fight for a multi-role ship because you never know how the world changes. We said: 'The world changes.' But we were told: 'Oh no, it doesn't, we have a war against Russia coming, you stupid navy people – you haven't got a clue.' But we persevered because if you have a multi-role ship then, if things change, it is not a waste of money. So, at the end of all that, we got a capable and useful ship. It is still not optimized to deal with asymmetric warfare so what we have done is we have put in train a series of measures to try and make it better. We have put on more machine guns, we are looking at adopting a 7.65mm Gatling gun, and we are looking at changes to our 30mm guns so they can be used against surface targets. We have got sailors with body armour and we need more weapons training for them. All of these things are coming along. I have no doubt at all that, compared to when I took over as Commander-in-Chief in 2000, we are way, way better than we were. But I will be a lot happier in mid-2005 when a lot of these projects will have been completed.

Swarm attacks have been an issue for a while. It was thought that the Iranians, for example, might adopt these tactics so, when I arrived in 2000, I wanted to know what we were doing about this. What I don't want is my first chap through the straits of Gibraltar, having been notified of a terrorist threat, overreacts, and I find out that one of my ships has wiped out a yacht full of topless lovelies that was just coming along to pass the stern and wave to the lads. You have to come up with a risk assessment. At the end of the day, if you have got somebody who is absolutely intent on killing themselves and killing other people, then it is quite difficult to stop them doing some harm. What we must do is put in hand mechanisms so that they do not do fundamental damage to somebody. We were quite fortunate in the Gulf.

JC: *Most of the volunteers just melted away . . .*

AW: Yes. There was an attempt to come out of the Shatt al Arab and in fact the Iranians helped us there. They shot a few up and others got lost. The other thing that people forget is, even if your target is close to the shore, if it is out of sight then it is very difficult in a small boat to find anything. Your situational awareness in a small boat is terrible. At night it [visibility] is zip, and we now have boats where we put in GPS, very clever secure comms, patrol boats with marines or Royal Navy boarding parties in them. People often forget about the sea, but we are used to operating on it all the time. Once you start getting a bit of a swell up, your suicide bomber in his small boat is going to struggle. This, coupled with seasickness, might make them less willing to go through with it. Although, for some people, being seasick makes them feel like ending it all anyway!

JC: *In Operation Telic your headline-grabber was the amphibious attack on the al Faw peninsula. Something we said we would never, ever do again – an opposed landing – yet we still keep doing them. But was it amphibious? After all, only two companies flew from ships and the rest came in via helicopter from land bases.*

AW: It very definitely was amphibious. It was a hook. We bounced into Viking and bounced through. Initially we were going to use a single Commando, but I was told we needed a brigade-minus out there so we deployed another Commando. So it definitely was a brigade-minus plus all the heavy equipment. The landing craft were due to attack red beach but there was a delay in that because the LCAC couldn't manage the gradient so it became easier to go up the KAA and come in from the top. But for ten days these guys were fighting on the al Faw without any bridge or anything with the main force. Now for all of those ten days everything was being brought in by helicopter and landing craft – it was totally amphibious. All the men, the light guns and the ammunition, initially came from aboard ship. Indeed, we initially were providing a lot of support for 1st Armoured Division.

JC: *But would you have been able to do it without the use of land bases?*

AW: The answer is yes, but I would want *Albion*, which I have now got, plus everything else as well. Part of the reason for not going from the ship was the sequencing of the battle. We needed to take the two big offshore oil terminals which had radars on. And we wanted to take those as the very first thing so that they couldn't blow them up and spill oil into the Gulf. The fact that we can operate from a land base or at sea underlines the flexibility of amphibious forces, plus our ability to move and strike along a coast where we choose.

JC: *But I have heard this argument with MCM [mine counter-measures] too – if there are mines then we will just go somewhere else. There comes a point where there may not be a 'somewhere else' to go.*

AW: Sometimes you have to go where you are. I would like to have a fleet of remote vehicles, ideally launched from a submarine that will allow me to quickly check an area and say: 'That's mined.' And we won't go there. But there is going to come a time when you say: 'That's mined. I don't want to use it, but I am going to have to.' That's why you need minehunters. You can't not have minehunters because you will have to clear a defended beach at some point. We were in that position in Iraq. But, in a sense, although it was only a small shoreline, we were flexible.

The other interesting thing that came out of it was, of course, air. We were assured by the air taskers that we had so much air that we didn't have to worry. If one of our guys was shot at they would wipe them out with so many air-launched weapons it would be fine. Our planners said that we would take a bit of naval fire support along just in case. The Americans said: 'You won't need it.' But our guys said: 'Well, we'll just put it in there.' What happened on the day? Weather was not very nice. There was no air. Now the marines really loved having naval fire support and we didn't have to fire that many rounds. That is because of the sort of battle it was. When they came across a strongpoint, instead of attacking and possibly losing people, the marines called in naval fire support because there was no air available. And we had a few accurate salvoes. The Iraqis thought 'I don't like that very much' and gave up. That happened in at least five locations. Talk about efficiency. With such a small number of rounds it was an excellent way of doing it and the weather was absolutely terrible. The light gun battery [on Bumiyan Island] was able to contribute even more. It was a very flexible and classic sort of operation.

It was a good tip for future operations. If someone had asked me, for exactly those reasons: 'Is this a good place to do a classic amphibious operation?' I would have said: 'Not really.' Actually it turned out very amenable and the business of riverine operations again proved to be very valuable. Looking to the future I would like to have a small cadre of people who would specialize in riverine operations. Indeed it was an issue I identified as we were building up to the war. We talked to CNO (US Chief of Naval Operations) about borrowing some boats but it is something I would like to do in the future. When one looks around the world there are other places where a similar situation could occur.

JC: *CEC [Cooperative Engagement Capability] is an area we are investing in, a technology that is only currently planned by the US. Are we not in danger of struggling to keep up with the US Navy yet, at the same time, leaving our European allies in our wake?*

AW: Certainly this is an area of concern. If you go back a few years we almost got ourselves into the ludicrous position of just being able to talk to the Americans, barely. And we had moved so far away from the Europeans that we were in danger of losing our ability to talk to them. That has all changed. The Americans now understand, very clearly, that coalition operations are the thing. They are looking at their communications architecture to enable them to communicate with others. We're very conscious of that and we have to be careful that there are two-tier, three-tier and four-tier systems that allow us to communicate with the French, Germans and Dutch, which we are pretty good at. But then you find the Bulgarians have come along and you have the Romanians who are just about to join NATO and then we can find ourselves, suddenly, dealing with someone outside of that loop. There is a real difficulty but it is something we are applying ourselves to see how we can coordinate ourselves with other countries.

If we look and see whom we see ourselves fighting alongside in the future, that would be the Americans, that is our primary focus. But the key message is: we fight with our allies, not like our allies. Who knows what will happen a year or so down the line? This whole area of connectivity moves at lightning speed; you can't have a twenty-year lead-in time on this. CEC is now fitting into the common integrated air picture and is very much a part of that. It is very exciting, classic, network-enabled capability. But we are very conscious of keeping in touch with all our other allies. The French, for example, have Hawkeye aircraft and Link 16. I went aboard the *Charles de Gaulle* recently and all the battle group had Link 16. We haven't yet got all our ships with Link 16. So it is a bit of a curate's egg this one and we are going to have to watch it very carefully.

JC: *There seems to be a bit of an obsession in the press about defining capability in terms of numbers of ships but there comes a point where a ship, no matter how hi-tech and capable, can only be in one place at a time.*

AW: It is an area where I have to think quite hard. I am very much aware where my priorities lie in the area of maritime operations in the UK. I have to arrange my priorities so that if the resources are stretched then I know where to ensure that the money goes. I am quite clear that it is the CVF and the JSF, then the attack submarine programme and amphibious shipping on a level. However, the amphibious shipping is now coming on stream so there is not a lot of new money required there. The attack submarine programme is different. We need a drumbeat of production there to make sure that we continue to press forward. One of the reasons we had problems over Astute was because we stopped making submarines and there was a gap. If you do that, as in any industry, the very bright people go off elsewhere. Those are my top priorities for the UK. In amongst there are battle winners and war winners.

Just below that is the Mars [military afloat reach and sustainability], the replacements for the Fleet Auxiliaries. A lot of my Royal Fleet Auxiliaries are getting terribly old and we want to be expeditionary. Logistic capability is important for that and thus important to UK defence. Then you say: 'Well what is left?' Well, you have the MCM capability, but we can't go much smaller with that. It is a capability we are probably the best in the world at. It is important. And for what it is, it is not that expensive and the balance is about right. What does that leave? Well, that leaves escorts.

I started this on the basis of having a limited amount of money and what are the top priorities. If we were absolutely purist we would say that we actually need more escorts. But you have to take risks. We have reduced the number of escorts dramatically. If you compare the average escort when I joined the navy with the escort of today they are chalk and cheese. Even the new ones, the Leanders, they were just about able to tell that something was about to blow them out of the water but couldn't do much about it. It had a gun that could fire not quite as far as the Mk8 now. It had Seacat, which was pretty iffy and it had Wasp, a single-engined helicopter, and they had no surface-to-surface missile. Compared with ships in service today the difference is immense. One could say that they are now more light cruisers.

But we are now getting to the stage where we have to ask ourselves: 'How low can we go?' You can have only one ship in the West Indies doing its mandated task from the government of making sure our dependencies are looked after, dealing with natural disasters and join in the war on drugs. You need a ship for that. Actually, you need three ships for that because you need to have one working up and one in training. What is the level we are looking at? Although we calculate the number of escorts we need by reckoning up what we need to escort a task group for a medium-scale operation plus two small-scale operations, that number sometimes come to less than what we have deployed as our presence in parts of the world. At some stage, if we keep driving down numbers, we are not going to be able to fulfil all the tasks required of us. So I am concerned. The other thing is, in wars, and it hasn't happened recently – touch wood, you lose things. In the Falklands war we lost four ships. If you lose a ship then your ability to undertake tasks decreases.

One interesting discussion, looking to the future, is the possibility of producing some ships of lower capability to do these lower-end tasks. Now Type 45 is a cruiser – let's not kid ourselves that is a cruiser. It is an 8,000-ton ship. If it gets tactical Tomahawks, which is what I want it to have and militarily makes absolute sense with the capability it has got – the ability to embark special forces, the AAW capability, the gun it has and I would like to give it a longer range gun in the future and a Merlin helicopter – then Type 45 is a very big cruiser. That is what it is.

Up Tempo – Lieutenant General Claude Christianson, Chief of Logistics, US Army. He provides a refreshingly frank account of the difficulties of operating in Iraq.

Lieutenant General Claude Christianson is a man at the top of his profession. Recently promoted to Deputy Chief of Staff G4, he presides over the US Logistics capability of the US army. In many respects it is difficult to get to grips with the scale of Lieutenant General Christianson's command, or the challenges he faces dragging US logistics kicking and screaming into the twenty-first century battlespace.

Sons of the desert

Operation Iraqi Freedom (OIF) tested the flexibility of the US system, and it was Lieutenant General Christianson, then Chief, Logistics, Coalition Land Forces Command, who had the job of organizing not only US logistics, but coordinating those of the coalition as a whole. But when did he first get involved in the planning process?

'I arrived over there in October 2002 to be the Chief, Logistics, for the Combined Land Forces Command,' the General said. 'At that point the operational plan, Tango 3 Victor, had been written, had been exercised several times and was in its final stages. The plan had been modified. It was being modified as I arrived, as force structure was being defined and as the mission was being developed.'

There had been a lot of speculation, and feverish diplomacy about Turkey. Did the drop-out of the Turks cause any problems?

'The plan did not have Turkey in it originally,' the General said. 'Turkey came into the plan around December and remained in the plan well into March. The decision to use – or not use –Turkey was taken very late. We had logistics forces in Turkey establishing a force reception capability and logs bases and getting the roads cleared to move the tanks and stuff from the ports.'

Step on the gas

Fuel supplies were one of the things that went well because its use is fairly predictable, but it didn't go so well in 1990–91. Then some units came close to or actually ran out of fuel because the rapid armoured advance took everyone by surprise. What had changed in the predictability model in ten years?

'In the first Gulf War there was an issue about understanding what these long [time] locks meant,' General Christianson explained. 'When a manoeuvre force moves so fast, even if it is 100 miles, I don't think we grasped the impact of that on a system that was designed to support troops from a more fixed location and a slower rate of movement. What that means, for example, is if I am setting up tactical field storage sites with bags on the ground and delivering fuel to those storage sites with tankers, I can reach from those bags to support the forward elements

111

but only to a certain distance. If they move much beyond that distance I end up with fuel but I can't reach far enough fast enough. To be able to come back to the fuel storage sites, refill the tankers, and get back up to the front; we couldn't keep up. The manoeuvre forces were still moving forward at a pace and the trucks could not catch up and that was the problem.

'We understood that this time around and we used some of the same techniques by placing some tankers well forward with the manoeuvre forces. The first couple of refills of fuel came from the theatre tankers that would come back then and fill up. Secondly, we stored fuel as close to Iraq as we could. That was a lesson we took from Desert Storm. We had 11 million gallons of fuel stored in tactical storage facilities just south of the Iraqi border. Then we used pipelines in order to minimize the use of trucks inside Kuwait. In addition, as we attacked forward, we used pipelines to move the fuel as far forward as we could to take the strain off the trucks.

'We have had the issue before, but how do you change your force structure and your processes to accommodate this type of manoeuvre warfare? Our change in logistics has always been a pace behind the operational change. Our folks did a great job of remembering Desert Storm and trying to take the tools that we had and using them a little differently. An extremely successful lesson learned. We had installed over 250 miles of pipeline for this operation.'

The US army had the luxury that they knew the theatre they were going to be fighting in and had a good ten years to prepare, rather like North Korea today. The issues that arise from less predictable circumstances mean that many on the logistic frameworks that were available in Kuwait and the Gulf may not be available.

General Christianson was aware of the issue: 'Well, if we use petroleum as the example, we know that the army pipeline system takes time to put in. The first element to go into Iraq was the marine hose-reel system. That is a flexible hose on big reels that can be rolled out and can be installed in a quarter of the time, or even less, than these fixed pipes. We realize that we are not going to have the time to build a robust pipeline structure if we have to rapidly respond so we are pursuing something similar to the marines but with a little more capability. That is because we can't get enough fuel through the marine hoses for a big army operation. We have the same technique called the Rapid Inland Fuel Distribution System, which we are working on now.'

112

Fuel was a success. But there were media reports that US forces were getting a bit short on food and ammunition at certain stages of the campaign, the appearance in the Western media was of a slow-down, and speculation that the campaign had got bogged down. Was this the case and were supplies failing to get through? Apparently it was more complicated than it first appeared.

'In the case of food it was a case of distribution, primarily,' General Christianson admitted. 'Water was more complex than most people would think. First of all we decided that the initial water supply would be based on bottled water. As the forces moved forward we intended to set up our water-making capacity and distribute our bulk water. Once again there were a couple of issues involved. The pace of movement created distribution problems. Even though we were able to start making water exactly how we planned, when we planned and in the quantities we needed, as the forces continued to move forward it became harder to turn the trucks around and get them to the units. Because the forces were widely dispersed, finding them in these different places became a huge problem. Our system was designed for a more 'fixed' operating area where you don't have these disconnected operations that are not necessarily contiguous.

'Where you go out to small units it is much easier to provide bottled water than it is to bring these big bulk containers. We don't have the right kind of trailers and water trucks to do this the way we want to do it. We are changing that now. Were people going short of water? The answer is yes. Our plan was to provide four bottles of water per person, per day. Then, as we started to produce water, we would reduce that to two bottles and augment with bulk water. Our whole supply plan was based on that. Now when the time came to reduce to two bottles we were producing enough water so it was not a problem of availability; it was a problem of distribution. The people needing water were a long way away and were still moving. We ended up with bottled water being much of what people got in the forward areas. When you go from four to two, with no bulk water, obviously you just got your water ration cut in half.'

Ammunition posed challenges too. There were media reports of US units running low on small arms ammunition that could not simply be written down to the more trigger-happy nature of US troops. So how had the US got into this problem?

General Christianson was frank: 'The mix of munitions that were consumed was different from the mix of munitions that were packaged up based on mission analysis,' he said. 'As the consumption of munitions continued, being able to see which munitions are consumed the most is very important. Because we didn't have the connectivity, we would send packages based on the plan. When we got feedback, and this was never in real-time as there was always a delay, it was 'We don't need that many tank shells; can you reconfigure the packages?' As a result of not having that information we were always late in adjusting. I don't think anyone ran out of ammo at all but in some units small arms ammunition got ground down to a very low level whereas tank ammunition stayed high.'

Pause for thought

But was the operational pause caused by these logistical problems and the need for the supply chain to catch up or were there other reasons?

'That operational pause was in the plan,' General Christianson said. 'It was in the plan because of operational needs. In other words at the point when it was done you had the Medina Division and the Hammarabi Division outside of Baghdad and intelligence had shown us that they were in a certain disposition. In order for the forces to prepare for the attack they knew that they would need some time. They had planned to do a couple of aviation missions and some missions with cavalry before they commenced the attack. So there was a plan to have what looked to you to be a pause, but – as this was going on – aviation, the cavalry and lead elements of the marines and recon were all doing the forward things. If you were on the other side of the line you wouldn't have felt much of a pause.

'Secondly, there is a requirement to have a sort of rhythm to your logistics. Ideally, we would like to synchronize that rhythm to the operational rhythm. So there really were two reasons, operational and logistical. Had the operational requirement been to continue forwards then the rubber band would have been stretched very tight. There wasn't much flexibility left when we got to this point and it was caused by several reasons. The first was the sheer length and speed of the movement. Secondly, the weather was incredibly bad. We had a re-supply convoy sitting in the support area and I could see them through ITV [In-Transit Visibilities] but they couldn't find them on the ground. It took almost a day and a half to find them. The young captain who was in charge of the convoy was one of those heroes. She could have got scared and done something wrong but she said: "I'm in the right place, I'm staying here", and they finally linked up.'

A problem of ownership

The US had been investing heavily in asset-tracking before the war to make sure that logisticians had a clear picture of where their supplies were and what was on the trucks or containers from arrival in theatre to delivery to units. This did not go according to plan in OIF, but the General is keen to stress that this was an organizational and a cultural rather than a technological problem.

'It is important to understand that there was not a problem at all with the technology,' he said. 'The issue is how you use the technology. How does the capability that comes with this technology enable a process? In this case we are talking distribution with RFID [Radio Frequency Identification] as the technology. If you look at a distribution system and you look at the roadmap and the internet in theatre and you ask "Where would I want to see the cargo as it moves through it, where do I need to have some controls over it?" and then you look at these points on the ground – these are different organizations. The arrival point where the supplies are delivered would be an army unit that probably belongs to a support battalion, a brigade in 3 ID for example. If you go back down the chain there is a cargo transfer location, a distribution hub so to speak, that is run by a transportation command that is nothing to do with 3 ID. Further back in Kuwait, at the theatre distribution centre, you have an operation run by a different transportation organization and then, at the airfield in Kuwait, you have an air cargo terminal run by the air force.

'So as you watch a piece of cargo come through you say: "I want to see it when it comes to Kuwait airfield, I want to see it when it gets to the theatre distribution centre, when it passes through this cargo transfer location in Iraq and then I want to see it when it arrives." So you are talking about four different organizations not linked commonly by anything, but they are sharing a process. The responsibilities of those four locations, if you believe in in-transit visibility, have to be clearly defined and they need tools to execute those tasks and they need to be resourced. Then you need performance metrics to see how you are doing. We had some success at the aerial port in Kuwait. We built a theatre distribution centre and formed an organization out of whole cloth, to give them some capability, but that was all from scratch so they didn't have any tools or training. The transportation guys who were running the cargo transfer had not been trained, nor did they have the tools as part of their authorization or the kit to do the task we wanted them to do. So we had to give them the kit: the tools, the antennae and all that kind of stuff and some kind of training.'

This was quite a remarkable set of circumstances. The admission was that all the kit was there but the haphazard nature of training and a lack of process ownership culminated in system failures that were wholly unnecessary.

'Well, it's not unusual,' General Christianson said, 'when you have these new technologies that get inserted from the outside. So if you have a good idea and great technology it needs to be brought in as an enabler to the process. If you own the process you embrace the technology and I guarantee you that it will get embedded across everyone who plays. If it is an outside idea and people come in and say: "Hey, it's a great idea, you guys should use it", and all they see is extra work. In other words, I am down here and I have got my hands full and you are telling me: "You need to use this computer system, put up these antennae, oh, and by the way, you need to burn all these tags so I know every part that is in that container." This is just extra work. You don't see the value of this. You are only responsible inside that hub; that is your area.'

Soldiers first, logisticians second

But logistics units are vulnerable. In Desert Storm, and again in the recent Iraq war, vulnerable convoys came under attack and casualties were taken. How could these units look after themselves better?

'First and fundamentally every logistician has to understand that before they are a logistician they are a soldier,' General Christianson said. 'The individual skills required to survive on the battlefield must be maintained. I think that over the last few years we have allowed that to slip a little bit. We have taken risk in some of our logistic forces, probably without the right kind of thought. We had been thinking that we may have been in a more secure environment, we thought we were going to be in this very structured battlefield. We have taken some risks by maybe not providing the right equipment, maybe not having as many bullets as we need for those logistics forces so they can maintain a level of proficiency.

'That has all changed. In training for this operation we required all our logistic personnel to go through live fire exercises from convoys, which is not a mandatory requirement, but we did that before they went out there. That is the most important thing: every soldier must understand that they are a soldier first. Beyond that, when you have a

116

battlefield that looks like our battlefield, with its non-contiguous nature, you have operations here and there and I have to bring sustainment to them across an area that was secure yesterday but may not be secure tonight, how do you do that?

'The movement itself looks a little different to how it did before. Before we would send some trucks out with a small communications element. Now we have satellite communications so we can talk to those movements. We are augmenting them with some kind of force protection, either a vehicle with built-up capability in it or accompanied capability such as military police or air cover. Then we have got some hi-tech stuff to block out mobile phone transmission – people using cell-phones to set off munitions as you are moving. You shut everything off in the area. So we are using a combination of methods to try and provide protection to the movements because, in this new battlefield, you know you cannot secure the route. So we have to secure the movement.'

Partners in grime

The US army had to stitch together the USMC logistics and those of the coalition partners as well as organize itself. With partners arriving some-times at the eleventh hour, how could this flexibility he hoped for be broadened to accommodate allies?

'The most important task I had from the very beginning was to lay out for the coalition partners how we were going to operate,' the General explained. 'And it wasn't just for the coalition it was also for the US Marines. We sat around a table, looked at the maps, talked about the concepts, and said what we were going to do. Each of the coalition or joint partners would be looking at this and, if they had an issue, either they couldn't do it that way, or didn't do it that way, or not having the capability to do the things we were asking them to do, we would lay all those out and deal with them separately to find resolutions.

'The challenge, first and fundamentally, is to have nothing hidden. If somebody is in charge, then they are in charge and they lay out the concepts for everyone to understand. Then everybody lays out on the table what they can and cannot do inside the context of that concept. The danger that we have is if nobody is in charge, and everybody does their own thing – you can't get any kind of synergy and you can't get any kind of effectiveness. It is unrealistic to expect that the nations of the world will ever fully harmonize their systems but, on the ground, we have got to learn to work together.'

[John Chisholm interviewed General Christianson in February 2004.]

Red lessons – Lieutenant General Ronald Keys, Deputy Chief of Staff for Air and Space Operations, on what the Iraqis should have done. Interviewed by Gwyn Winfield in March 2004.

The US has a reputation for putting things right. While other countries hope for work-arounds, or good luck, when the US acknowledges that it has done something wrong it fixes it. When I heard Lieutenant General Keys speak at the recent Air Power 2004 conference, the candid nature of the Americans to put right the things that went wrong, in an operation that went so right, was sobering. He and his staff have been working on Task Force 'Enduring Look' since the beginning of the campaign and the work is still ongoing.

It is amazing that so many lessons came out of Operation Iraqi Freedom (OIF) when you consider that the USAF and RAF could not have asked for a better scenario. Coalition planes had 'air-occupied' Iraq for twelve years, there was an accurate assessment of what the threat was, and most of the assets were already in place. The lessons learned are not so much about what the Iraqis did as how the US forces operated. 'We did not see a major war fight. There were pockets of fierce resistance, pockets of Iraqis who fought well but in the end they were overpowered by our training, technology and the ability of our commanders to take control of any opportunities that presented themselves,' said General Keys.

'So from that standpoint I don't think any earth-shaking things happened that we hadn't anticipated, other than the fact that they didn't stand and fight in large numbers and that the organization collapsed. There are some things we didn't anticipate but as far as they operated, when they did operate, it pretty much followed what we anticipated.'

General Keys suggested that we were approaching a new paradigm for many countries of 'they win if they don't lose'. If they can put off losing for long enough for the international community to step in and stop the conflict, they can then try and change the political and military environment to a more profitable situation and that is their 'win'. What sort of military lessons do we take from this sort of military scenario then?

'We ran lots of models, we looked at what we believed to be the adversary threat scenario,' said General Keys. 'We ran various war games on – what if he attacked us before we attacked? What if he used WMD? All the way to the things that he doesn't control – what if the weather got bad? In fact, three of the issues that we had going into Iraq – what if the weather gets bad, what if we don't get all the basics that our initial plan requires and what if he slimes us by using chemical or biological weapons – the first two of those three happened. But because we had looked at our options we had back-up, to the back-up, to the back-up,' he concluded.

As well as lessons learned on how the organization functioned (federated bomb damage assessment didn't work, for example, because the reach-back could not cope with traffic in the thousands), there were also some interesting red team lessons – what the Iraqis could have done that would have seriously hampered the USAF. General Keys enumerated these as: prevent lodgement, prevent air supremacy, protect your own C2, attack enemy networks and 'use-or-lose' weapons of mass destruction.

It is an interesting side issue of the focus on NCW [network-centric warfare] that while it might be an potent enabler, its potency makes it an attractive target to disrupt. 'We realize an asymmetric strength may be an asymmetric weakness. If you are depending on something to a high degree then it becomes a vulnerability,' said General Keys.

'We spent a lot of time looking at the old cliché that if you are going to put all your eggs into one basket then you better guard that basket! We looked at robust networks and self-forming and self-healing networks so if a portion of the network goes down for one reason then the entire network doesn't go down and you have a backup system. You have to attend to those sorts of things. You can't just assume that your adversary is going to give you a free ride to play to your strengths. They are going to try and get you to play more to their liking. We spent a lot of time in our lessons learned saying how did we do it? And then red teaming it with experts in those particular sectors saying "what if?". What if someone got into our networks? What if someone contaminated our fuel? These are all mundane sorts of things that have a big impact. We recognize that, so we build work-arounds, or protection, or surveillance, to make sure that what we do well will not be subverted because we have overlooked something.'

The issue with weapons of mass destruction, that some nations such as the UK took to be a *casus belli*, has become even more charged. General Keys suggested that they have now become a 'use or lose' capability. If other countries on the 'axis of evil' do have these devices they should think about using them before their regime is destroyed and their weapons confiscated. 'Precision, identification and location are absolute must-haves. You have to have developed the ability, if you must, to attack those areas and do it safely,' said General Keys.

'The one thing you don't want to do is attack some storage site of WMD and have a plume that comes out and kills 300,000 people. It is very difficult because these are relatively large countries with something that they don't want you to find. Even if you find it they are going to make it very difficult to strike. You need to develop persistent and precise intelligence, surveillance and reconnaissance to find out where this stuff is, how is it stored and when is it moving. There may be a lesson on the other side that says if one of the reasons we are actually in this conflict in the first place is over WMD maybe the way to throw this operation off balance is to use it. Then, if they use it, there would be hell to pay.'

There has been adverse comment on the amount of missions that were tasked to hit WMD. If the threat had been as real as it was portrayed in the media there would have been far more. General Keys doesn't believe that this is necessarily so. The amount of ordnance that can be carried is far higher than could be read from ATOs [air tasking orders] and that the best way to stop WMD might be through hitting their C2 nets rather than their NBC dumps. 'How many [ATOs] do you think ought to have been tasked? Remember now we are talking about one airplane having the ability to hit multiple targets, one airplane with precision. We dropped 1.3 bombs per desired main point of impact in OIF, whereas if you go back to Desert Storm we dropped a lot more bombs per desired main point of impact. So if you've got a B1 that could hang on for hours and hours with a large number of JDAM on board, then that's two or four or six or eighteen smaller airplanes. The calculus has sort of changed when you start talking about weight of effort. Weight of effort is not necessarily the number of sorties you put against the target,' said General Keys.

'You have to understand what you believe your adversary's *modus operandi* is and target his command and control, for example, so the codeword doesn't get transferred to the people who actually have the weapons and employ them. You have to try and understand at what point is that authority released to the field? Is it a failsafe or is it a fail unsafe? Is it one of those: "If you do not hear from me do not use WMD." Or is it: "If you don't hear from me you are authorized to use it on your own?" '

This would seem to be another one of those red lessons that will be taken to heart by future opponents. They can expect to have their C2 or C4i system closed down in a very short space of time so they need to have a well-rehearsed low-tech system that can provide a limited capability. 'It's clear that I'm going to attack your command and control because I don't want you to have all the options that you started with. I want to slow down the way you make decisions. I want to know more about your situation than you know about your situation,' said General Keys. 'If you know that, you are going to try and make a robust command and control network that uses multiple avenues to move information. Iraqis, in most cases, were using couriers for their command and control. There is a downside to couriers, however. Couriers get lost, couriers get killed and couriers are late. It's cumbersome, but that is an approach. You have got to look at the problem and say: "If I did this what likely course of action would my adversary take, what would my backup be?" You have to look at what the country is like, what's the communication like, the infrastructure, and so on and think how will they get around this? You may not be able to totally kill their command and control, for example. When you finally get to the point where you have come to direct action, at least their command and control has a reduced potential to react to your manoeuvres.

'The better his C2 survives, the more of his force will be able to co-ordinate as a group when they meet you. That's where technology and training comes in. If we have to we can fight one on one. We can fight strength on strength, and we will win, just because of the training and technology that we have. But there are better ways of doing it. You try to influence the decisions he makes so his decisions are wrong for him but right for you. You try to slow down his decisions so he is paralysed. You try to clog up and kill his command and control so he doesn't get information. Without his eyes and ears he is now essentially frightened of the dark. He is trying to guess what you are doing from the very frag-mented pieces of information coming in. Through the speed of a very integrated joint operation we have a tremendous advantage,' he concluded.

One of the biggest factors of OIF was the issue of fratricide. There is a need in the media to believe that we have moved past this, that war can be dictated to such a degree that we can eradicate our own mistakes. Despite all the advantages that technology can bring to the battlefield it is unlikely to eradicate this as a problem, instead it brings new issues to overcome. 'It's a fast moving game,' said Lieutenant General Keys. 'It has some dangerous weapons and it can still get very confused. Even the fact that you have little blue dots roaming around on your cathode ray tube, you are down on the ground, there is a shape in front of you, you are in your Bradley and there is some kind of vehicle across the street there and it turns to you. Now the question is how do you resolve that in the half-second you have before you shoot?

'We had infantryman engaging infantryman – blue-on-blue. We had tanks engaging tanks, we had Bradleys on tanks, we had airplanes engaging infantry and vehicles. In some cases we were talking to the people we bombed! Somehow we didn't get that right. It's a very difficult situation. If you look down with your eyes and you are talking to the guy who wants you to deliver ordnance and somehow it doesn't come out right and you end up dropping on him rather than dropping on the description he gives you. You look with your eyes at the cross-roads he is describing and you are convinced it is the cross roads he is describing, but it isn't, it is one crossroad down . . .

'Technology can help,' continued the General. 'We are working hard to get a common system. The problem you have is 'red registration'. If I'm dropping a bomb from seven miles away, for example, a half a degree of red registration can be quite a distance. If I've got 15,000 people in a division moving around, and they are all not being tracked 100 per cent of the time (they send a message every fifteen seconds or forty-five seconds or three minutes), then how far can they go from the last known position from my display?

'How do you equip, how do you size the widget, how can you field it, where do you put it, what kind of band width does it require? Is it jammable, how much information will it provide, is it one way, will it work at 100 yards, will it work at 100,000 yards, is it going to work across the entire force? It's making some progress. We had eight systems in OIF, but if you have eight systems then you don't have a system because they're not all interoperable. We need to make sure we understand what the requirements are,' he said.

These problems are not made any easier by the sorts of scenarios that coalition forces are likely to encounter. With 30 per cent of the littoral being urbanized it is likely that urban conflicts, requiring close air support, are more and more likely. Yet it is exactly these sorts of conflict that are the most dangerous for blue-on-blue. Red targets are fleeting and require instant response, positive target ID is all but impossible and the area is full of civilians. This starts to breed the problem that even though the airman is told that the target at the junction is a red force by people 100 metres away, it may well be a blue force. The pilot who has red and blue dots interwoven on his display has no choice but to fulfil the urging of the ground resulting in a fratricide incident. General Keys agreed with this sort of scenario. 'We had one instance of people on one side of the river taking fire and they said there were no blue on the other side of the river. It turned out that there *were* blue on the other side of the river! It is a command and control issue, knowing where all your people are. It's much, much better than it has been in the past. We do have better communications. We know much more clearly where our scouts are and where our detachments are. But again, because of some of the scenarios that we are getting into, because of the environment and the opportunity to get lost in the canyons of the city, there is a lot more of that opportunity to get pinned down. Giving detached units a capability to provide precision coordinates to an airplane, a laptop and a radio that you can squirt your position through, would start to solve the problem.

'It also goes back into training. We had an unfortunate [situation] where someone changed the battery in their GPS system. When they changed the battery it then reverts back so it memorizes your position instead of the target position, so it transmitted his position. When you looked at the percentage of the force that we've lost to fratricide it's extremely low. When you look at the percentage of the losses that are fratricide compared to our ability to sweep into a country and win with limited casualties, then fratricide starts to make up a larger percentage of your losses. It's devastating to lose good people to your own weapons. One situation we had was when one group called in air support on another group. One of the problems was they couldn't get up and see what was going on. They were pinned down and were being shot at such a high volume of fire they couldn't even move, so they didn't have the ability to know or the capability to communicate with anybody else. We're currently trying to figure out what went wrong and how to fix it. Is it technology, is it training, is it tactics, techniques, procedures? This is a very confused situation. Having perfect knowledge would be nice, but we just don't see that, certainly not in the short term.'

The real stars of the show in OIF would seem to have been the B1 and A-10. Certainly Air Marshal Glen Torpey, Deputy C.-in-C. Strike in the UK, rated the B1 as the star platform for persistence, payload and precision at the Air Power 2004 show. Similarly ground troops were impressed with the AC130 Spectre gunships and the A-10. It would seem odd then that two of these platforms, the B1 and A-10, were destined for mothballs before OIF. That situation has been reversed now and A-10s are being upgraded and the more modern B1s are being brought out of the desert.

'We're starting a programme now to look at the A-10 because there are certain subcomponents of the A-10 that we are going to upgrade. We are going to up-engine and put some more technology on it for those special occasions where you need that kind of airplane. It's starting to get a little long in the tooth, like a lot of our fighters are, so we pick the ones that don't have fractional bulkheads, wing boxes, and put pods on them and look at re-engining. We are going through that project now to understand how many we need, what level of sophistication do we want to bring them up to. We're looking at the STOVL JSF because the great thing about the A-10 was its ability to work in shorter runways. For example, in Afghanistan and Iraq we could get those into runways that we can't get our other airplanes into. So we're looking at what is the right mix of STOVL and CTOL JSFs for when we get to the point where the A-10 goes the way of the buffalo.'

The lessons of Iraq for the British army – Brigadier R.A.M.S. (Mungo) Melvin, the Director of Land Warfare, spoke to Paul Moorcraft in November 2003.

PM: *Some of the main lessons of Op Telic have been published by the MOD in their First Reflections report. What would you add to that?*
MM: When I reflect upon the future of land warfare as a result of operations such as Op Telic everyone is looking for shifts and changes, whereas I would like to emphasize what is enduring – the nature of war and how we command in war. For the British Army and the armed services as a whole our general approach to warfare is broadly sound. My reasons for saying this are as follows. Firstly, for anyone who was involved in the planning or who was there [in the field] the chaotic nature of war, the Clausewitzian friction, has come home again. If people think that war is tidy, well organized and everything is under-stood, then that's just not the true nature of war. Secondly, our manoeuvrist approach to war – looking for and exploiting oppor-tunities, seeking the enemy's weaknesses – has been validated yet again. Thirdly, and even more importantly, our method of command which underpins that approach – mission command – has been validated.

Mission command is a pragmatic solution to the chaos of war. But it evolved not just because we needed to know what to do when the radios broke, but rather on account of our understanding of the fundamental nature of war and of people who fight. Commanders will continue to devolve responsibility to subordinates empowered to take the initiative, and who are able to lead and motivate their commands by personal example. Mission command is based on developing a bond of trust and mutual understanding throughout the chain of command.

Speaking to the senior and middle-ranking commanders in Iraq, you get the impression that they enjoyed a good deal of tactical freedom and had the opportunity to exploit local success, which then became more significant operational success. So an overall war-fighting ethos, a manoeuvrist approach and mission command, for me, are the big three aspects of the enduring nature of our approach to war.

PM: *Well, I would expect you to toe the official doctrinal line, but in coalition warfare the different American approach to say, mission command, does complicate matters.*

MM: The Americans do have a similar approach to manoeuvre warfare but it's a fair point to distinguish command styles. The evidence of those people on the ground, however, is that the British division under the US marines and the [strategic command of the] US army-led headquarters was given a great deal of freedom and the [British] commanders did enjoy mission command. Indeed, in coalition warfare, whether we are under another nation's command or other nations are under our command, mission command uses a robust system that allows people to get on with it. So mission command and coalition warfare are not incompatible. Rather, they work well together.

PM: *OK, we are talking about the main thrust into Iraq, but it is clear that there are very big differences in the US and UK approaches to containment in the post-war phase. Some of the issues are tactical – for example the methods of street patrolling and intelligence-gathering – but they have strategic and political repercussions.*

MM: I am not disputing there are very different approaches to command. My view is that the British system has worked well. And it's still compatible with working with a large coalition. In a coalition it doesn't mean that everyone has to be the same.

PM: *Let's take the broader issues of compatibility – or lack of it – in coalition warfare; I am referring to the British problem with equipment, particularly digital communications. We can't keep up with the Americans.*

MM: There's lots of work-arounds and exchanges of technology in place. We're doing a lot to cooperate with the US to improve that interoperability. But I'd be the first to say that it is a big challenge, although it's not as if we're not doing anything about it. The digital exchange is a huge challenge; as both armies are fully digitized, we have to be very careful. It's not so much actually talking to each other, but sharing the situational awareness. The key to compatible tempo will be the appropriate sharing of the blue picture. That's a big area we're working on.

PM: *And especially the IFF [identification friend or foe] dangers.*

MM: No one can ever condone incidents where there is a tragic loss of life. Having been in a number of very near misses and accidents myself, I come back to the frictional nature of war. It doesn't excuse it, especially where there have been errors of drill or procedure. Those need to be corrected. But there's work to be done to make sure we have the right combat ID. We're involved here [at the Directorate of Land Warfare] in quite a lot of the procedural, as opposed to the technical, side of combat ID. There is no unique technical solution that is absolutely 100 per cent. A combination, however, of the right doctrine, right procedures and the right technical means should certainly go a very long way not to eradicating the issue, but to really driving it down. If you look at the incidents in the last Gulf War in 1990–91 and the most recent conflict, there has been less of a problem.

PM: *Can we examine this issue in terms of close combat in urban terrain – for example, Basra?*

MM: Too many people regarded urban operations as a front for light forces. There's a big difference between doing urban operations in training, where very few people get hurt because of the odd accident, and urban operations for real, where it is a very deadly environment.

PM: *But in training there are always very high theoretical casualties in urban ops.*

MM: Yes, very high. But what has been validated by operations in Basra and Baghdad is that the urban fight is a very much heavier fight than people had considered beforehand. Historically, this is a truism: if you wish to fight in urban areas, you've got to be prepared to use armoured vehicles. Armoured vehicles alone of course are very vulnerable but it's the combination of light and heavy forces in the urban environment and, crucially, having the right intelligence picture as well.

You ask how we can avoid unnecessary casualties. It's the combination of having people with the right protection, using armour where appropriate, having the right intelligence to know what they should be directing their fire at, and being able to move from one posture to another, at the appropriate stage. The lessons of Basra are [the effectiveness of] this more flexible approach rather than an all-or-nothing approach: the combination of raids into Basra, to pick up information, precision attack to exploit that information, to start dominating particular routes, to start attracting people to checkpoints, to build up a human intelligence picture of what's going on. The combination of active and passive means and a willingness to proceed flexibly, but also when things were going well to exploit quickly, gave a new nature to urban operations.

PM: *What are the lessons here for future infantry soldier technology?*

MM: In terms of protection, for the foreseeable future, it does show us that we should retain a good mix of heavy armour, armoured infantry – Warriors, Challenger 2s, AS90s, and heavy armoured engineer equipment. That combination is still very valid. New technology will come in two ways. One, the improvements to intelligence, surveillance, target acquisition and reconnaissance – Istar – will mean that all involved in this fight will be better informed. Secondly, when we get the future technologies which will be available to the dismounted infantry, we will be able to give them better situational awareness. Theoretically, we will be able to give them the opportunity to look around the corner, and will reduce their overall vulnerability with a picture of what's going on, where their colleagues are, blue forces to the right and left and behind them, and where their potential opponents are. They will also have the communications to call upon the entire firepower available in the joint force.

PM: *When will this technology be available?*

MM: By the end of the decade. Some of the equipment, such as the Personal Role Radio, is in now and has been very, very useful. It's being used not only by the British army but also by the US Marine Corps as well. And they are hugely complimentary about it. Giving each man in the section the opportunity to communicate with his peers is very important. It means that, at very low-level, people are fighting in far more coherent teams.

PM: *PRR is great when it works, but it's very short range.*

MM: It is short range but that is the nature of that particular fight. And being short range means that an enemy can't intercept it. It seemed to work very well in Iraq.

PM: *You referred earlier to the achievements of the Challenger 2. Some experts are saying that, while the armoured helicopters' role was disappointing for the Americans, the success of the Challenger 2 marks 'the return of the tank' to the top hierarchy of the battlefield.*

MM: Over the last fifty years experts have delivered premature prophecies about the demise of the tank. We were of the view before Iraq, and remain of the view, that for the foreseeable future heavy armour – the Challengers, Warriors, AS90 and armoured engineer equipment – remain essential on the battlefield, not just for the big manoeuvrist sweeps across plains but actually in the close urban fight. But those forces are potentially vulnerable if they are not being accompanied by dismounted forces. It's the balance between light, medium and heavy forces that is essential for us. That's where we are going in terms of our force development: a better balance between light, medium and heavy, achieving more usable and strategically deployable forces. Until 2020–25 we will see our heavy forces retained as a part of the army. So it's not a return of the tank, it is the tank *remaining*. With eighteen potential threat armies in the world, with over 1,000 tanks each, we simply cannot afford to ignore our heavy armoured capability.

Regarding attack aviation, armed helicopters, we didn't of course employ any of our Apaches in the Gulf. We used our two armed Lynx, which performed very well. The big debate on the air manoeuvre is: should we use our attack helicopters deep or close, and the relative vulnerabilities of using them deep or close. There are so many lessons which have come out of the Gulf which have not been properly analysed. We need to investigate carefully that close/deep balance. There's going to be a very good rationale for our helicopters being used both in the close role and for raiding in a deep role.

PM: *I get the impression that the Americans were rather disappointed with their Apaches' role.*

MM: They had one very spectacular incident where it was very disappointing. But it's also a matter of record that subsequent use of the Apaches was a lot more successful.

PM: *But there is a cautionary tale here for the British Apaches.*

MM: There are always cautionary tales about using any equipment without employing it properly. Having been involved in a great many exercises and studies of this, the temptation to underestimate the ability of the enemy is great. So you sometimes get caught out. We need to strip away the headlines to analyse carefully what happened. Where you underestimate the enemy and don't use your normal drills, you might take a lot of damage. If you put attack aviation, the Apaches, with the right sort of package for the right kind of suppression of enemy air defences and coordinate it properly, the success can be outstanding. There's much evidence from the Gulf War, from the American point of view, that shows outstanding success. Of course that has not attracted the publicity compared with the less successful outcomes.

PM: *But there were major failures in both Afghanistan and Iraq for attack helicopters. In Britain, I suspect there was an overselling of what the Apaches could do. I now sense a certain rowing back of the gunship supporters, both for technical reasons and because of what has happened in recent wars.*

MM: Those apostles of deep air manoeuvre have been challenged.

PM: *That's nicely, and politely, put.*

MM: But those of us, who saw a more balanced use of the Apache, both close and deep, would say that nothing happened in Iraq that was totally unexpected. If you are over-confident in anything you do militarily – be it air or ground manoeuvre – you may get caught out. On the other hand, if you are not confident enough to exploit the situation you will be forever pedestrian.

PM: *You've talked about ISTAR, but at the moment we've just got Phoenix and it's a bit of a joke.*

MM: I challenge that. It was not a joke. It was an outstanding success. You've got that completely wrong. The evidence is that Phoenix was used very aggressively; that Phoenix allowed for some very good use of artillery. It was designed as a target-acquisition system and in that role it was superb. That doesn't mean that we feel that Phoenix is enough for the future battlefield. We need more modern systems, and hence our focus on the procurement of such systems as Watchkeeper.

PM: *But the Phoenix is embarrassing compared with US UAVs. It looks like a toy.*

MM: It's not what the kit looks like. Look at the effects. The combination of Phoenix and precision fire-power from AS90 was devastating.

PM: *And there were no overheating problems with the AS90s?*

MM: The lessons of Saif Sareea were learned. The equipment – Challenger 2, Warrior and AS90 – worked extremely well. Kit has been a big success story for the British army.

PM: *Well, you would say that, wouldn't you? I might well agree with you on heavy equipment, but the logistics of other kit left a lot to be desired.*

MM: It's in the public record that there were problems with the supply of some kit. This indicates the scale of the enterprise: sending so many servicemen and women in such a short time, it was almost inevitable that not everyone would have the right equipment. It was done on a very compressed timescale. With such a large expeditionary operation – unless you have a long period of in-theatre/in-country preparation – it is almost inevitable that there will be some problems. There is absolutely no cause for any complacency. We are looking at a rigorous review of our logistic concepts to make sure that those problems do not happen again. Some of it depends on when the decision is taken to deploy, and when the financial authority is given to buy extra equipment. The whole point about what we are saying about a balanced force – balanced not only in terms of the fighting elements but balanced between those at the front and those in the logistics tail – that we deploy on expeditionary operations the right combination of capabilities that not only allows us to fight but also to be sustained and supported properly. And there's more work to be done on that.

PM: *I know there's an MOD reluctance to talk about cluster bombs and depleted uranium shells, but perhaps we can talk about the general effects of artillery during Operation Telic.*

MM: We saw a combination of greater precision in the use of air power and greater precision in the use of land-based indirect fire-power of artillery. There's a lot to be analysed there in terms of having a better understanding of what effects we are trying to achieve and how a combination of direct and indirect approaches, the combination of manoeuvre and firepower, the combination of information operations and manoeuvre. There is a huge amount of analysis to be done from the emerging lessons from Iraq.

PM: *There was a massive technological overmatch, laid bare by the media, which played badly in the Muslim world. Many in the Iraqi army simply ran away. High-tech manoeuvre warfare against a backward opponent can be counter-productive politically.*

MM: There can be a technological overmatch in one area but, more than likely, future opponents will counter that with asymmetric means. That's why we have done a lot of work looking at asymmetric warfare. Human intelligence, as opposed to technical intelligence, will remain absolutely key. Because, if our opponents do not offer themselves as massed formations of enemy armour, which our technological overmatch could deal with very quickly, then we have got to understand our enemies may confront us in different ways. We will have to adapt our current doctrine and concepts and use our technology in a slightly different way. We need a sober analysis of not just the last Gulf War but Afghanistan and other conflicts in order to predict and prepare for future war.

PM: *There is always much theoretical debate in staff colleges about what constitutes the centre – or centres – of gravity of an enemy's strength. Once the armed forces in Iraq started to collapse, what precisely was your manoeuvrist approach trying to destroy?*

MM: One of the key issues in south-east Iraq was the local population's fear of the Ba'athist regime. One of the keys to success was to begin to deal with that perception and, once people started to understand that the regime was doomed, then it became a virtuous circle of people providing more and more human intelligence. And therefore we could proceed [to deal] with the problem. If we fail to understand that war and peace are ultimately about the hearts and minds issue, then we will be surprised and disappointed in the conduct of war.

PM: *During the fighting weren't some of the senior commanders deluged with data? Isn't information-overload becoming a real problem?*

MM: With modern technology there's always a danger of overloading everybody, commanders and staff, with too much information. Our basic principle, however, of mission command – of giving people the right intent and then let them work out themselves how to do it – means you can reduce the amount of detailed information required. A discipline in applying an established system of command can alleviate this problem, but it cannot get rid of the problem. It's a matter of education and training to try to reduce this surge growth of information, which if unchecked, threatens to slow down command and reduce tempo.

PM: *It seems as though the Brits have a better handle on what the Americans are now calling 'three-block war'.*

MM: There was a greater understanding that, once you advanced one metre into Iraq, a humanitarian operation and a potential counter-terrorist operation started. Three-block war is not a stage of war, it is the war. Therefore, the war is not won just by the war-fighting end. It's a combination of dealing with those opponents who wish to fight with you in a symmetric manner, the war-fighting, and being prepared to deal with the asymmetric fight, counter-insurgency; it is also acknowledging that war takes place in the human environment and you will probably have to deal immediately with humanitarian operations. And if conditions of peace are established then you have got to keep that peace. So a combination of the Balkans, Northern Ireland and our war-fighting ethos has led not only to a confirmation of doctrine but to a broad understanding among our military that this is the real nature of war. Although we haven't formally incorporated three-block war into our doctrine, all the elements of it are already there.

PM: *There is an old military saying that those who fight the war shouldn't be asked to keep the peace. Three-block war contradicts this and may demand that soldiers do all three in the same day.*

MM: It may be inevitable that in future wars there will not be a matter of choice; that those who were involved in the war will have to be peace-keepers. Over time, those who have been involved in hard, sharp, very decisive engagements may not be best to be there at the end of the campaign. But there may not be the luxury of choice. I think doctrine will develop far more along the lines of – this is what we have to do, so we jolly well have to get on with it.

THREE

Imperial Overstretch

Policing the World – Dr John Mackinlay teaches in the War Studies Department, King's College, London. The former British army colonel is an expert on peace support operations. Interview with Paul Moorcraft in October 2003.

PM: *There used to be a great debate about separating peace support operations – both doctrinally and practically – from war-fighting. Where are you now in this debate?*

JM: There was a very narrow definition of peacekeeping which was a result of the Cold War where you couldn't have a peacekeeping operation except with the consent of the powers between which you were keeping the peace. And in that situation there was a separation between that [peacekeeping] activity and, more or less, any other low-level activity. The problem was that when we went into the post-Cold War scenarios of the Balkans, Somalia, West Africa and so on, people continued to use that formula in situations where it couldn't be used – because the consent factor was absent.

Separation, then, was something which your pure traditionalist peace-keeper wanted to maintain. I maintained, along with most people in the British army, that once you got into a complex emergency scenario, where the preconditions for traditional peacekeeping were no longer there, you couldn't sustain the separation because you'd have to get your men to behave in an escalating scale of violence. Where one minute your man is Mr Plod in the streets with his beret on, acting as a soft target being nice and friendly to all the people in the street and, when the shots ring out, you've got to be able to go straight into being able to return that fire accurately, and acting as a hard-edged target to the people who are trying to destroy him. So you have a continuum from being Mr Nice-Firm-and-Friendly right through to being able to carry on an effective counter campaign involving factors such as supporting fire and all the hard aspects of war.

PM: *You have said that peace enforcement involves the 'military task of restoring a monopoly of violence in a crisis zone which has much in common with the deeply unfashionable principles of counter-insurgency'. Is that just limited to the Iraq experience?*

JM: No, given the fact that after the Cold War the majority of your contingencies took place in countries where the monopoly for violence had collapsed, where the government no longer controlled the state. You had to restore that monopoly. To take guns out of the hands of the local militias. To take power off the streets and local leaders and centralize it back into the hands of the government. That's more or less what you are trying to do in an insurgency. Where the insurgent forces are resisting the government and trying to set up an alternative state within a state, whereas you are trying to revert to the status of a central-ized state.

We were no longer acting in the traditional old war peacekeeping role, we were acting in a new war scenario where the problem was the integrity of the state.

If that's the starting point of your campaign, it's absolutely wrong to regard peacekeeping as the solution. You need another form of military campaign to restore the central authority of a government. The obvious structure was counter-insurgency (Coin). All the principles were there. In Coin you are trying to win over the population to support the govern-ment, but in this case you are trying to win over the population to support the peace process.

PM: *Kosovo was seen as a new type of peacekeeping, but has 11 September changed this model as well?*

JM: I have described Coin in an idealistic form which no one actually does at the moment. Instead you had this bastardization of peace-keeping . . .

PM: *In Kosovo?*

JM: In all those Balkan campaigns. And also to some extent in East Timor and Mozambique. There was a bastard version of peacekeeping which wasn't quite peacekeeping. You had a number of different agencies such as UNHCR, Médicines sans Frontières, SAVE, Caritas, all the big agencies, whose task was to sort out the development side of the state, and blistered onto the side of that would be a military force whose task was to create a secure environment in which they could work.

The problem was the military had its long-term strategic aim and the stove-pipe organizations, which were all autonomous such as Caritas and UNHCR, all had different long-term strategic aims. The impact was when you are trying to squeeze the opposition out of the state and squeeze the ability for them to use force out of their hands, you've got to use everything to do that. You've got to secure the opponents with military force and you've also got to bribe them and pressurize them with the conditional use of development. That is how you do Coin in this context; you've all got to be singing off the same sheet of music.

The reason I say 'bastard' form is because that wasn't happening. You didn't have a director of operations on the ground in Kosovo who controlled the entire shoot.

It's telling you that there isn't a very big sense of conviction in the international community to really achieve that Clausewitzian monopoly once again. They're just containing the situation. They didn't have the political energy to do any more than hold the lid on top of the pot; as long as the population of Kosovo didn't spill out into the Balkans and upset the Serbs or Albanians or whomever. OK, quite a large part of the population did spill out and ended up in places such as Switzerland and Germany. But it was no big deal – you could bear it.

But the problem with 11 September is that Osama bin Laden – bang – reaches out from the depths of Afghanistan and smacks the Americans right in the centre of New York in the most dramatic way. Thus he torpedoed the whole containment policy because it was absolutely obvious to people in rich safe countries that containing the thing was no longer an option. You could no longer imagine that you could sit back in London or New York and have this safety curtain between you and that Kosovo place. All you had to do was keep the lid on the place. Now you really have to go for gold.

Afghanistan is a demonstration of where you aren't going any longer for old-fashioned containment; they actually went there to sort the place out and restore that monopoly [of local power] and make the place absolutely untenable as a future terrorist development centre which is what Afghanistan effectively was.

PM: *But in Afghanistan you have ISAF just about containing the capital, while US forces are based in Bagram, fighting a pretty hopeless border war and ineffective internal Coin campaign, with resurgent warlords undermining the penny-packets of development work done by the NGOs. Is this really a new kind of peacekeeping?*

JM: You shouldn't worry about calling it peacekeeping.

PM: *So what do we call it then?*

JM: You don't need to call it anything except intervention. If you chart international forces from 1948 onwards, during the Cold War when the world was completely dominated by this East-West rivalry, the only thing that really worked was peacekeeping. In the period directly after the Cold War, when the East-West conflict was finished, and we were rather uncertain of the strategic framework, you had containment. After 11 September you have intervention.

The way I explain it here, it looks as if you have three wonderful stages of development. It appears that one stage succeeds the other. In reality, all manifestations continue to co-exist. For example, I was lecturing to a group of officers recently who were going off to peace support operations. Some were going off to traditional peacekeeping operations, some to containment operations in the Balkans and others were definitely going to an intervention operation in Iraq.

There are so many actors now in the operational space, more and more than ever before. And many are independent actors. The idea that you can just trip from one thing to another in an evolutionary sense will take forever and a day – to move the old juggernaut out of containment into intervention is impossible. Because a lot of the baggage from containment moves with you into the intervention phase.

Your criticism [of the Afghanistan policy] is correct. Intervention is what they wanted to do, but the actual character of what's on the ground has a great deal of containment about it. This resolve which they should have is not there. It's a screwed-up operation: you've got ISAF on the streets of Kabul, with vertical command back to NATO; you've got JTF-180, vertical command back to Tampa. Do they ever speak to another? I don't know. And then you have a bloody great development programme, which is like a multi-headed hydra – bits of the UN, bits of EU and USAID, and NGOs, and they all have their own agenda.

In an ideal intervention the Yanks would say: 'We are going to do a regime change in country X and it's going to be very swift. We are going to provide the framework for the military force. Then, folks, we're going to provide all the money for the development. So that means, Médicines sans Frontières, if you want come in here and set up a number of surgical units, we're going to pay you. And, Médicines say fine, but they start their own agenda, well, that's not on, guys. There's a contract. You want our money, you whistle to our tune.'

PM: *Where is that actually happening?*

JM: It's happening just about in Iraq, and just about in Afghanistan, but not very convincingly . . .

PM: *Tell me about the Afghan model and what more should be done?*

JM: The problem with the Americans is that they have no track record of success in this field.

PM: *In nation-building?*

JM: In imperial policing. That's the old-fashioned term, but call it 'nation-building' if you like. They have no track record in Coin. Of success. Washington is not a government town which is configured for imperial campaigning. Why? Because there isn't the equivalent of an effective cabinet-level government. What happens is that – besides Condoleezza Rice – you have these two monstrous departments – Defense and State, headed by two monstrously powerful guys, Rumsfeld and Powell, plus one or two others, and they are all big jungle creatures, who are completely independent. They have their own constituency and they talk mainline to the president. And so Rumsfeld comes in with a plan for the president which says we are going to do this, and he will independently put all his operatives out into the operational space. Powell will do exactly the same thing on the other side of the house and he will send his operatives out. So, in this rather fractured government town, you don't have a coherent policy at the top level. And Condoleezza Rice is not powerful enough to say to these guys: 'You've got to sit down and hatch a joint plan.'

Tell me: who is the joint director of this thing? There isn't one. OK, the President. And if it is the President, who is the joint director in Iraq? Is it the civilian or the military commander? And if it is the civilian, if he is the director, you go one tier down to brigade level, are you really telling me that when the brigade commander comes in for the weekly security meeting, the guy at the head of the table is an Iraqi adminis-trator? Rubbish. The guy running the town is the military commander. It tumbles upside down as it goes down the chain of command.

In the British system, in Northern Ireland for example, you had a director in Belfast who was the chief guy. He was a civilian and at the table sat the Chief of Police, the Chiefs of the army, intelligence, Home Office and all these people. And one level down, at the brigade, you had a replica of that meeting taking place: the local Special Branch guy, local government officials and so forth. This vertical structure went down to the ground. And it all emanated from the Cabinet Office, because the Cabinet Office spoke with one voice because they had already buried all their interdepartmental differences into a cabinet strategy and policy.

PM: *I agree – this is the development from the old Robert Thompson Malayan strategy. So the lack of central security command in Afghanistan and Iraq is a result of the fractured government in Washington?*

JM: You can't do anything if Washington is all over the shop.

PM: *So that explains why there is no real political will to extend ISAF throughout the country.*

JM: They've got to have a major disaster because the Americans are a very trouble-shooting nation. Once they know they've got something wrong, they have a great capacity for putting it right. They trouble is the problem is fundamental [in Washington] that nobody is going to let go of the reins of power.

PM: *Would you summarise the key differences between the US and UK approach to – let's call it 'peace intervention'?*

JM: The Brits have a cost-benefit approach to establishing security in an urban area, which the Americans don't fully understand. I'll define that: you've got to take a risk about the protection of your troops in urban areas if you want them to communicate with the population. You've got to take a risk and go out soft-target patrolling, with your beret on, in amongst the people, looking them in the eye and exuding this firm and friendly approach. And the benefit of that is that they will start to relate to you and start to talk to you about giving you information and you begin to find out about the fabric of the community. Then your patrols really start bringing home the goods.

If you don't take any risks at all in the streets, you go hard-target the whole time – as the Americans do it – the downside is that you bring back nothing at the end of the day. In the TV coverage of American patrols moving around Baghdad, you can see when they pass through the populated areas there is no visual contact or any kind of emotional contact between the patrol and the people they're moving through. They've got these very dark sunglasses on and they move through with a weapon-pointing posture, weapons at the ready. It's a very confrontational body language they're using. You've got to take a risk, go in soft target and you get the benefit of doing that.

Whereas the Americans have always got this huge whip being cracked over them from Washington: no casualties, no risks. So the local commander will say, damn this, I'm not going to expose my guys to any risk, and we're going out like an armoured fortress. If the Americans can do it, they won't even go on the streets – they'll do it from behind an armoured vehicle or from a helicopter. And that's even worse because your benefit there is absolutely zero if you take a cost-benefit approach. That's the absolute difference between the British and American approach. The Americans are less much less able to delegate down to the corporal in the street. The Brits learned that lesson in Northern Ireland.

The other difference is this: when you have a contact, instinctively the Brit soldier knows that when he gets back to barracks he is going to have to account for every round he's fired because that's what you have to do in Northern Ireland. If there were any rounds missing a soldier would have to explain what he used them for. And if you'd hit anybody, the next thing a lawyer would come around and start making a case for your defence. You would definitely have to go into some sort of enquiry – hitting somebody would be a civil offence.

Take Iraq. A [recent] example in Fallujah. When the Americans killed those eight policemen they had been firing at them for three hours . . .

PM: *I thought it was forty-five minutes . . .*

JM: Even if you're right, there were thousands of empty cases on the street. It was a disastrous use of force in an urban area. They even killed a Jordanian guarding a hospital. Can you imagine the Bloody Sunday committee [the inquiry into the shootings in Northern Ireland in 1972] trying to work out who had shot what at whom, when you've fired thousands of rounds over a period from forty-five minutes to three hours, whatever account you take? It's unaccountable behaviour.

And the Press collude with this in never publishing the casualties. OK, we know that eight policemen were killed but how many people were injured? The hospitals all over the city were absolutely full of wounded people. If you fire 4,000 rounds – let's make a modest estimate – into an urban area – and pointing at 90 degrees, then the rounds would be bouncing all over the place. There will be casualties all over the city, but you don't hear that score. Generally, all you hear is that there have been a few people killed – usually American.

PM: *We're also not hearing about the number of American casualties as opposed to fatalities.*

JM: Yes, it's a large tally.

PM: *So what is the answer in Iraq? Is there one?*

JM: Yes, but not a very hopeful one. Incidents such as Fallujah are a gift to the other side. This is happening out of sync with the nation-building programme. It's very easy for a reporter to go into the streets of Baghdad or Basra and talk to a civilian who will tell you water is still not connected and the lights are still not on. If you had a district committee, say at battalion level, in a small village and the same man controlled the security and the development programme in this same area. If you wanted to get the population of this village on-side you would secure this environment so that they didn't suffer robbery and rape. And you would make bloody sure that the electricity was turned on. And the water. The two issues are interconnected: the reason why the electricity is not working is because thieves nick all the copper. The reason why the water is not working is because they've stuffed up the pipes.

You've got to think about it in a holistic way. If you really want to get the population of this village on-side, you've got to have a unified approach. If water is the priority this week, you get your troops to sort out the water mains and protect them. You tell the locals: Number One priority this week is to get you the water. So they will understand if they have to watch out in case someone comes in through the back door with an AK to rape their daughter. Stage by stage you slowly win over the people.

PM: *Aren't the Brits trying to do just that in the Basra region?*

JM: They can't possibly succeed. The poor battalion commander is stranded in a place, say, the size of Petersfield [a small town in Hampshire, UK] but the guy who is trying to fix his water is sitting in Baghdad whose budget is controlled from some aid office in America. The priorities are scrambled. It's hard to see a coherent strategy going on there. I might be wrong, but what I interpret from the media interviews is that you don't have that kind of cohesion – and it comes right from the top.

PM: *The Brits, say in Umm Qasr, have been working from the bottom up, by setting up local councils. But they can provide only band-aid – until there is security they can't get help from the international NGOs.*

JM: They were setting up the local councils but they weren't resourced in that unified way. The local council might say the main priority is water, but the guys who were going to switch the water on were in Baghdad, and they haven't arrived. And the Americans said that, for example, building the airstrip was more important. All this is a gift to those who condemn the intervention; they say: 'Look these guys can't even switch the water on'.

PM: *My impression in the south was that there was a lot of local military support to the councils, and there wasn't a lot of money – and hence bureaucratic impediments – coming from Baghdad, but of course the Brits didn't have much money to throw around compared with the Americans.*

140

JM: The reports I am getting is that conditions in Basra are improving.

PM: *Are the Americans making the same mistakes as in Afghanistan by inadvertently encouraging warlordism or at least Lebanonization by backing tribal chiefs and religious militias? This alienates the urban elites who are less tribal, religious or ethnic in approach.*

JM: Iraq is a post-modern society in the urban areas and a pre-modern society out there in the sticks. Somehow, you've got to merge these societies into a modern state. And it's hard to see how you can do that in the lifetime of the ordinary soldier on the ground.

PM: *Does Britain have the political will to maintain a five to ten year policing role in Iraq?*

JM: I don't think so. It's a hell of a commitment for a country like America. It should be a global responsibility.

PM: *Perhaps a new UN resolution might achieve that.*

JM: In the end, they [the Anglo-Americans] will shrug it off and secure some kind of UN resolution that will allow them to withdraw gracefully in a number of years' time. And it will become like the Lebanon, which slowly corrected itself after about thirty years, including a disastrous civil war. And you've got a scenario for civil war in Iraq now.

PM: *That sounds very pessimistic. So the Brits and Americans will leave within five years?*

JM: I should think so and they will hand it over to a UN mandate and then the whole thing will collapse, after a civil war, just like Lebanon – a Balkanized Arab state. Unless a global solution can be found. Because what is happening in Iraq is extremely offensive to your average moderate Muslim.

PM: *Do you accept the latest notion of Washington adopting a so-called 'flytrap strategy' of deliberately making Iraq a terror magnet?*

JM: This is an idiotic idea, just a spin on failure. You cannot ignore the size of the Islamic radical movement. You cannot contain it in one place. It's a completely irrelevant way of looking at it. The radicals can manifest themselves wherever they want. The Americans don't choose the battleground. If Osama bin Laden had the capability to fight in the streets of New York, he would go there.

The Long Haul – The US Deputy Secretary of State, **Richard Lee Armitage,** discussed Iraq and the war on terror with Paul Moorcraft in November 2003. The tough ex-Marine became irritated by the line of questioning – luckily, it was a phone interview.

PM: *How does the US plan to bridge the French-German position and the longer view of the State Department regarding the full handover to Iraqi control?*

RA: I didn't realize French-German had a hyphen in it and that they were holding identical positions. The French position, as I understand it, wanted sovereignty to be turned over immediately and then their more recent pronouncement was 'as soon as possible'. And we would in a major way agree, but we need to hand over to an administration which can exercise the sovereignty. As soon as we can stand up something that can exercise that sovereignty, we'll do it. In theory, there's not much difference [from the French position]. In fact, we have the responsibility to leave this place better than we found it, and we intend to do that. That means that we won't be turning it over tomorrow.

PM: *There have been numerous comments on the differences in approach between the British and American peace-enforcement in their respective zones. Any views on this?*

RA: Yes. First of all, British troops are very well-informed, having had the experience of the Northern Ireland conflict for many years. It has stood them in very good stead. Equally, the two zones are quite different. In the so-called Ba'athist triangle, we're having to deal with the Sunni, former regime loyalists. In the south, there is a different situation where the Shia – if you will allow me to use the expression – freed from the recent boot on their necks by Saddam Hussein – are revelling in their new-found freedoms and are organizing themselves in their cities and towns. And that's very much to be saluted. But it also, in the short term, makes the security problem slightly easier.

PM: *The American troops in Baghdad tend not to go out on the streets on foot. There is a deficiency in human intelligence sometimes if you go around in armoured vehicles using helicopters and so forth. In contrast, the British usually patrol in their berets on foot or in soft-skinned vehicles, and so there is a difference in the intelligence flow.*

RA: Much of that is true, but let me come back to my point that you have a different security threat in the areas where primarily the US is patrolling. I don't accept that we don't go out on the streets. My understanding is that each night there are 2,000 patrols. So it's not that we're not out there but the intelligence problem we have is a more difficult one. Getting back to the issue of the Ba'athists, who have dominated, and the Sunni, who have even longer dominated life in Iraq; these groups have suddenly found that their ability to have the lion's share has been eliminated.

PM: *Do you have hard evidence of foreign Islamic extremists coming into Iraq, perhaps via Syria or Iran?*

RA: I am a little out of date with my numbers but not many weeks ago there were several hundred foreign fighters held in detention by the Coalition forces. They had among their number Saudis, Syrians, some Iranians, a Jordanian or two, Sudanese and Yemenis. So that's enough evidence of foreign fighters. One of the failed bombers of the other day [in Iraq] had a Syrian passport. But I don't think anyone has a good handle on the numbers or the percentage of problems which is caused by foreign fighters.

PM: *A few commentators have suggested that there was a plan – even before the Iraq war – to create a honey-trap or fly-paper strategy that would attract extremists and thus create a central front against Islamic terrorism, using trained soldiers, rather than fighting terrorism on the West Bank or endangering civilians in London or Washington. Is there any truth in this speculation?*

RA: It's absurd.

PM: *I agree with you, but there have been newspaper articles arguing that it's better to fight in Iraq – choosing your own ground – rather than fight elsewhere and let the terrorists choose . . .*

RA: Wait a minute. No disrespect to you, but no one can say that to me. These [American troops] are young men and women who give their lives in some cases. To suggest that this is a honey-trap, to think that we would do that [deliberately] is to fly right up my nose. To any of these rubbish articles to which you refer I would reply in even stronger terms.

PM: *It's good to get a formal refutation of that allegation. Can we move on to WMD? As a result of the Iraq Survey Group, has the US government essentially given up on finding them in Iraq?*

RA: No, on the contrary. David Kay's interim report . . . seemed to show – without question – that there was a programme of WMD and a programme of missile development, which would carry these weapons. So he's gone back to Iraq with his colleagues to investigate [further].

PM: *There is a feeling, certainly here in the UK, that the apparent failure to prove the WMD case in Iraq suggests that, when the authorities warn of major unconventional attacks at home, that they are crying wolf – even though the terrorist threat may be even greater now than before the Iraq war.*

RA: I was under the impression that the UK had a policeman sacrifice his life recently to terrorism. So I am a little surprised at the question. Our view is that our intelligence and the British intelligence which led

143

us to the decision that we were in danger will be seen to have been correct. Further to that, although it's not directly on the WMD point, and as I am talking to you I am looking on my monitor here, there was that torture film which was recently 'exploited out' of Iraq. Those that don't like the involvement in Iraq would do well to review that film.

[I was in loyal opposition at the time], but during Bosnia and later Kosovo the whole world watched genocide. In Bosnia a couple of hundred thousand people were sacrificed. It took us three years of standing around and dumbing ourselves to death before we finally decided to move on Bosnia, and it took another year and a half in Kosovo where we saw the same type of genocide. We didn't do those operations under the UN Security Council resolutions, did we? No, we did not.

Iraq is the same question. We had dumbed ourselves for twelve years, and seventeen resolutions. One must ask oneself how many Iraqi citizens would be alive had we actually moved sooner. I wanted to get that off my chest.

PM: *I spent a long time in the Balkans and I understand your viewpoint.*

RA: What about *your* viewpoint?

PM: *I agree with you. I believe it was the right thing to remove Saddam Hussein, but there are political problems with the WMD rationale. As for battlefield WMD, I think they will find evidence in the end.*

RA: We'll fix it.

PM: *There hasn't been much progress on the road map in Israel/Palestine. Presumably, until the issue of the so-called apartheid wall is resolved and more pressure put on the Sharon government by the USA, there won't be?*

RA: There is no moral equivalency here. Bombers going in and placing themselves next to buses full of women and children and blowing them up will bring forth a reaction every time. At the same time, Chairman Arafat has been cynical in allowing Abu Masan to put forward a government; and then to fail to empower the entire security forces to go after the terrorists was another act of cynicism. And now we're witnessing Abu Alaa who may or may not be able to form a government and then the question will come back to whether Mr Arafat will allow the security forces to actually work against terrorism.

The only vision that's out there is President Bush's road map. He's the only US president who's spoken about a two-state solution. And *both* parties have to summon the political courage to move forward on that. But I can guarantee you the Israeli government is not going to move with women and children being blown up.

PM: *Until there is a UN-sponsored and effective international 'separation' force interposed, can there ever be peace?*

RA: We've had various times when violence has been brought way down. If both sides were seen as wanting to – on the Israeli side to live up to the tenets of Resolutions 242 and 338, and trade land for peace; and on the Palestinian side to eschew terrorism as a political means to an end – then they could work it out. Look how close they got in the final days of President Clinton; unfortunately Chairman Arafat couldn't take yes for an answer.

PM: *Mr Rumsfeld has just been compiling a scorecard. What's your overview on two years of fighting the war on terror?*

RA: Probably in Afghanistan a realization that nation-building from the failed state is a long hard slog, as Mr Rumsfeld said in his recent, now famous, memo. The fact that the main actors in the international coalition have been able to hold the coalition together and to have people add to it . . . in fact the UAE [United Arab Emirates] representatives were in here [the State Department] today saying they were going to increase their number of forces in Afghanistan. It's pretty remarkable. And the way to bring that about is to continue with that hard work, with the diplomatic and political effort. In Iraq it's too soon to make a call.

PM: *But the two key figures – Osama bin Laden and Saddam Hussein – are still on the loose. The tribal areas on the Afghan/Pakistan border are hard to police, but maybe more effort is needed by the Pakistan government to hunt down al-Qaeda.*

RA: There are two different cases. In the case of Osama, I agree with you, but I would not want it said that the Pakistanis haven't been turning up the heat. I was out there again, a couple of weeks ago, and they had just finished what I thought was a fabulously successful operation where they killed or captured eighteen to twenty al-Qaeda, Chechens, Uzbeks and I think they had an Algerian. And they have started to move against the Talibs. Now, after two years, they have been able to make some inroads – some actual roads and schools and clinics – in some of the tribal areas. It's not as if nothing is going on.

The question of Saddam Hussein is a little bit more complicated. Although it would be a great day when he is captured, I do not believe that in itself would end this insurgency. To some extent the fact that he allowed his nation – in the eyes of nationalists at least – to fall almost without a fight would deprive him of real legitimacy. We would still be faced with some Ba'athist resistance, whether he was dead or alive.

PM: *There seems increasing evidence of concerted resistance to the Coalition, especially the example of very recent attacks.*

RA: Six bombs going off in forty-five minutes and another five or six that did not go off would lead you to believe that there is a certain living, thinking organism behind this effort. This is not just a series of independent one-off attacks.

PM: *Do you think the war on terror will last as long as the Cold War?*

RA: Like you, I have a muddy crystal ball. From about day two of the Afghan conflict President Bush was preparing the United States for a long haul. He said it. Most nations – most recently nations such as Indonesia and the Philippines – have seen they have problems in their own backyards and now they realize the truth of those words: that we are going be at it for a while. I don't know how long.

High-intensity warfare – but only with the Yanks – Paul Keetch MP, the defence spokesman for the Liberal Democrats, on current crunches in British defence.

When seen against the backdrop of the December 2003 White Paper, the recent disputes reported in the press between the MOD and the Treasury point to a deeper division about the future strategic direction of UK policy. British defence policy is at a crossroads.

The New Chapter to the Strategic Defence Review announced in 2002 outlined a vision of UK defence policy similar to the strategy outlined in the recent White Paper: a focus on network-centric warfare and effects-based operations as opposed to sheer numbers of troops and firepower. In this view, deployability and flexibility are the key concepts and the defining criteria. It also places a premium on US cooperation since the technology is designed to work in tandem with US systems and focuses on high-end operations while at the same time effectively ruling out UK participation in high-end operations without the United States.

These goals for our armed forces are worthy and in large part correct but they risk obscuring the other tasks that our armed forces perform and undermining our ability to carry them out.

While the New Chapter and the White Paper outlined this new vision of combat operations they assumed no changes to the UK's ongoing post-conflict operations. This is in fact the primary task of our armed forces at present: in Iraq, Afghanistan, Bosnia and Sierra Leone. The risk of the focus on high-end combat operations is that other vital tasks decline in priority.

This risk is all the more acute when resources for security and defence tasks are squeezed. There is always a limit on public spending but in the current climate it looks as though the Treasury is trying to trim the defence budget yet further. With less money the hard choices become harder.

Of itself, the focus on effects-based operations is sensible and appropriate. Arguably it is an analytically sound approach whatever the strategic environment – the effect we are trying to achieve should always be the starting point for discussion about the use of force.

Following this line of thought, the effects the UK military is trying to create in most parts of the world (particularly Iraq and Afghanistan) are stability and a democratic peace. What is needed to create this kind of effect in both these countries is large numbers of well-trained troops. Britain is acknowledged as a world leader in this field. It would be a shame if we were to relinquish that reputation because we were unable to continue fielding sufficient troops in multinational operations. The force to the Congo is a good example. There was a clear role and need for the EU to assist but the UK was able to provide only seventy-odd non-combat troops.

One key lesson from the recent conflict in Iraq is that the UK is certainly seen in the Pentagon as an ideal partner nation for the US in military campaigns. Indeed, the White Paper goes further, arguing: 'The most demanding expeditionary operations, involving intervention against state adversaries, can only plausibly be conducted if US forces are engaged.'

The newly increased US defence budget of more than $400 billion compared with under one tenth of that for the UK defence budget tells its own story. It is clear that the UK cannot compete with American resources and cannot therefore match the rate of development of US defence systems. Inherent in that assumption, and in the White Paper's assertion, is the understanding that in high-end warfare the UK won't engage except with US support. The government seems happy to follow this path, but having 'support for the US' as an MOD mission statement presents its own challenges. The counter to this is that if the US is going to war anyway, the UK contribution is mainly symbolic and could be of mutable size.

Fighting the Treasury

There will always be competition for resources within the MOD and an external fight with the Treasury and other departments which have a different view of where public spending priorities lie. The trick is to make sure that the process by which internal priorities are set is sound.

At present, it seems as though the technological changes are the priority and the welfare of the troops is secondary. Turning these priorities on their head might be a better way to approach the tough decisions.

If we take the peace-building role of UK forces as the most important task, which – given the need for large numbers of troops in Afghanistan and Iraq for many years to come – is inarguable, then the balance of forces' equation should be the primary driver in decision-making. I would prefer to see troops coming first before we consider the question of what technology we can afford.

Nation building takes time and security. With fewer troops to keep the peace afterwards we may be restricted in our ability to successfully manage the aftermath of future conflicts and thus contribute to ongoing insecurity. This will bring the problems in recruitment and retention increasingly to the fore. If fewer troops are asked to do more and spend longer away from home they may be even more reluctant to serve for long periods of time.

The government's own target, set during the Strategic Defence Review of 1998, was for an interval between tours of duty of twenty-four months. The Defence Secretary himself said on the radio before Christmas [2003] that the average tour interval is now down to nine months. This is a measure of how far the armed forces have been forced to compromise. Among key specializations – such as medical personnel, aircrew and signals – shortage of numbers is extreme.

Vicious circle

Overstretch is a vicious circle since as pressures increase more people leave. Shortfalls are then taken up by reserves who themselves feel the strain and leave the ranks. Medical reservists are now under similar strain to regular personnel and are called up even in peacetime.

It is no wonder that when asked 'How much does the effect of operational commitment and overstretch affect your current intentions to stay or leave the Army?' 44 per cent of respondents said that overstretch increased or strongly increased their intention to leave. This is a worrying figure for the MOD and for anyone that cares about the welfare of our troops.

Recent answers to my parliamentary questions also show that 85 per cent of members of the RAF think that overstretch is causing serious problems in the RAF as a whole and that 68 per cent think that overstretch is causing serious problems in their service. No one strongly disagreed with the statement that overstretch was causing serious problems.

Ministers themselves do not deny the problem but the government could do more to alleviate the strains on forces and their families who feel under increasing pressure. Looking after our armed forces is good security policy because if troops leave, who will defend us?

While UK commitments remain as they are, force numbers need to be maintained at the levels set by the Strategic Defence Review. The SDR targets have never been met, and the establishment has been adjusted downwards as the size of the forces has shrunk.

The budget crisis currently facing the MOD will make it particularly hard for the government to square the circle of overstretch and meet new funding requests for technological advances. There is a tension between funding the new technologies required to match US forces and participate in high-end joint operations and between providing ground troops with the support and equipment they need to conduct stabilization operations.

There is no easy way through this dilemma, but the initial thinking of the government displayed in the White Paper seems to put equipment first and troops second. Finding the right balance will be one of the biggest headaches for the MOD and the Treasury in coming months. Through this difficult time, the government would do well to make the men and women of the armed forces the unequivocal priority of policy by boosting numbers and improving their welfare, since, without them, no amount of high-tech equipment will make us safe.

This article was written in March 2004, before the big defence changes announced in July 2004.

'I wasn't going to cut your throat' – Lord Guthrie, formerly General Sir Charles Guthrie, was the Chief of the Defence Staff from 1997 to 2001. In this exclusive interview – the only one he has given since he left office – the former SAS commander talked to Paul Moorcraft in October 2003.

PM: *How do you think the gap can be bridged between the Franco-German position and the US approach to the internationalization of the Iraq situation?*
CG: In my experience – I was in the army for forty-four years and was

involved in rebuilding nations and terrorist operations – conflict was very much easier than conflict prevention or conflict resolution. The latter always goes on for very much longer than the conflict itself. It needs large numbers and a great deal of money and it always takes very much longer than people think.

I can remember one of the prime ministers I served asking me, before we began a particular campaign, what my exit strategy was and I said I thought he must be joking. It is extremely difficult to say what the exit strategy should be until you have gone into a place and found out what it is really like. And then you might be able to get some idea of how long you are going to stay, and even then you are probably likely to stay much longer. Think how long we have been in Cyprus. Those who launched allied forces into Bosnia didn't think it would go on for years and years. But if you've studied post-conflict resolution in places such as the Balkans then it's not the slightest bit surprising that we're still there.

The worst thing you can do is go in quickly and then rush out before a peace has settled on the country. Because the killing will begin again and it's likely to be twice as bad as before you went in. What complicates the issue is the culture of dependency that emerges in the countries in which you intervene. The peacekeepers also constitute a third party who, by keeping the sides apart and stopping the killing, can create an atmosphere in which negotiation and dialogue can take place

Everybody talks about the US Army – this enormous machine – but we're already seeing that it is going to be difficult in Iraq and they do need other people to help them. Because even the American army can't carry out all the tasks.

PM: *How do you rate the British performance in Iraq?*

CG: I have not been to Iraq but all the reports I have heard are that the British have done extraordinarily well. It's invidious to make comparisons about who's been doing best – that's rather a simplistic approach. The Americans are facing different problems. Everything I hear about the British there confirms my feeling that they are very, very high-quality people.

The speed with which the conflict was resolved – and I stress that that was the easiest part of the problems of Iraq – was really astonishing. And that went unremarked upon by very many people in the media. One of the reasons for that is that nowadays there are so many journalists who are really unversed in defence and security. They have not made a study of it. They didn't realize what they were witnessing – an astonishingly rapid operation. When people talked about delays and reverses and fierce firefights, they were using terms which I wouldn't have used. That's not their fault. There was a huge surge in the number of embedded journalists – and I've not had much experience of that. As someone said to me the other day: 'You wouldn't send your wine correspondent to cover Wall Street if there was a crisis there.' Defence is complicated, as is Wall Street.

PM: *Two years on from 11 September, what is your view on the progress of the so-called war against terrorism?*

CG: With hindsight, before 11 September there were many signs that terrorism would become a very serious problem. Those signs were not picked up by governments in the way they should have been – certainly by the American government. I don't like the term 'war' in this context, although I can understand why it's been labelled as such. Wars usually have clean endings – starts and peace treaties and so on – and we're not in that sort of business. I can understand why people use that emotive term, but I call it a long-term struggle rather than a war.

Many good things – such as agencies working more closely together – have come out of it. I think but don't know – quite rightly because it shouldn't be broadcast on the streets – that our own intelligence services have probably done surprisingly well in thwarting some of the attacks. The police, the military and the intelligence services are pulling together. They all have important parts to play. I still hear people talking about this as a military confrontation. It's not, though the military have an important part to play. It's about intelligence and policing, examining the causes of terrorism and in some cases trying to put that right; and perhaps having a much greater understanding of terrorism and what terrorists are trying to do. Terrorist organizations are very different from each other, but they often – although not always – have aims in common.

As far as al-Qaeda is concerned – which is said to be operating in over sixty countries – it is a pretty loose organization: it hasn't got a structure of headquarters and communications and commanders in chief like an ordinary army. We did know a lot about al-Qaeda before 9/11 and perhaps we did not do so much as we could have done.

PM: *If the intelligence services are so good why were they so wrong about Saddam's WMD? I had been told by so many sources – in Britain, Israel and America – that Saddam had them. I was surprised when nothing was found.*

CG: Like you, I am surprised that WMD haven't been found. It's hardly possible to say anything new on this subject, but he *did* have WMD. He actually used them – on Iranians and his own people. We do know that he had a method of delivery – he fired Scuds into Israel. It was the likely conclusion to come to that he still had them because he did everything to go on convincing everybody that he'd got them. If he had cooperated, he could so easily have shown people that he hadn't got them. I wasn't close to the intelligence but I can understand exactly why on his past record and his attitude to the inspectors and the flouting of the rest of the world at the United Nations most sensible people who had thought about it would have come to the same conclusion. But we haven't found them. I can understand why that's an embarrassment for some people.

But it was right to go to war. In 1991 the allies should probably have finished the job. And in 1998 when he kicked out the inspectors they should probably have taken action. If we want to have world order we can't have people like Saddam flouting the UN resolutions that had been agreed to. There were more reasons to go to war than just the WMD. We were dealing with a monster. His malign influence in the region was apparent for all to see.

PM: *Maybe the simplest explanation is that nearly all the experts got it wrong. That there was a cock-up not a conspiracy.*

CG: The thing about intelligence and different interpretations is that people have different views. You have to see what evidence is available and then it comes down to judgement and advice. But it's very unlikely that if you're trying to put the jigsaw together that every piece will be available. There will be missing pieces. In this case, there *were* some pieces missing.

Throughout history there are many cases of misinterpretation of evidence – mistaken judgements. That doesn't mean to say that those who made the judgement were being dishonest. It just means that we are all fallible. The Battle of Arnhem is a good example. So is Waterloo. It is usually impossible to have the whole picture. I can think of many historical examples of the necessary intelligence not being there. You have to be careful not to interpret the available intelligence in the way that you want it to be. For instance, it's very easy to convince yourself of something if your prejudices and your instincts lead you in that direction.

The British system of the JIC (Joint Intelligence Committee) is admired by most nations around the world. Lord Hutton is investigating this process now. When it works properly, it pulls together strands of intelligence, discusses them and gives advice. It's not infallible, it makes mistakes, but you do need that sort of organization. In intelligence you very rarely have 100 per cent of the picture.

1. A Palestinian woman sits outside her battle-damaged house after the siege of Jenin, May 2002.   *Paul Moorcraft*

2. Jenin refugee camp, after the fighting of May 2002. *Paul Moorcraft*

3. The former palace of the British governor general in Khartoum; the site of General 'Chinese' Gordon's last stand and now government offices. *Paul Moorcraft*

4. A Harrier rises from HMS *Illustrious* during the Saif Sareea 2 Exercise in Oman, 2001. *Gwyn Winfield*

5. HMS *Marlborough* during Exercise Saif Sareea 2, 2001. *Gwyn Winfield*

6. Geoff Hoon, UK Secretary of State for Defence, with British troops in Kosovo 2001.

Gwyn Winfield

7. British forces helped to set up this girls' school in Kabul, 2002.

Paul Moorcraft

8. British troops helped to feed children in this orphanage near Kabul, 2002.

Paul Moorcraft

9. Shades of the Raj. British troops occupy a former Soviet gun emplacement overlooking Kabul, 2002.

Paul Moorcraft

10. British soldier on patrol in Kabul, 2002.

Paul Moorcraft

11. German ISAF troops in Kabul.

Paul Moorcraft

12., 13. and 14. London's emergency services during a CBRN exercise in the heart of the City of London, October 2003.   *British Transport Police*

15. Mother of all Battles Mosque, Baghdad. Saddam built this to celebrate his 'victory' in the first Gulf war.

Paul Moorcraft

16. Tariq Aziz, interviewed in Baghdad, September 2002.   *Paul Moorcraft*

17. British troops patrol near Basra, May 2003.   *Paul Moorcraft*

18. Desert Rat on patrol near Basra, May 2003.   *Paul Moorcraft*

10. Hearts and Minds in Basra: Military Police on patrol in a Basra market, May 2003.

20. US Marine Corps gunner in Baghdad. *Tim Lambon*

21. Burnt-out Soviet-era Iraqi tank destroyed in the Second Gulf War. *Norwegian MOD*

22. Donald Rumsfeld, US Secretary of State for Defense, in Mazar-I-Sharif, Afghanistan, December 2003. *Gwyn Winfield*

23. Alleged Iraqi mobile bio-weapons lab. *US Department of Defense*

PM: *When I interviewed the current CDS [chief of defence staff] recently, he talked cautiously about the different US and UK approaches to the notion of a 'three-block war' in Iraq.*

CG: There is a mistake sometimes made in the UK armed forces - that of criticizing allies. That's a very dangerous thing to do – certainly in public.

PM: *I must emphasize that the CDS did not criticize the Americans – he said that they had a different approach.*

CG: Of course they have a different approach, because of the nature of their army which is enormous compared with ours. For historical reasons they have developed along certain lines, which are different to us.

PM: *Dr John Mackinlay – who, when a colonel, helped to formulate the British army doctrine on peacekeeping – says that the Americans just don't have a tradition of successful imperial policing. This is what is important for the Brits, not just Northern Ireland.*

CG: Well, they didn't have the kind of empire that the British had. But I don't want to get involved in this debate.

PM: *How long should – or could – the Brits stay in Iraq?*

CG: I haven't a clue.

PM: *They could stay there for ten years?*

CG: It depends on how things turn out. It would be a very brave person who put a date on it. Not just brave – foolhardy. I believe – along with most people – that as soon as Iraq can run itself, the better.

PM: *By implication, then, they could be there – as in Bosnia – for ten years?*

CG: Iraq is different, a much bigger and greater country, a very old civilization considerably older than our own. What emerges will not be on the Westminster model or like Capitol Hill. Whatever it is in Iraq I hope it will come quickly.

PM: *Some experts have suggested that the downfall of the secular centralized Ba'athist regime could lead to a tribal, ethnic or religious Lebanonization.*

CG: Saddam Hussein held the country together with an iron hand. Just like Tito kept Yugoslavia together. But very few Iraqis seem to want Saddam Hussein back. A system of government will hopefully emerge and be capable of standing on its own feet as soon as possible, but nobody should expect that system of government to be like ours or America's. It will be an Iraqi version and you cannot impose or import democracy. Democracy is something which a people finds for itself.

PM: *Sir Robert Thompson developed in Malaya the model of a centralized police, military and civilian control to fight insurgency. There is a sense that there isn't this type of coordination in Iraq.*

CG: I knew Sir Robert Thompson well. He was a great colonial servant. But to compare Malaysia with Iraq seems wrong: a different age. We already had a structure of police there – of district officers, commissioners and courts, and regional and central government. When the insurgency came there was a real structure to build upon. That is different from Iraq.

People who look at the past often think that history repeats itself; well, it very rarely does. But what you can do if you study history – as Professor Sir Michael Howard would say, is to study in depth and in width – and you read a lot, you can learn very valuable lessons. But comparing Iraq with other campaigns is not terribly helpful.

PM: *Iraq was doable in military terms, but what of North Korea?*

CG: There does seem to be dialogue developing. It's difficult but I hope this will continue. I hope the Russians and the Chinese will engage more fully than they have. It's difficult to get inside the mind of the North Korean leader.

PM: *You had a reputation for being one of the toughest commanders in the British forces.*

CG: I may have had that reputation and, if I did, I am certainly not ashamed of it. Soldiers respect tough leadership, as long as it's fair. I've never known an army organization which is fit and tough that wasn't a good one. And people like knowing where they stand. The services are designed for when times are really bad and when it's frightening and when people have to do things they don't want to do. Not that they must be bullied into doing it. They need a firm framework to operate. It is misguided to think about the services only in peacetime. War is difficult, but if you train hard, you fight easy.

PM: *In peacetime the oddballs such as Orde Wingate don't fit, but they excel in war. In peacetime perhaps the talented – and tough – oddballs can go into the SAS?*

CG: I was in the SAS and I am Colonel of the SAS, and I can assure you that there are talented people who never go near, or want to go near, the SAS. That's as it should be. It's wrong to think that the SAS is the only part that matters in the army. Certainly somebody like Wingate would have found it difficult to have managed peace. I would have thought he would have been a nuisance in peacetime. But there are still a lot of great characters in the army. A lot of rather strange people; although the army doesn't exactly mirror society, and there are not as many extremes as in civilian life.

The Duke of Wellington, who is a hero of mine, never passed a promotion exam, never went to a staff college, bought his commissions and yet beat the greatest army in the world – the French, who had a very different type of army. Would Wellington have achieved what he did achieve if he were alive today?

Today, there are strong characters in the army. The business of soldiering – working in all the services – has become very much more complicated. Servicemen and women need to train for so many different kinds of war and peacekeeping. The qualities and skills required in war – such as ruthlessness and decisiveness and speed of action – are quite different from what you need for certain types of rather benign peacekeeping: issues such as mediation, law, human rights and political considerations become paramount. So you are asking an awful lot of the military now. That's why the British are so good because they can cope with this wide spectrum – from all-out war at one end to benign peacekeeping on the other.

PM: *No matter how good they are, do you think they are overstretched?*

CG: Yes, I do. They are overstretched, under funded and tend to be taken for granted.

PM: *You have this tough reputation but can I risk suggesting that you seemed to have mellowed?*

CG: I don't think I have mellowed at all. If we were having this conversation over the last thirty years, I don't think you would have found me any different.

PM: *But you have adapted to now working in Rothschild's bank.*

CG: Clearly, I never sought confrontation with people in Whitehall, politicians or civil servants. I believe people should work together about most things. And we did. Discussion and dialogue are the best ways of taking these things forward. I worked for two prime ministers and four secretaries of state. They were all very different. All had different strengths and I was able to work for all of them.

I don't think I have mellowed in the slightest. If we were back when I was in command of an SAS squadron, sitting around a table in the middle of the jungle, we would have had a very nice friendly chat – I wasn't going to cut your throat.

PM: *But have you mellowed – adapted – enough to write your memoirs? I hear you have been offered nearly a million pounds. Or is the de la Billiere precedent off-putting?*

CG: I must make it absolutely clear: I haven't mellowed. No way. I have not written my memoirs, although I have been offered a great deal of money to do so, but I am not going to do it. I might do an unofficial diary one day, just for my own interest. I am too busy to do it at the moment.

The reason why I have been offered a lot of money is because they want gossip about what Tony said to Robin and Robin said to Gordon and Alistair came in . . . I am just not in that business. I do think – until a long time has passed – that it's wrong. If the Prime Minister thought that I would write down everything he said in private to soldiers, like me as CDS, he would, quite rightly, be less frank and willing to have a dialogue with me. It's astonishingly disloyal how people rush into print, convincing themselves they are doing a service to history, and spill the beans and dirt the moment they leave.

And the less people know about the SAS the better.

PM: *You were considered to be a very politically nuanced CDS, but that's presumably part of the job.*

CG: It would be barking if CDS went out of his way to have disagreements with the Prime Minister. I had two prime ministers and I got on well with them both. That doesn't mean to say we didn't have heated arguments, but I am not going to tell people about that for the reasons I have just outlined about writing my memoirs.

PM: *But some of the books on the SAS – Bravo Two Zero, for example – must have been good for recruiting.*

CG: Yes it was. But I don't think it's right.

PM: *Anything you would like to add?*

CG: Despite what some people say, the military has huge public support and sympathy. Not that everybody wants to join the military. This support was a tremendous help to people like us, when we were trying to do the right thing.

PM: *It is the only organization in the country which has not suffered from a decline in respect for all major institutions of the state.*

CG: Considering it's overstretched and under funded, it's one of the principal parts of the state which really does work. And you can't say that about many of our state and national organizations.

Teaching UAVs to Dogfight? – General John Jumper, a former combat pilot and now Chief of Staff of the US Air Force, discussed Iraq, space programmes and the future of unmanned aircraft with Paul Moorcraft in April 2004.

PM: *In the 2003 air war against Iraq, how important was the British contribution? Did the problems of interoperability, especially fratricide, outweigh the benefits of coalition warfare?*

JJ: It's always reassuring and a pleasure to have the RAF by your side when you are in this kind of conflict. There's no other air force in the world which thinks more alike and with whom we can operate so closely together. In this conflict the RAF flew over 2,500 sorties and released nearly 1,000 precision-guided munitions – they were mostly precision-guided munitions. Plus a variety of other contributions on the ground and at sea. We felt very much at home with the Brits by our side.

Fratricide is one of the lessons we keep learning from. Even one or two of these incidents is unacceptable. We had one with the RAF having an aircraft shot down. These things are going to happen in war. War is all about confusion, fog and uncertainty. It's our job to analyse why and try to minimize that.

PM: *Why was the air campaign so short before the land component went into Iraq? Some of the timing seemed premature.*

JJ: Everybody starts their clocks at a different time. Reporters are ready and poised for some big whistle to blow and the event to start. In fact, we had been working the skies over Iraq for ten years. Air superiority was already there, especially since the previous July of 2002. We had flown hundreds of sorties focussed on the Iraqi air defence network. From a commander's point of view and mine, we had been working on this air war for a long time. Which meant that when you have the situation in hand, it's your choice of when to start the ground war. So I am rather amused by the notion that people's expectations weren't fulfilled, when we had been working the air problem for a very long time.

PM: *The air war was a special case in that the Iraqi air force essentially refused to fight or was incapable of fighting, so does this undermine any general lessons from the war?*

JJ: First of all you still need air superiority. The fact that we got it in a rather unconventional way is a credit to the coalition, who over the ten years of the no-fly zones made their presence well known. The Iraqis understood that they would have virtually no chance if they did choose to fight. That part [of the coalition strategy] worked very well.

The other part is, when the operation kicked off, there was mass confusion in the Iraqi command and control. I'm not sure that any orders ever got down and that left commanders in the field isolated and not knowing what to do. I don't know how much of this burying of aircraft and not flying any sorties or not shooting very many surface-to-air missiles was due to mass confusion and a breakdown of their communications.

PM: *We hear a great deal about the role of the US Army and the Marines, but how important is the USAF in stabilizing the current situation in Iraq [in Mid-April 2004]?*

JJ: We are flying more than 150 sorties a day in Iraq and another fifty or more a day in Afghanistan. There are a great number of UAV [unmanned aerial vehicles] sorties. Our fighter aircraft and our surveillance aircraft are there. When you see the 500 lb bombs that are dropped, most of them are dropped by airmen of the USAF. So we are there every day. The fact that we are not in the headlines I am not going to make any excuses for. Certainly the guys on the ground are bearing the brunt, but we are there by their side. The air component commander is engaged with the ground component commander every single day. We are working together to find these bad guys. We still have fourteen bases open in that area that we are flying from. There are more than 200 aircraft stationed over there. We are very active.

PM: *You were reported to have been shocked when you visited Afghanistan to find that the A-10 Thunderbolts were the only strike jets which could fly from such rugged terrain. Hence the decision to buy some STOVL [short take-off and vertical landing] JSFs [Joint Strike Fighters]. Presumably the 'A-10s on steroids' will be the stop-gap. Longer term, can the JSF fulfil the close air support role?*

JJ: Since Afghanistan, if you count up the number of bombs dropped and the number of enemy killed with close air support, you will find that the most effective close air support aircraft we've had is the bomber . . .

PM: *But you can't use bombers against cities such as Najaf or Kerbala . . . at the moment.*

JJ: Well, you could use them to put a very precise bomb anywhere you want. In fact we're not dropping 500 or 1,000 lb bombs in Kerbala with anything right now, including A-10s. There are many ways to do close air support. Right now, the aircraft we are relying mostly on are the F-16s and A-10s. The A-10 still has plenty of life left in it. We are going to continue to upgrade the A-10s, and then bring the Joint Strike Fighter in as a dedicated close air support airplane in the future . . .

PM: *I know this question annoys combat pilots such as yourself, but can you imagine that in a decade or so the sky will be full of UCAVS [unmanned combat aerial vehicles] with the majority of pilots sitting on the ground?*

JJ: It's nowhere near that simple. We have pilots flying Predator today. Any time that you are responsible for putting weapons against an enemy and putting people's lives in danger, it's going to take an operationally qualified person to do that. We have to remember what makes unmanned aerial vehicles valuable to us: it's when they can do things that people cannot do. For example, stay airborne for twenty-four or thirty-six hours and be just as sharp in the twenty-fourth hour as you are in the first hour. We are not losing so many airplanes that we can say that it's worth the billions of dollars it would cost to take the pilots out of the airplanes, because of the risk to the pilots. Look at Kosovo: we lost two airplanes in 38,000 sorties there.

We have to be very careful as you approach this UCAV issue. Pilots like UAVs because they can help them find targets; because they can persist over the battlefield for a long period of time. You have to remember that if you are going to replace all airplanes with UAVs somehow we have to invest in the technology to have those UAVs be able to defend themselves. Are we going to teach them to dogfight? Or are we just going to make them very stealthy and fly them at night? If we fly them only at night then why are we investing in a twelve-hour a day air force? Those are the kind of questions we have to wrestle to the ground before we decide that it's OK to turn the whole of the air fight over to the aircraft that are unmanned.

PM: *You speak with the passion of a combat pilot! May we move on to the issue of overstretch? Clearly that is a problem for US ground forces, but how is the USAF coping with the problems of constant high-tempo duties in places such as Iraq and Afghanistan, especially in terms of rotation?*

JJ: Everybody is busy. Back in the mid-1990s we transitioned ourselves into a rotational force, what we call the Air Expeditionary Force. Our whole air force has been broken up into ten equally capable packages, and we have those forces on rotation. We are manning our posts around the world through our AEF. Everybody is extremely busy and some people are being deployed longer than our normal policy, because some specialties are shorter of people than others are. But generally our AEF concept is working. So I cannot argue that we do not have enough people, as long as we are using them as efficiently as we are and as long as our rotational policy is able to hold up. Of the ten AEF forces, we called eight of them forward to fight in Iraq. Then we reconstituted the force and we have started our rotation cycle again. It seemed to have worked fairly well.

We take very great advantage of our Air National Guard and our Air Force Reserve and they are very much blended into our day-to-day USAF operations. And they help as a great shock absorber when we need to surge

our activities. Right now, I can't go and argue that we need more people.
PM: *But the continuing use of reserves in high-tempo warfare – especially urban campaigns in Iraq – is bound to have an effect on the morale of the armed forces.*
JJ: Over a long period of time, you are absolutely right. But while we are able to rotate the people in and out and give them a break, it has less of an effect. But it also has an effect on the employers. When we activate our Air National Guard and our Air Force Reserve, we are taking those people out of their normal civilian jobs. We have to make sure we don't overuse that. If we have to continue to activate National Guard and Reserves for an extended period of time, of course that's not what they are designed to do. But we haven't reached that point yet.
PM: *What are your future programmes for space? And other air projects that are being planned?*
JJ: We have a programme that we are kicking off called Joint Warfighting Space that will take advantage of rockets that you can launch very rapidly – in hours instead of weeks, as it takes now; with payloads in the vicinity of a 1,000 lb, where we could put up a rapid capability over a specific part of the Earth, as far as communications and other space-related surveillance equipment, using micro-sat technology. This is something we will try to get off the ground in the next year or so.

We are continuing to work on the next-generation of long-range strike technology which answers the question of what are we going to do to replace the bomber eventually. Will it be something from space or something that we launch and flies in orbit and then comes down and attacks and then comes back again? Will it be one-way or two-way? Will it be manned or unmanned? There is a lot of research going on into the proper answers to these questions. That's exciting.

Another concept is the Battlefield Airman – this is what we were talking about earlier with close air support. What are those things which we dedicate to the forces on the ground – the whole notion of upgrading the A-10, its replacement for our airmen who are working closely with the army guys on the ground all the time? Their equipment – is it state of the art? What do we need to do to upgrade [CAS] etc? There is lots going on to deal with working with the army – positive ID of what's on the ground, the fratricide issue, the BDA [battle damage assessment] issue etc.
PM: *The more you talk about technological advances, the more difficult it will be for interoperability with your allies. You may be going too fast for your allies to keep up!*

JJ: I fundamentally disagree. There are three things you need as an airman to get into the fight. One: secure communications. Two: some means of precision delivery. And, thirdly, and this is in the next six or eight years, you are going to have to work inside a data-linked network. That's the way we're going to pass information. None of those things is extraordinarily high-tech. And none of those things, in my opinion, is outside the reach of any of our allied air forces.

What we are doing as far as the information technology is concerned is arranging all of our space, manned and unmanned vehicles to be able to provide information. All we need our allies to be able to do is to *receive* that information. This notion that we are going too fast and outpacing our allies – I don't buy that argument at all.

Afghanistan

Ending and Resolving Wars

'The battles fought during a war, of course, contribute to its aftermath; but it is the way in which a war is brought to an end that has the most

decisive long-term impact.' Professor Fred Icklé's dictum is a crucial part of UK staff college training. Two terms are, however, often confused. *Conflict termination* is the process that ends the hostilities phase – truces, surrender of forces, repatriation of POWs, immediate medical aid etc. – whereas *conflict resolution* is the much wider process which aims at achieving the strategic goals of the original war aims. Think of the ending of the Second World War. Officially, Britain went to war to protect Poland, only to hand it over to Soviet domination as a result of the way the anti-Nazi war ended. There was no formal peace treaty in 1945, just a separation of forces that engendered a Cold War which lasted over forty years.

We may be entering another long war: a world-wide conflict against terrorism; a war without a defined end-state. The first campaign of the conflict has been terminated – perhaps – in Afghanistan, so that it is important to understand how coalition forces are generating a possible resolution to that long internal civil war.

Afghanistan: a personal perspective – Paul Moorcraft went to Afghanistan in mid-2002.

'There are 11 million mines in this country – almost one for each person living here.' The sergeant's voice booms in the briefing tent at Kabul airport. It is 02:30 in the morning and freezing cold. He also warns of the endemic diseases including anthrax and cholera. 'Afghanistan has eleven types of venomous snakes and there are scorpions everywhere.' He goes into some detail about a scorpion hiding in an Italian officer's trousers. The sergeant also notes: 'The driving is terrible. And, by the way, prostitutes are available, but it's illegal. And, remember, the police are heavily armed. They use RPGs for traffic control.'

I had forgotten what a nightmare Afghanistan can be. I was here during the 1980s at the receiving end of a major Soviet offensive. Now it is May 2002, and a British general is commanding a nearly 5,000-strong force from nineteen nations – the International Security Assistance Force (ISAF). It polices Kabul, the capital. Elsewhere, tribal leaders and warlords hold sway. ISAF is a peacekeeping operation, separate from the war-fighting missions of the US troops and UK marines to the south of Kabul. But the thousands of remaining insurgents belonging to al-Qaeda, Taliban and Hekmatyar Gulbuddin regard all Western troops as fair game.

The heavily mined Kabul airport had been attacked by rockets three hours before the RAF's giant new C-17 touched down. A broken-backed Russian cargo plane slumps near the entrance to the terminal building, a victim of the previous civil wars, not recent US bombings.

Another high-level briefing is launched at 04:00. 'Kabul is like Berlin during the Cold War,' says Colonel Richard Barrons. A good comparison. Four different parties, of different tribal and political allegiances, make up the interim government, headed by President Hamid Karzai, but the Northern Alliance holds sway over the key ministries because they have the guns and tanks in Kabul. ISAF's mission is to hold the ring in the capital until a national convention – the *Loya Jirga* – organizes a more permanent, and ideally more democratic, government. Meanwhile, coalition troops are training a new national army, of possibly 50,000 men. The first element is the 1st Battalion of the Afghan National Guard, helpfully abbreviated as Bang.

The Karzai government directly controls roughly 10 per cent of the country. It has to negotiate with the rest. In Afghanistan negotiation is normally about force or money. Coalition troops are reluctant to engage in factional issues. And very little of the promised international donations has reached the government's coffers. The UN has estimated that the five-year cost of reconstruction will be at least $6.5 billion. The Kabul government's mantras – disarmament, demobilization and reconstruction – need money, and quickly, if the Western-backed interim administration is to survive.

Nevertheless the British-led forces have stabilized Kabul. Crime has dropped, although not to the level enforced by the draconian Taliban regime. Many schools, including classes for girls, have reopened. Commercial life – at a basic level – has resumed. Kabul's streets are bustling with cars and market stalls, often accompanied by long-forbidden music.

But the infrastructure is weak – many buildings are destroyed by years of war. Radical Islamic opponents of foreign intervention are active: there have been four concerted attacks on ISAF by political opponents, and a larger number of attacks by 'bandits'. The diehards are hoping to disrupt the quasi-democratic reforms leading up to the *Loya Jirga*.

There is not much to do in Kabul; the locals visit the central zoo, which has few animals left. The centre of attention today would appear to be the two UK female officers who are escorting me. *Burqa*-clad ladies are astounded (as far as I can see) by two blonde uniformed women sporting weapons, driving and commanding armed men. This is culture shock with a vengeance. British troops have responded by naming their mess tent the 'Burqa Bar'.

British troops are heavily into hearts and minds. I visit schools and orphanages where soldiers hand out pens and writing paper, although female soldiers are tasked with donations to the girls. Later, a patrol with the Royal Anglians is transformed into a Pied Piper parade, as children flock around the troops. Some squaddies are even enticed into an impromptu football match. This is no PR fix: the troops are obviously very welcome. But for how long? Over the last 160 years, British troops have often gone into the country in large numbers – sometimes by invitation – and it has nearly always ended in mayhem and massacre, including Britain's worst imperial defeat.

British troops are not taking any chances in an isolated observation point on the top of a large hill overlooking the southern access from Kandahar. This was a former Russian defensive position. The new occupants have been harassed by occasional artillery and small-arms fire. A squaddie from the Royal Anglians tells me. 'When I arrived I was told to look out for armed men, but – bugger me – all the men around here are armed.'

Kabul is a pleasant town to visit if you like people who haven't heard of David Beckham, and Manchester United shirts are unseen (although you can buy fakes in the bazaar for $50). Football, though, is being played in the national stadium, where just a few months back the Taliban were amputating and beheading their victims.

There is little doubt that ISAF has achieved a near-miracle in a very short time, but apart from the occasional humanitarian foray – earthquake relief, for example – its writ extends to no further than the capital. Elsewhere, banditry, warlordism and drug-running are rampant. This is a fertile breeding ground for the return of those who still support the Taliban and al-Qaeda. Britain has emphasized that nation-building must apply to the whole country, but the US is extremely wary of such a massive expansion – the dreaded mission creep.

Britain is scheduled to hand over command of ISAF to the Turks in June, provided Ankara receives enough US military and financial support. Up to 500 of the more than 1,400 UK troops may remain. To prevent a return to anarchy, financial and military stability needs to be extended far beyond the capital. Otherwise, the Loya Jirga and consensus politics will have no chance to take seed in this utterly war-weary, but highly tribal, feud-ridden society. For decades, especially since the fall of the king – whose return has brought fresh hope –

whenever one group has sought to dominate, the result has been civil war. The communists, the Northern Alliance and the Taliban have tried it and failed.

Many Afghans do realize that this may be their last chance to settle their internal differences peacefully before a resumption of hostilities. And, for once, nearly all the external players – especially neighbouring states – are benign. Coalition forces have imposed peace, partly because Washington managed to end the war by bribing and cajoling nearly all the neighbouring states into acquiescing in the American design. But the USA's powerful legions may soon be called away for duty in the Middle East, not least against Iraq. Meanwhile, the Afghan conflict remains, arguably, in the termination stage; there is not yet resolution.

Commanding the 'peace' – Major General John McColl, the British commander of the International Security Assistance Force, was interviewed in Kabul in May 2002 by Paul Moorcraft.

PM: *How do you rate the success of your mission?*
JM: On 15 December [2001], when I first arrived here, there was considerable doubt being expressed about whether or not sufficient consent existed from the [interim government] to allow us to deploy in the first place, or whether or not we would receive the support necessary to allow us to operate here in the way that we are. There were some suggestions that we should deploy a limited force, remain out of the town, and only come in if there was a problem. That was never going to be acceptable for our modus operandi, which integrates us completely with the Ministry of the Interior and the police. We [also] have a good liaison with the [Afghan] Ministry of Defence. As a result, the environment here in Kabul is extremely secure. When I look back on our statistics – I don't claim that they're authoritative, but they are certainly indicative [the general shows some impressive charts] – the murder and other crime rates in Kabul have fallen since our arrival, so that they are now comparable with other cities across the world, particularly in Central Asia. So you've gone from having a city that was pretty lawless (it didn't really have a police force) to an environment that, for Central Asia, is a reasonably secure place to live. It's not [just] me saying that; if you go out and talk to the population about how they feel regarding security, they will say it's as good as it's been in the last twenty-three years.

We've now done over 2,000 joint patrols with the police, and a number more on our own. So, in terms of success, we've exceeded our expectations (and those of the interim administration). The security situation has underpinned a commercial resurgence in Kabul – it's a remarkably busy, normal place now.

PM: *How good is your intelligence gathering?*

JM: A key part of what we do is interface with the police – putting company bases next to district police stations, joint patrolling, combined intelligence gathering etc. We've drawn a great deal on our experiences in Northern Ireland. That experience, which we tend to take for granted, stands us in enormously good stead. It worked in Pristina and is doing so in Kabul.

PM: *What about the attacks on ISAF troops?*

JM: [The general explained that there had been thirteen 'joined-up' attacks on ISAF. Nine had been law and order issues.] What I haven't spoken about is terrorism. British patrols have encountered four terrorist attacks, politically motivated. I put them down to a combination of al-Qaeda, Taliban and Hekmatyar [Gulbuddin's troops]. They're trying to create an unstable security environment to reflect badly on the IA [interim administration] and the international community, implying that we're incapable of running a secure environment.

PM: *Are you expecting anything in terms of what the IRA used to call 'spectaculars'?*

JM: No, I wouldn't describe them as spectaculars; what I'm saying is that I think there will be more terrorist attacks, especially before the *Loya Jirga* [national quasi-parliamentary convention] is held.

PM: *Do you have enough in the way of force protection? ISAF doesn't have many armoured vehicles, no heavy metal.*

JM: Because I think the major threat is terrorism, I don't think that heavy metal, artillery etc. would particularly help. The reason that most kids are all over our patrols downtown [we had previously discussed my favourable impressions of how the locals had warmly welcomed British patrols] is that we're open; we don't drive around in tanks.

PM: *The UK government has done its best to separate the British-led ISAF peacekeeping mission [Operation Fingal] from the war-fighting mission of the Royal Marines [Operation Snipe], but I wonder whether the average Afghan understands this distinction, especially as some of them seem to think the Russians have come back?*

JM: First of all, I think there is some distinction. In some areas, the distinction between the different roles may have some effect. I suspect, however, that the al-Qaeda, Taliban and Hekmatyar regard all coalition and ISAF forces as legitimate targets.

PM: *May I ask about Cimic [civil-military cooperation, humanitarian aid]? Much of what I have seen is laudable, especially in schools in Kabul, but isn't it rather cosmetic compared with the long-term needs of the whole country?*

JM: From the point of view of the humanitarian requirement, as you well know, the UN takes time to get going. Because we're out in the streets every day, we have no difficulty identifying demand, and we can very rapidly implement it. So as a tangible symbol of international engagement, early action, when people's opinions are forming, it has a critical role to play. It certainly improves the quality of people's lives – the majority of schools we've repaired would not have been repaired had we not done it. So there are at least 4–5,000 children in Kabul now going to school thanks to our efforts. That's got to be good news.

Most importantly, it very eloquently tells the people that ISAF is a force for good. Therefore, I think Cimic, combined with the information operation, is the most important element of force protection that we have. You are never going to convince the hardened [al-Qaeda or Taliban] supporter that the presence of a Western force is a good thing. What we can do is influence the less extreme (but nevertheless conservative) groups who are opposed to our presence in the city. Despite their protests they have to admit that we are a force for good; by our enforcement of the laws, the security situation has improved as has the quality of people's lives. I've spoken to conservative leaders – such as Professor Sayyaf – who have admitted as much.

PM: *In view of the debate in the UK about women in the frontline, may I add a cultural issue? How, in your estimation, have the numerous female soldiers and officers I've met been treated by the Afghans?*

JM: I've been surprised how easily the Afghan males have related to our female soldiers and officers. The female officers are very authoritative. [The general mentioned a specific female Cimic officer.] In fact, she's quite bossy, but very, very effective with Afghan males; everybody jumps to attention. The fact that she's a woman is completely irrelevant – which is quite extraordinary.

PM: *Is there any sort of specific lesson you've learned from your command of ISAF?*

JM: There is one. We went for multi-nationalization of headquarters on 18 February [2002]. It was under sole British control before then (British two-star headquarters, 3 Division and 16 Brigade). We went for a

German tactical command at the one-star level. We're all very used to multi-nationalization in the Balkans. But, in operations in a volatile situation, it is essential that a strong lead nation is established to provide command and control and coordination until such time as the operation stabilizes itself.

PM: *So you've accomplished your mission?*

JM: I am very proud of what we've achieved here in the past six months . . . When we deployed on 14 December the question was: are we going to do it at all? It's quite difficult to imagine that now.

Building work ahead – Gwyn Winfield went to Kabul and Mazar-I-Sharif to examine the work that is being done to rebuild Afghanistan.

Afghanistan would seem to be on the cusp of a decision that will decide the fate of the country: whether or not to accept that NATO and the US are sincerely trying to make the country better. This sort of decision is one that the Afghans are used to making, in 1842, 1878, 1919, 1979 and 2001 to name a few examples. Their solutions have all followed the same path – breaking out the jezzail or Kalashnikov. The decision is not limited to the foreign troops. If the feeling is that they are occupiers rather than liberators then the Karzai administration will be seen as a puppet regime to be swept aside for feudal warlords to fill the vacuum.

There are a number of groups trying to ensure this happens. The Taliban, al-Qaeda and *Hezb-I-Islami* are all pushing to ensure that a moderate Islamic state is not a viable future. Instead they seek to replace this with a hard-line version of the *Koran*. The warlords have not been wholly compliant in ensuring that the road to Afghan peace is smooth. They have vested interests to secure, knowing that if they are seen as weak they will not be able to get concessions from the West. Their activities range from mischievousness – kidnappings, assassination, drugs and general sabre rattling – to serious attempts to destabilize the region.

While there has been a political vacuum in Afghanistan for the past thirty years as the people fought the Russians or the Taliban, there has been no shortage of political groups. In some areas these are a new name for previous tribal loyalties, but in others they have a manifesto and an agenda that would be recognized in any country. In the area around Mazar-I-Sharif alone there are five parties, polarized by *Jumbish* on one side and *Jamiat* at the other.

Jumbish is the political party of 'Great Leader' General Dostum, a mainly northern Afghanistan party that speaks for Uzbeks. *Jamiat* is a pan-Afghan party with General Attah as the most senior figure around Mazar, but with major representation in the Karzai administration through figures such as Abdullah Abdullah, Mohammed Fahim and Mohammed Qanuni.

Between these, and with tortured lines of influence and allegiance, are other political parties such as *Harakat, Wahdat* (1) and *Wahdat* (2). As opposed to firing insults at each other on different sides of the ballot box, *Jamiat* through 7 Corps and *Jumbish*, through 8 Corps, have been firing artillery and tank shells at each other. This came to a head in October [2002] as the two sides squared up to each other in what promised to be a major incident. Thanks to the help of Interior Minister Jalali and the presence of the UK PRT (Provincial Reconstruction Team), the situation was defused and normal political sniping resumed.

Both *Jamiat* and *Jumbish* were part of the winning side in the war against the Taliban and are keen to remain so. If public will turns against NATO and US troops, there is little doubt they will too. It is the battle for hearts and minds that needs to be won now and the PRT is doing a good job. The military component of the PRT polices only the police and keeps a strategic hand on the direction of the province. The real battle for Afghanistan is now being fought in the corridors of London and Washington.

When the Northern Alliance was recruited to fight the Taliban it is clear it was told, or allowed to believe, that when the war was over paradise would be built in its devastated country. Every village you visit is waiting for the trucks full of money to arrive and the bounty to be forked out of the back. When it is pointed out that they now have running water, or more power, this is quickly batted aside. This bounty does exist though. USAID, the American aid organization, has been allotted $30 million for the north of Afghanistan in 2004 alone. While $30 million may not bring a great deal of change in the US or Europe, in Afghanistan, with its low labour and raw material cost, it could make a huge difference. Yet this is where the problems that could see a descent into conflict begin.

Even though this money has been approved by the US government, it is not in the power of the USAID staff out in Mazar to spend it. The process of spending the money runs from USAID in Mazar to their office in Kabul, then to the International Office of Migration (IOM) and up to the State Department and Senate. There has also been the suggestion that a new level of bureaucracy may be introduced. This means that aid

– a new school, for example – moves at a glacial pace. There is a lobby of opinion at both a high and low level that this needs to arrive soon.

This is not to suggest that there is not a great deal of work going on, as Miriam Simonds, of USAID, said: 'There has been a lot of reconstruction but not a lot of new construction. For example, a local school that was the HQ of the Taliban and was pummelled into rubble has now been rebuilt as a school.'

The biggest change to the whole region is DDR (Demobilization, Disarmament and Rehabilitation). This is where militia soldiers are paid $100 for their weapon and taken from their units and trained for a new job so they can be rehabilitated. This has proved a great success and is a positive way of stabilizing the region and moving relatively quickly towards safety. This is despite apocryphal tales suggesting that one enterprising soul traded his jezzail for $100 and then went and bought three Kalashnikovs!

The police force in Mazar-I-Sharif is slowly becoming professional. Some of the aid money that the UK's Department for International Development and the Foreign and Commonwealth Office allocated has gone into making sure the police have official uniforms and transport. It is a lucrative business in Afghanistan to impersonate the police and set up a roadblock. The show of support and muscle behind the police has enabled some key arrests of prominent terrorists. But one of the most telling successes is the lack of guns on the street. One year ago a trip to Mazar would have been like an arms jamboree, but thanks in small part to DDR (confiscating the weapons) and the police (providing the security to allow guns to be left at home), the localized security situation is improving. There is, within some parts of the Afghan police service, a naïve confidence that everything is going to fall into place very quickly. While this is misplaced in its estimates of timing, it is correct in terms of the overall direction.

Whether it is police, schools or fresh water, a positive change is coming. It just isn't coming quickly enough. 'The Taliban have also been spreading the suggestion of "See, they've been here two years and they've done nothing. Trust us instead,"' said Miriam Simonds. When Donald Rumsfeld visited in December [2003] it was the one issue that Generals Dostum and Attah agreed on – the money that was promised must be turned on. There is a mass of good work happening in Afghanistan; it just needs the extra money behind it to ensure it is a critical mass. There is no administrative middle class, for example. At the moment Afghanistan is forced to be a cash administration; if you want to be paid for government work then you better go to Kabul. The police are a perfect example. They used to be poorly paid and had to raise revenue with illegal roadblocks. Now their wages are far better than ever before, but the actual cash is often months late.

This transition from one system to another is where disaffection breeds. The forces raised against a moderate democracy are not slow to realize this and there has been an increase in al-Qaeda and Taliban activity to make sure that the process is reversed. There has been an increase in shootings at aid workers (some of these are drug related rather than politically motivated), but the murder of the French aid worker Bettina Goislard and the series of explosions aimed at military targets show that there will be opponents to the change all the way.

Thankfully, though, the forces of realpolitik look like they are going to help save Afghanistan, as this year is US presidential election year. While there are many excellent reasons for aiding Afghanistan ranging from the humanitarian – a deprived country that has suffered thirty years of civil war – to the military (depriving al-Qaeda and the Taliban of a base for their operations), it would seem that the need to keep George Bush Junior in the White House is the most compelling. State department sources have suggested that the money started to flow normally in August last year and has improved steadily since.

Donald Rumsfeld has now made six trips out to Afghanistan, and more are expected. And with Iraq looking worse and worse from month to month there is a need for foreign success. Currently George Bush's scorecard looks like a score-draw. Two military successes but two foreign losses (neither country is safe or stable) and an Afghanistan that is well on the way to peace, combined with the suggested withdrawal of US troops in the south, may well provide him with the necessary patriotic wave to land him back in office. This is not to suggest that Afghanistan will be helped just because of the US election campaign. All the other reasons for a solution are equally compelling. What it will do is act as a catalyst and ensure that it is done sooner rather than later.

Perhaps this is too cynical and the recent increased attention is due to a carefully planned strategic plan. If it is not, once the election is over, Afghans may find themselves wondering where the largesse has gone.

Gwyn Winfield visited Afghanistan in December 2003.

Any old iron – Colonel Richard Davies, head of the UK's Provincial Reconstruction Team, on taking the weapons off the warlords in Mazar-I-Sharif. He was interviewed by Gwyn Winfield in December 2003.

GW: *There were a series of incidents in Mazar-I-Sharif throughout October last year that looked like they might spiral into a full-scale conflict. How bad was it and has that been the main focus of your work?*

RD: We have been engaged in the north since June and a large amount of the work has been involved in security centre reform. We have conducted a number of local-scale disarmaments to try and resolve the problems in the north, including one we did August to September in the Shulgarah valley. The principal reason was to provide voluntary disarmament and to allow the weapons to be collected and held in a factional armoury.

This summer there was an amount of tension in and around Mazar. There was quite a bit of tension in May, and there was nearly some quite serious fighting in August, which we managed to prevent. During October the situation was raised to quite new levels and both [Generals] Attah and Dostum deployed a large number of troops, tanks and artillery and there was some limited fighting.

The fighting was not as bad the press suggested. They had figures that showed estimates of 60–100 killed. We checked extensively in all areas of conflict and got confirmation on only seven dead and twenty-seven wounded, of which only one was serious. It is possible that there are twos and threes of people which are suspected kills, but I would say they were not technically killed by the fighting. But they did deploy tanks and artillery, and this was a significant step.

GW: *What was the reason for the conflict?*

RD: It is not a simple question to answer. There had been a series of assassinations and kidnappings on both sides that led to a general raising of tension. This in turn resulted in the *Jamiat* kidnapping of a *Jumbish* commander. That really built the tension up. August's problems were the result of an ambush of a *Jamiat* convoy by *Jumbish*. The October incident was the result of another kidnapping of two *Jumbish* commanders by *Jamiat*. You basically had tit for tat kidnappings that wound both sides up until it came to a use of force. We put a lot of pressure on them to calm it all down.

GW: *How do General Attah and General Dostum fit into this?*

RD: General Attah is the commander of 7 Corps and, while General Dostum has no formal military position, he has considerable military

172

influence over all of the units of 8 Corps and influence over some of the units in 7 Corps. So 19 Division, which is formally part of 7 Corps, is essentially *Jumbish* (which is headed by General Dostum). In October you saw the game raised to such a level that it had come to blows and Minister Jalali came up to Mazar with the British and US ambassadors and organized the ceasefire that the PRT oversaw.

But central government realized this would happen again, further stabilization methods were needed, so came up with a document which Minister Jalali brought up to be signed by Generals Attah and Dostum. This has led to the cantonment of heavy weapons as the first step, followed by the creation of 15 Corps, to help create peace in the region. 15 Corps will only be an intermediate step because you have the disarmament project (DDR), the third such pilot project (there is one in Kunduz and one in Gardez), coming to Mazar.

What you'll see is the formation of 15 Corps, with its 7 and 8 Corps parts, that's about 1,000 soldiers, going through the DDR process. As the DDR process continues then in subsequent months the whole of 15 Corps will be disbanded, so it is a temporary step that gives you better control of the forces. There are some problems in both camps that would benefit from a new HQ and rationalization

GW: *How many heavy weapons have been handed in to the cantonments?*

RD: There are about 200 pieces of equipment in the eastern site and there must be about forty pieces of equipment in the western site. Some people have pointed out the discrepancies in numbers, but sitting in the eastern site is the equipment from 19 Division which is a Dostum division, for example. So you can't compare the sites as one being Attah and one being Dostum.

GW: *Will these weapons be made safe?*

RD: The idea is that the weapons going to the cantonment sites will be formally under ANA (Afghan National Army) control. What will subsequently happen to the weapons has not been decided. Some people would support these weapons being handed over to the ANA, equally some of the weapons may go into the DDR process. What happens will be subject to detailed negotiations. The important thing is we're able to have an early effect — control of the weapons — and that is what we have achieved.

GW: *Is there the possibility that if things escalate again, either General Dostum or Attah may turn around and say, 'I want my kit back'?*

RD: Most of the weapons have been temporarily disabled.

GW: *Any idea of how many useable weapons are out there?*

RD: We have a very good idea of the number of heavy weapons because there was a MOD census done at the end of 2001-02 which, checking with our own observations over the past six months seems to have been very accurate, though some of the equipment was damaged. The difficulty with weapons in Afghanistan is knowledge of smaller weapons. There are a lot of RPGs and machine guns knocking around and you cannot find anyone who doesn't have a gun. But when you are dealing with tanks and pieces of artillery, I think we have a reasonably good idea of what there is.

GW: *There have been stories about people using the $100 they receive from DDR, for an old Lee Enfield, to go out and buy three Kalashnikovs.*

RD: I have spoke to the DDR team and they are very clear that if someone turns up with a nineteenth-century musket, as we've seen in some of the villages, then that does not count. They need to bring us a modern, serviceable weapon. While some of the heavy weapons we have accepted are damaged beyond what would be accepted under the DDR scheme, a lot of the heavy weapons are better than anything that has been given to the ANA. So it will be for the DDR team to look at what is in the compound and decide what can be allowed into the scheme and conduct detailed negotiations with the units that are handing weapons in.

We have kept very detailed registers of what has been handed in, who handed it in, the serial numbers, and the state of serviceability etc. We can make sure that the right sort of information is supplied to the DDR team to link the two processes together. What we [the PRT] are not doing is collecting light weapons. The DDR process is mainly about the collection of light weapons which is why, if they are run together, it can be a very complementary process.

GW: *Are we seeing cherry picking in the weapons that are handed in? Do you receive just the old or unserviceable weapons?*

RD: In terms of divisions, we have had all the weapons, but not all of them are working. After all this is Afghanistan not the US or UK! Things we would regard as unserviceable, the Afghan ministry will look at and say: 'Actually you can make that serviceable, you should collect that.' Probably 80 per cent of what is in the cantonment is reasonably serviceable. The reasons that figure is so low stem from the early days when we just collected everything. Quite soon I said to the guys: 'Look there is no point just collecting scrap metal, just collect the serviceable bits.'

174

Some of the broken stuff you see dates back to the start of collection.

GW: *Have there been more T55s handed in than T72s for example?*

RD: We have seen mainly T55s and T52s with a couple of T62s, but we are seeing a lot of ZU23s, the twin-barrelled anti-aircraft guns. They were used a lot in the conflict.

GW: *It would seem that the warlords are getting more canny, realizing that power is no longer going to flow out of the barrel of the gun but out of the resources and land controlled. Is this the case in the north?*

RD: The north will probably be sorted out because of the oil and gas around Shulgarah. They are probably the biggest natural resources up here. The oil is not likely to be much to write home about, but the gas field is quite significant. We looked after the US geological survey to allow them to build on the Russian data that was valid as far back as 1981. Clearly that data, when it is available on public websites, will be of huge value to investor companies, and it is the investor companies that will kick-start regeneration. The reason they won't come here yet is that they are worried about the security situation. We will look after them and make sure that they can do their job.

GW: *In terms of the security situation, isn't having foreign oil companies coming here to take their oil and gas going to make matters worse? Isn't it just going to confirm suspicions that we are just here to strip Afghanistan?*

RD: Who said it had to be foreign companies? This is going to be in four or five years' time and you can't make investment decisions on the oil and gas fields until you know what's there. It will be up to the Afghan ministry of mines as to how they want to utilize that resource. It will be a central government decision. It will never be exploited by foreigners unless that basic decision has been made.

Divide and Rule – General Mohammed Attah and **General Abdul Dostum** on some of the complexities of reconciling warlords with the central Kabul government.

9 October 2003 saw a ceasefire arranged between the two opposing forces of General Dostum and General Attah that had threatened to spill into the sort of regional fighting that has been endemic in Afghanistan. It was not the first time that these two individuals had faced up to each other. Following the killing of Rasul Beg in May 2003 there had been some light skirmishing between the *Jamiat-I-Islami* and *Jumbish* groups

of General Attah and General Dostum respectively. Prior to this there had been a longer history of antipathy between them, with General Dostum waging war on behalf of the Russians against the *Mujahideen*.

This antipathy is unlikely to disappear, especially in a country that takes blood feuds so seriously, but is now taking on a political veneer. 'We want a credible government that compares well with other governments. Dostum wants a local government and anarchy,' said General Attah. 'We want a credible government to work with the world. Dostum wants his own government backed by his guns. We fought for the freedom of Afghanistan and he fought for the Russians.'

What both of them want is a stable north Afghanistan. The area around Bulkh, Sheribgan and Mazar-I-Sharif is likely to be rich in oil and gas and there is the prospect of wealth and power far beyond the cave dreams that occurred fighting the *Mujahideen* or Taliban. This wealth can come only with stability, which guarantees that outbursts such as the one in October are going to be very rare indeed. Especially so since the Karzai administration has set up a process to disarm the two groups and shatter their power base in 7 and 8 Corps. It is too easy, however, to point to the two corps and allot them a leader. The two corps are politically led and, while Attah is nominally in charge of 7 Corps, there are divisions in 7 Corps, for example 19 Division, affiliated to General Dostum.

The creation of a new 15 Corps should break down these tangled webs. While undergoing the DDR and PRT disarmament process, 7 and 8 Corps will be disbanded and amalgamated into 15 Corps which will later be disbanded or subsumed by the Afghan National Army (ANA). Both disarmament and 15 Corps are sore points between the two factions. There have been suggestions that the cantonment of heavy weapons is not a fair structure. General Dostum's advocates point out that *Jumbish* is a regional power, while *Jamiat-I-Islami* has a national following. If Dostum and Attah completely disarm, then *Jamiat* has not lost a great deal, while *Jumbish* has lost everything. General Dostum puts it another way: 'As the special advisor to the President on security and military affairs I submitted a proposal about the disarmament process and the formation of the national army. I have made an auspicious start on disarmament and the collection of heavy arms. I am keen on the proposal and we are cooperating with the process of disarmament and cantonment of arms and we will continue to support the DDR. But we believe that this process should not just include 7 and 8 Corps, but all army corps throughout Afghanistan.'

General Attah, meanwhile, has a different view: 'Dostum has handed in only twenty to thirty pieces of artillery. Just the ones around Mazar. Every time Dostum has spoken about disarmament it has not been true. When Dostum gives up his weapons he will no longer be a general, so he wants more privileges from the government. If I gave the excuse of Kandahar and Dostum gave the excuse of Herat [that others have not handed in their weapons so why should I?], none of this would work.'

While this may be true, it does not escape from the fact that the cantonment allows a political opponent of *Jamiat* to be defanged, a process that General Dostum would no doubt like to avoid. General Attah is adamant that this is above party politics: '*Jamiat* is not insisting that Dostum must disarm. The weapons are the property of the government and *they* are asking him. If Dostum is giving excuses it is just to change the situation. Dostum has neither the weapons nor the influence compared with *Jamiat*. Regardless of whether he hands in any weapons he has far less power than me. When we took Kunduz he took 30,000 light weapons and he has support from the Uzbeks too. All this is unaccounted for.'

Both Generals confirmed that the dissolution of 7 and 8 Corps and the creation of 15 Corps was a good idea. That just left the problem of the Corps commander. While both sides are happy that the other's power base be taken away, the last thing they want is for a commander allied to the other to take control and be the pre-eminent force in the north.

General Attah laid out his views on who the candidate should be: 'Whoever the candidate is, they must be committed, educated, not black, not a Soviet war criminal, not to have contributed to the civil war, not myself, Dostum or any member of our group and he must be agreed by central government.' General Dostum was strident in denying that he might be interested in the post himself. 'No. I am not going to be the Commander of 15 Corps,' said General Dostum. 'I have been the commander of several corps in my time. We have been discussing my cooperation at a central level, within the defence ministry or the national army. I am not interested in taking a regional military command,' he said.

There is also a drive to win laurels in the continuing fight against the Taliban and al-Qaeda. Since the end of the war in Afghanistan a lot of international interest has been focussed on Iraq and sorting out the security situation there. With only so many resources in the US arsenal, it would seem that some of the effort that might have been expended on

Afghanistan has gone elsewhere. General Dostum has been convinced by Donald Rumsfeld that that is not the situation. 'I have found from talks with Donald Rumsfeld that the US has neither neglected the reconstruction nor the war or terrorism in Afghanistan. On the contrary I have found that there is a suggestion of enhancing the fight against terrorists in Afghanistan. I think that those Afghan commanders who fought against terrorism, together with their international anti-terrorist coalition, were not being included in fighting with the remnants of al-Qaeda and the resurgence of the Taliban. There are issues such as why is the international community fighting the terrorists in Afghanstan and losing their lives? Why shouldn't the Afghans take a more active participation in this? And experienced commanders must be included in this fighting. The commanders in the north do not just belong to the north. We belong to the whole of Afghanistan, so we do our duty wherever there is a problem, whether it is Kandahar or any of the complicated places bordering Pakistan.'

While security and stability are big issues, another is the need for reconstruction. General Attah mentioned his dissatisfaction that the British 'have not followed through on everything they said on reconstruction' and there is a lot of reconstruction needed. With the lack of an educated middle class to run the regime there is a pressing requirement to train up Afghans, whether from home or abroad, to run their own country. 'Reconstruction is needed for everything,' said General Attah. 'For example, in education, to raise the literary level, we need more buildings, more schools. We have placed the foundation stone of the university but do not have the finance to finish it. We are also short of resources, chairs, tables, pens, notebooks etc. In healthcare, for example, we need more physicians, we also need more hospitals. And then there are the roads, bridges, electricity.'

Yet these are all medium-term projects. Some of the major road building will take months or years. General Attah is sure of the first steps. 'Collection of heavy weapons, then the DDR process,' he said. 'The DDR process would be better if those that handed in their heavy weapons were also rewarded. More training centres for the ANA and police. Now that most of the heavy weapons have been handed in we need all the support that has been promised. If we destroy the roots of the Taliban, kill Osama and Mullah Omar, then the rest of the tree will fall,' he promised.

It is clear that with so many problems facing Afghanistan it requires a strong man to lead the country. Yet both the Generals are reticent about how large a part they could play. 'As for the politics, I feel myself to be a good man. We are moving towards a lawful system,' said General Attah. And General Dostum? 'The vital thing for us and the people is to have a successful constitutional *Loya Jirga* and constitution and, according to the constitution, elections will then take place. And then it depends on the will of the people, the path that people will decide for me.'

The last round of fighting and the subsequent war of words that followed have all been about power. The Karzai administration, backed by US muscle and cash, is now recognized as the fount of authority in Afghanistan and the recent sabre rattling has been directed at gaining its attention. General Dostum needs to convince Kabul that he is still a strong figure who commands men and respect and General Attah needs to be able to prove that he is more than a match for General Dostum and a capable soldier and administrator. This jockeying for power is likely to be seen in all the provinces of Afghanistan as the centre makes itself felt. Quite how this is going to impact on General Ismail Khan and Herat, which has never had a close relationship with Kabul and Afghanistan, will be interesting to see.

Interviewed by Gwyn Winfield in December 2003.

Tracking the Taliban – Donald Rumsfeld, US Secretary of State for Defense, and **Lieutenant General David Barno,** Commander US forces in Afghanistan.

There is a simplicity about the rhetoric surrounding the conflict in the south of Afghanistan that is designed to lull you into a sense of security – none of the problems are insoluble and the problems the British had on the North-West Frontier can all be ameliorated with technology and the US will prevail. When Donald Rumsfeld is asked whether he is afraid that the Taliban is making a comeback in Afghanistan, the answer is fired back. 'Am I afraid? I wouldn't use that phrase. Those that have previously been removed would like to come back and they will not have that opportunity. In the case that they assemble in more than ones and twos we will find them and they'll be killed or captured.'

It is not proving that easy to do, however. There have been a number of tactical blunders where the Taliban have tried to do conventional attacks and been wiped out, but by and large they do what the Afghans have always been good at – staying in the hills, sniping and falling on weak targets. 'Our combat forces are continually conducting operations against the Taliban,' said General Barno. 'We had a great success against the Taliban in September in the Orguz region where the Taliban, in a great tactical mistake, came out in large numbers and we were able to kill numbers of them in a several-days engagement. So they have learnt that that is a way in which they cannot be effective and they took tremendous casualties.'

It is very difficult to win a strategic victory in this sort of conflict without the attendant outrage that follows the clearance of guilty, and innocent, to capture the insurgents. There is also the problem of Osama bin Laden. There are weekly suggestions that he has been sighted or, as Donald Rumsfeld puts it: 'There is a suggestion today? Almost everyday, somewhere in the world, he has been spotted.' General Barno has made comments to the effect that he feels that Osama will be caught this year. Yet Pathan code makes handing over a guest a mortal sin. Without effective intelligence the troops are left with the option of being lucky or depopulating the area in the hope that he is there. 'Oh goodness, it would be wonderful if he was captured,' exclaimed Donald Rumsfeld. 'But most of the militaries of the world are trained and equipped to fight armies, navies and air forces, not to track down some individual. It will take time, but it will happen.'

This is not the first time that this has happened. In 1936 Mirza Ali Khan, better known as the Fakir of Ipi, led the British forces and subsequently the Pakistani forces a fine dance for decades. So success, even considering bin Laden's parlous state of health, is not guaranteed. Yet the capture of bin Laden is not going to bring an end to the troubles. Unlike states, terrorist organizations don't collapse with the loss of the head, as the adherents are bound together by a sense of purpose rather than geography. The US rhetoric of military action is backed up by the work that is being done across Afghanistan through the PRTs (provincial reconstruction teams).

These are a long-term solution to the security problem and are part of what could be called a hearts-and-minds strategy. There are PRTs in Herat, Bamiyan, Kundun, Gardez, Mazar-I-Sharif, Parwan, Jalalabad, Ghazni, Logar, Ghor and Kunduz, with another four or five planned for the summer. Their combination of humanitarian aid and low-level military presence has been seen as the best way to combat the situation in Afghanistan. This is not to say there is a template for PRTs. The UK PRT in Mazar-I-Sharif has a particularly British bent – berets, soft skinned vehicles and low force posture – yet this is not a template across the PRTs. The Americans, New Zealanders and Germans all have different approaches to the same problem.

While the British approach may be diametrically opposed to the US style it has drawn a lot of praise and acclaim from both General Barno and Donald Rumsfeld. 'The Mazar-I-Sharif PRT run by Colonel Dickie Davis is the model provincial reconstruction team, in the country,' said General Barno. 'If I look at what they are doing, and I look at the incredible impact they have had in an extremely difficult situation, I can see it is the ideal of what a PRT should be and what it should be able to deal with. It is an impressive operation and we have told people that leadership, when everything is routine and normal is one thing, but leadership in a very difficult situation, the last two months in particular, brings the best out of the soldiers and civilians working in this PRT.

'We can see this in the impact in Maz [Mazar-I-Sharif]. If you had been here six weeks ago there would have been guns everywhere and there would be police who were doing things that were not correct under the rule of law. Today you walk out there and you see no guns, you see police treated with respect and you'll find that they have collected in heavy weapons. I have been in Afghanistan for two months and spent the first part of that dealing with the conflict that was threatening to erupt here in Maz. The government stepped up and made bold moves to resolve the factional fighting, to lay down the law. The Minister of the Interior fired some of the recalcitrant officials and brought some national police up to use them to restore regional order. It was a very bold move on their part and the PRT enabled all that to happen.'

The conditions for the PRT to 'allow good things to happen' are not the same in every part of the country. While Herat may pose some problems, due to the traditional antagonistic relationship between Herat and Kabul, the security situation is at least stable. When you look at the southern and south-eastern areas you quickly understand that berets and a low-force posture would only be a recipe for casualties. PRTs, by their nature, succeed because they improve the local situation which filters into improved intelligence and helps settle the security situation. In the tribal areas this is less straightforward as the borders used to determine Afghanistan and Pakistan mean nothing to the Waziris or Chitralis.

General Barno disagreed, however, that part of the reason why the Mazar-I-Sharif PRT has worked is that there are firm borders. 'I don't agree that this PRT is successful because there is a formal border. The PRTs are different in Maz as opposed to the south and east, but it is no less difficult. Here you have some very serious battles and factions that have used artillery and tanks. You do not see that in the south. In the south and east you have the challenge of criminality in some areas and you have the challenge of helping to bolster the government down there. But I don't see the situation there as any more difficult than the PRT up here. We are putting a PRT into Kandahar and it has been welcomed by the people with open arms. We are looking at putting PRTs in Jalalabad, Khost, Herat. We have one in Gardez that is hugely successful despite being in a very bad, contested, area. We have seen terrific results there in a different situation with different threats, but it is the right model to take to other provinces down there.'

This is a view that Donald Rumsfeld agreed with and saw as integral to the growth of Afghan government. 'There is no question that the circumstances of every part of this country are different to any other part. There is not a single circumstance for the country of Afghanistan, it is all different. The PRTs do not have a fixed template that is then imposed on an area. The ones that have been initiated are all different in their own way and they are doing things that fit the local circumstance. This one here, with Colonel Davies, is doing an extremely good job. There is no question that they have made a very constructive contribution and the transitional government, the Karzai administration, is being felt and being reflected in the regions and that is a good thing.'

Certainly the PRT is working in Mazar-I-Sharif and there have been circumstances outside of the usual British peacekeeping experience that have been handled with aplomb. The problem will come in getting the posture right. Afghanistan is volatile and the security situation can shift both ways very quickly. Having the military, and more importantly the aid organizations, kept informed of the minute shifts is going to be critical to ensure that there is a build up and scale down at the right time. Once the number of PRTs are increased it will be interesting to see what sort of impact a Human Rights Watch type report will have on the PRTs' working relationship. The lessons that have been learnt in places such as the Balkans, Malaysia and Northern Ireland are essential for Afghanistan, as one mistake can quickly ripple through the whole country.

Interview by Gwyn Winfield, with correspondents from *The Times, The Telegraph,The Independent* and the BBC, in Mazar-I-Sharif in December 2003.

Not West Belfast – Colonel Mike Griffiths, Commander British Forces, on counter-terrorism in Afghanistan.

It is almost impossible to find a British officer above a certain age that has not served in Northern Ireland and that proving ground is showing its fruit in Kabul. The Afghan capital is currently acting as a honey-pot for terrorists. As the PRTs in the regions do positive work, the support for the terrorist disappears. No longer can the Taliban, al-Qaeda and Hezb-I-Islami (the terrorist organization of Gulbuddin Hekmatyar) rest behind passive insurrection of the 'what have they done for you lately?' variety. The interim administration is, with NATO and US help, finding its authority, and with the DDR process bringing hope and occupation to thousands of militia there is a real trickle-down effect.

This has forced terrorists to take a more aggressive stance, suicide bombing, vehicle bombs, improvised explosive devices (IEDs) and rocket attacks are becoming more commonplace. This is a two-edged sword for the terrorist organizations as they need to break cover to make their strikes. This has resulted, in the period October to December 2003, in eight arrests, all of various seniority. In December Milang Zafir Khan, who was rumoured to be a senior commander in Hekmatyar, was arrested. Indeed local police sources have said that his arrest 'has cut the left leg off Hekmatyar'. His arrest was a good example of the sort of cooperation between the security forces that is being fostered. Information was passed to NATO through local sources, this was corroborated, and the intelligence passed onto British forces. They then collaborated with local police forces and at a routine police check, Milang was pulled over and requested to produce his papers in an off-road site. Here he was greeted by a unit of Gurkhas and a Saxon vehicle. Coming to the obvious conclusion that resistance would be brief, the three occupants of the car, with a quantity of *matériel*, handed themselves to the British forces.

Major Malcolm Fox, Colonel Griffiths' Chief of Staff, explained that this was just one of many similar sorts of operations they run. 'We run a lot of these operations for our own force protection, because, as you can imagine, there are a vast array of threats. The organization that he is alleged to be working for is one of those organizations that have said that they will carry out these threats, from the suicide attack to the vehicle-borne IED – whether that is with a person attached or just left with it in. These sorts of operations are to protect ourselves and the wider ISAF community.'

While many of the terrorist cells are networked, ensuring that it is difficult to catastrophically damage the organization in one hit, this does not exclude them from having to replace quality people when parts of the network are hit. This requires accurate information on the league table of terrorists – who goes up and who gets relegated. 'Our intelligence community has a vast array of both names and locations of individuals who would be of interest,' said Colonel Griffiths. 'The difficulty is finding out who is active and interested in taking an attack into the city and against ISAF. That is one element, actually unravelling who is current. The other problem is, once one is removed, another one moves up into that position and it is how quickly we can identify who that is. We were lucky that there was enough intelligence, both from prior and during ISAF, for us to be able to target him [Milang Zafir Khan]. They tend to step up into empty shoes and we are reliant on being told who it is next.'

There is a change in MO over the past twelve months. Intelligence sources in Kabul have suggested that there has been a lot of tactical, technical and personnel transfer between Iraq and Afghanistan. There have been 'lessons learned' sessions for both blue and red forces, and much scrutiny of how the peacekeeping organization works. Local intelligence sources suggested that the level of sophistication has increased in a number of areas. 'The understanding of how to put together more sophisticated improvised explosive devices has improved, remote control devices, for example, so they don't need to be on-site using wire. They do it through radio signal. While they all use the munitions that are scattered across this country, instead of using one they are placing daisy chains so it has more of an effect. One was discovered linked to a rocket attack on a NATO camp. Later on, when they were clearing up, they discovered a remote-control IED close to the site. The vehicle bomb in the centre of Kabul, first of all they used a bicycle to carry the bomb, it was followed by a larger vehicle-borne bomb closer to the site on an IED. So as people rushed in to sort the first one out, the second went off and killed a number of people. Previously there have been isolated rocket launches where they have literally propped the thing up on two sticks. In September there was a coordinated rocket attack where two rockets were fired from a range of twenty kilometres, one impacted in the airport and one overshot the airport and struck a house in the residential area. That was the first time we have seen the equipment used as it should be, over its range with the right level of accuracy. There has been an increase in both frequency and accuracy.'

Hekmatyar, in the 1990s, terrorized Kabul with a semi-constant bombardment with these types of rockets. While they don't have the opportunity to increase the frequency, thanks to NATO surveillance and speed of response, they have clearly dug out both the technology and experience to make these sorts of strikes. There has also been the suggestion that a number of the suicide attacks seen in Kabul have not been by Afghan nationals. Suicide bombing is more the preserve of Chechens or Pakistani terrorists and while the identity of the bombers is unknown it would seem that they have been brought in from other areas.

Thankfully, though, the Iraq experience is not being successfully transplanted into Afghanistan. The battle for hearts and minds that is stalled in Iraq is proceeding well enough in Afghanistan to ensure that there is both a flow of information and a reluctance to aid the terrorists. 'People realize that the security situation is improving and individuals wish it to carry on improving,' said Colonel Griffiths. 'As the local community becomes more involved, that develops into not necessarily more intelligence but more information. As you get more and more it identifies the right people and by linking up information you can pull people in – they are all connected. As the coalition has more success in the regions it will bring them into Kabul more, because that is where the targets are.

'Nowhere in Kabul is there a sense of menace. The people of Kabul support ISAF; this isn't West Belfast. The terrorist has to work where he doesn't have local support – as he does in the south. What we do, we have to do in a sensible manner so we don't aggravate the local population,' said Colonel Griffiths.

Colonel Griffiths admitted that at certain stages of the counter-terrorist campaign the British have taken the lead due to their Northern Ireland experience. This is not to suggest that counter terrorism has become the British role in Kabul. Colonel Griffiths is keen to point out that this is a NATO-wide task. 'Commander ISAF [ComISAF] is looking to do more proactive operations in counter terrorism – the ability to dominate an environment and interdicting, preventing and lowering the level of violence – as soon as we get the right toolset. ComISAF needs to have the intelligence and the ability to move his forces around. He needs to have his own command-level intelligence. As with all these things we give and share whatever information we can, but, ultimately, we need to protect our sources.'

The challenge in Afghanistan is to keep the lid on the problem long enough for the work that the PRTs are doing to take effect. There are issues with the PRTs that suggest it might take more time than would be ideal, but as long as the work that they are doing can take the edge off the disaffection, ISAF can help patrol the honeypot of Kabul. Events in Iraq and Madrid show the levels of damage that can be done if terrorist groups are not continually disrupted and it is the lessons learned from the British in Northern Ireland that might make the difference.

Interviewed by Gwyn Winfield in December 2003.

Iraq

A War of unintended Consequences – Lindsey Hilsum,
Channel Four News International Editor, spent much of 2003 and part of 2004 in Iraq, witnessing the war and aftermath at first hand. She saw that the diplomatic and human consequences of the war might be both unintended and disastrous.

'History is the sum total of things that could have been avoided.' These words by the great German post-war Chancellor, Konrad Adenauer, were cited by US Defense Secretary Donald Rumsfeld in his speech to NATO foreign ministers on the eve of the war in Iraq. He tried to convince them that failing to overthrow Saddam Hussein would be more dangerous than going to war. Later, as Iraq burned, and George Bush and Tony Blair struggled to defend the stated reason for war, those who backed them may rethink the meaning of Adenauer's words. The conflict in Iraq has followed the law of unintended consequences, because the politicians who chose war failed to think through the likely impact of their bold plan to remake the strategic map of the Middle East.

The Iraqi political scientist, Gailan Ramiz, a graduate of Princeton and Oxford, had some inkling of this as he hid in the basement of his Baghdad house on 9 April 2003 listening to the rumble of American tanks overhead. 'Why could not the Iraqi army do this? Why did we leave it to the Americans?' he shouted. He knew that liberation came at a price: humiliation. In mid 2004 he was killed in his garden by an explosion in a neighbouring house which American troops were storming – ironically, he became an unintended casualty of the war he welcomed and abhorred in equal measure.

Vice President Dick Cheney's confident assertion that Iraqis 'would welcome as liberators the United States' showed a fundamental mis-understanding of the psychology of occupation and the nature of Iraqi nationalism. Iraqis welcomed the overthrow of Saddam Hussein, but that did not mean they wanted to be occupied, especially by the foreign power which they blamed for twelve years of sanctions.

For Israel and oil

Understanding that there could be no liberation without occupation is painful for Iraqis – they want an impossible situation in which Saddam Hussein has been overthrown but that somehow the Americans didn't do it. Their reaction to the Americans is therefore sullen, indifferent or hostile and frequently contradictory. An opinion poll carried out for Channel 4 News in July 2003 showed that 88 per cent believed the Americans came either for oil or to help Israel, while less than a quarter thought it was to liberate them. In other words, they believed that their freedom from dictatorship was merely an unintended consequence of the conflict.

Of course, the warnings were there – Anthony Cordesman of the Center for Strategic and International Studies was writing in December

2002: 'We badly need to consider the Lebanon model: hero to enemy in less than a year.' Britain's Intelligence and Security Committee, analysing intelligence made available to the Prime Minister and presumably available to the Americans, reported that back in February 2003: 'The Joint Intelligence Committee assessed that al-Qaeda and associated groups continued to represent by far the greatest threat to Western interests, and that threat would be heightened by military action against Iraq.' Documents leaked in October 2003 showed that before the war, the State Department had predicted many of the problems that occurred immediately afterwards, but the Pentagon and the White House blocked their collective ears.

The Iraqi exiles who cultivated policy-makers in Washington convinced them not only that winning the war would be a 'cakewalk' – which it was, more or less – but that winning the peace would be too. After months of deadly attacks on American patrols, and the continued effective sabotage of oil pipelines, electricity cables and water supplies, a note of tetchiness entered the debate. 'Just because the terrorists are trying to bomb us out of Iraq, it does not mean that we have to stay there,' wrote Edward Luttwak, an influential thinker who has advised the National Security Council and the Department of Defense. 'Most Iraqis simply do not believe that the occupation is benevolent, and therefore refuse to collaborate to make it a success . . . after two or three decades of relentless benevolence, Iraqis might overcome their incredulity – but that would require more blood and money than the entire Middle East is worth.'

Luttwak could have expanded his category of people who did not see US intervention as benevolent to include the leaders of most member states of the UN. 'Few things are more dangerous than empires pursuing their own interest in the belief that they are doing humanity a favour,' noted the historian Eric Hobsbawm. But for American policy-makers, the option of cutting and running simply did not exist, because they *do* think the Middle East is worth a lot of blood and money – that is why they are there. They didn't overthrow Saddam Hussein to make the Iraqis happy, but to change the strategic equation in the region.

The administration believed that by transferring US bases from Saudi Arabia to a newly liberated Iraq they could more effectively fight the war on terror. The pressures on the Saudi government from al-Qaeda sympathizers had made it increasingly difficult to operate from the kingdom, but Iraq would be entirely under American control. Moreover, it had the advantage of bordering two of the countries both the US and Israel see as potential threats – Syria and Iran. More extreme elements amongst the neo-conservatives may have even dreamed of a new puppet regime which would break the stranglehold of OPEC, but the Americans did not dare include oil in the mass privatization of Iraq's assets and businesses.

A tolerable occupation?

The strategic regional vision depended on Iraq being stable, which was predicated on the Iraqi population seeing the American project as benign, or at least tolerable, so it is hard to understand why so little attention was paid to analysing how Iraqis might react to their occupiers. Moreover, the way American marines and soldiers interacted with the population they were meant to protect reinforced prejudice and suspicion. One morning in July 2003, this writer saw an American armoured vehicle moving at speed the wrong way down a road in central Baghdad. An elderly man, slowly driving his car the right way up the street, did not move fast enough for the impatient marines, so they sprayed his bonnet with bullets. He had done nothing wrong, but they casually wrecked his car and drove on. Iraqis know they can, in theory, claim compensation for such cavalier acts of destruction but that does not dispel the sense that the Americans are lording it over them.

The Americans refuse to count, so we do not know how many civilians were killed as they tried to defeat their elusive enemies during and after the war. By mid 2004, the website 'Iraq Body Count' was estimating that up to 13,000 had been killed since the war began. The doctrine of 'force protection' translated into a policy of 'shoot first, ask questions later'. While British troops may shoot only if there is an *actual* threat, the Americans may shoot if they believe there is a *potential* threat. Any Iraqi who complains that a family member was arbitrarily killed in a raid for weapons or terrorists has little chance of redress. If the American soldier can say he believed – however erroneously – that the person was a threat, he is deemed to have acted properly. No-one could expect the 'bad guys' – whether they be former Ba'athists, al-Qaeda supporters or radical Shias – to stop attacking Americans, because they are beyond convincing. The aim should have been to persuade ordinary Iraqis that they have more to gain from helping the authorities to stabilize Iraq than from helping the saboteurs and militants. This has become a guerrilla war like any other, where the battleground is the hearts and minds of the populace, and the Americans are not doing well partly because they do not know how. The scandal of American troops and contractors abusing prisoners at Abu Ghraib did not help.

'A liberated Iraq can show the power of freedom to transform that vital region, by bringing hope and progress into the lives of millions,' said President Bush in February 2003. Optimists suggested that the 'roadmap' to peace between Israelis and Palestinians would benefit, ignoring the internal dynamic of that intractable conflict. More directly, the war was *pour encourager les autres*, notably the Syrians, Libyans and Iranians, all of whom were suspected of developing weapons of mass destruction. The Libyans did give up their putative WMD programme, but – despite President Bush's claims – this probably owed less to the example of Iraq and more to years of diplomacy, and Colonel Gaddafi's desperation for foreign capital.

Historic shift of power

Syria was probably at least chastened by the vision of American power on its borders, but the war seems to have emboldened Iran. The Islamic Republic may have drawn the lesson that America needs deterring, so a nuclear weapons programme was essential. Tehran continued to deny it was developing a nuclear weapon but traces of weapons grade uranium found at nuclear sites at Natatnz and Kalaye in early 2004 raised the suspicions of even European countries who favoured engagement with the Islamic Republic. The Iranian explanation that their centrifuge equipment must have been already contaminated when they imported it, convinced few. Under pressure from both the Americans and the Europeans, Iran agreed before a deadline in October 2003 to let inspectors from the International Atomic Energy Agency carry out spot checks on its nuclear facilities. In return, Iran hoped Europe would help with civilian nuclear programmes and formalize a new trade deal, but the Europeans edged towards the American position. Iran continued to play its cards carefully, revealing the names of just a few of the al-Qaeda leaders it had captured, but refusing to hand them over. Saddam Hussein had no bargaining chips, but Iran's rulers, especially the hardline mullahs who fear reform from within, are managing to ensure that everyone knows the Islamic Republic cannot be so easily dismissed or destroyed. By mid-2004, hundreds of Iranian agents were believed to be operating in Iraq, but they were working for multiple centres of power in Tehran and Qom. The rise of the Mahdi militia, led by the young cleric Moqtada al Sadr, showed how Iran could influence Iraq's potentially restive Shias.

The overthrow of Saddam Hussein was a cataclysm in the Middle East, maybe paralleled only by Israel's triumph and the Arab world's humiliation in the Six Day War in 1967. The Americans knew – even though they did not mention it – that they would disturb the equilibrium between Shia and Sunni power centres in the region. Sunni Saudi Arabia and Shia Iran eye each other uneasily across the desert, each mindful of the epic battles of centuries back which form the core of Islamic history and mythology. One reason the corrupt Sunni regimes in Egypt and Saudi Arabia were reluctant to endorse the overthrow of Saddam Hussein was their fear that Iraq's Shias, backed by Iran, would become too powerful. With the demise of the militant anti-Shia Taliban in Afghanistan, Iran was already feeling more confident. The leaders of Saudi Arabia's Shia minority, which lives in the east of the country where the oilfields are, felt emboldened to hand a petition to Crown Prince Abdullah complaining that they face discrimination in education and government employment, and are prevented from building mosques. There is a sense throughout the region that the time of the Shias has come, that the Americans have caused a historic shift, the significance of which no one, least of all those that caused it, can quantify. The emergence of a revolutionary Shia miltancy in Iraq in mid-2004 suggests this may be a violent shift, and certainly beyond the control of the Americans. The British envoy in Iraq, Sir Jeremy Greenstock, made multiple trips to Tehran to ask for help in containing Iraq's Shias – the Americans may soon find they need more direct channels.

The American administration acted as if the interests of Israel and America were indivisible, apparently accepting Prime Minister Sharon's assertion that America's 'war on terror' was equivalent to his own attempts to quash all opposition to occupation, both violent and non-violent. Some European politicians feared that Israel might even be emboldened to strike Iran's nuclear facilities as they attacked Iraq's in 1988, derailing European attempts to foster the reformists in the Iranian government. Iran's refusal to reward European diplomacy did not help, but Israel has been careful not to overreach itself.

Strategic aims

It is hard for democracies to go to war, because the real reasons for conflict – however valid – will probably not convince the voters, hence the concentration on WMD and the refusal to discuss strategic aims. In Britain especially, the failure to find WMD exposed the public case for war as false, but there was little debate about the real reasons. It is entirely possible that the British entered the war simply because they feared what would happen to the international status quo if the Americans acted alone. The price seems to have been much higher than expected, both diplomatically in the region and in terms of human life.

While diplomats and military planners like to work through scenarios, politicians are more comfortable with the unknown, understanding that too much analysis leads to paralysis. It is entirely possible that the politicians refused to contemplate the likely consequences of their actions, or followed the old mantra 'Yes we must think! Yes we must analyse! But first we must act!' Shortly after the conflict, one of its architects, Richard Perle, said: 'The war in Iraq has demonstrated the significance of strong, decisive leadership, bold military tactics coupled with advanced technology, and the possibility of spreading freedom and democracy throughout the Arab world.' That, then, was the declared result, but it is hard to avoid the conclusion that beyond the simple aim of ending the rule of Saddam Hussein, the policy was to throw all the pieces in the air and see where they landed.

Lindsey Hilsum wrote this article in November 2003, and updated it in August 2004.

Re-inventing the wheel – Former Ambassador **Timothy Carney,** who previously worked at the Office of Reconstruction and Humanitarian Assistance (ORHA), on the mishandling of the Iraq reconstruction effort. Interview with John Chisholm in November 2003.

JC: *In one or two US newspapers, you were described on your appointment as a long-time hawk on Iraq when your name cropped up, but what sort of new Iraq did you hope would emerge from the conflict?*
TC: First of all I could not possibly have been considered a long-time hawk on Iraq because I paid no attention to Iraq at all before [Deputy Defense Secretary Paul] Wolfowitz called me and asked me to join the mission. The only work I did on Iraq in December last year was aimed at drawing lessons from other UN missions and I participated in that. The only hands-on work I did on Iraq was what I did at the time.
JC: *So why do you think your name cropped up when it came to discussing who was going to make up the ORHA team?*
TC: Because I was Paul Wolfowitz's political counsellor when he was US Ambassador to Indonesia, and when he became Assistant Secretary

of State for Asia and the Pacific I was a specialist on Cambodia back when the Vietnamese invaded the place in 1979.

JC: *What sort of preparations did the team make before entering Iraq?*

TC: The focus was very much on various humanitarian crises such as refugee flows and starvation. When we got to Kuwait, because the whole effort was in Kuwait for more than a month, there was an attempt to look at everything from vetting – that is screening Iraqis for unacceptable activities (an effort that came to very little) – to very broad discussions on, for example, human rights issues such as how traumatized Iraqis might be having lost family members under Saddam Hussein. There was a fair focus on the economic side as well in particular looking at how to go about kick-starting the Iraqi economy.

JC: *From reading some of your recent articles there seemed to have been a fairly minimal interface with the military even in the preliminary stages.*

TC: There were military people with the team but they were civil affairs officers, as that component of command is called in the US military. All of us who were assigned to be ministerial advisors were expected to be introduced to the ministerial staffs by military civil affairs officers. That happened to a degree but in no way as effectively or as deeply or as broadly as we had hoped, partly because most of the ministry buildings were either totally looted, gutted by fire or destroyed by blast.

JC: *Do you think that more work could or should have been done before you entered the country?*

TC: No question, no question. They should have started much earlier. They should have started at the time that there was a serious consideration that there was going to be a war.

JC: *I recall that the ORHA plane got commandeered by a US general, but you did eventually reach Baghdad, and once there you were continually plagued by minor niggles such as lack of laundry provision, telephones that could only be used outside and so forth. There seems to have been a staggering lack of forward planning.*

TC: I think what happened there was that the structure and the organization of the civilian side got suppressed because Jay Garner was a retired lieutenant general and all his staff were retired military people so the organization was totally military. Now what the military has is an abundance of privates and corporals who are around to make sure things like that get done. The civilian mission, however, had too many chiefs and not enough Indians. As a result you had us chiefs, fifty-year-old-plus Ambassadors retired, lugging cases of water up to our room, sweeping up the hallway, putting out the garbage, that sort of thing. Once you are at a certain age and grade you work out what has to be done and you do it, but the mid-echelon people thought they had stopped doing this sort of thing once they got out of their twenties.

JC: *You described the reconstruction process in general as re-inventing the wheel – claiming that no lessons seemed to have taken hold from Bosnia and Kosovo. You mentioned nation-building in several articles but Donald Rumsfeld, only recently, said that Iraq didn't need nation builders because the Iraqi people are going to do it. This seems to be a rift between the executive branch and what is happening on the ground. Why?*

TC: Damned if I know! It is the most dispiriting thing to observe and to have been part of. I expect you have followed the news that the National Security Council has been appointed to take a prominent role in coordinating things?

JC: *Yes, I spotted that, but you have to question whether Condoleezza Rice has the political clout to draw in all the separate strands . . .*

TC: That is supposed to be the role of the NSC as defined: to broker disputes between cabinet offices. It should not have a policy role but it often assumes that role if there is a weakness within the executive branch.

JC: *Or if there is a disagreement . . .*

TC: If there is a disagreement then they should broker it. If I were writing my after-action report I would look at the NSC and see why that role failed.

JC: *You have said that private contractors were something of a curse initially . . .*

TC: Yes, I suspect they still are . . .

JC: *So why was this reliance there, even from the early stages? Was it an ideological need, a belief that private enterprise would be more efficient or was it a recognition that the US army was not capable of fulfilling all those requirements?*

TC: I think it was a recognition that the whole ball of yarn, one strand of which was what I have already alluded to – the lack of civilian capability to do the things we needed to – even our own communications were poor. Another was the desire to get private contractors in to do the job as quickly and as efficiently as possible but this did not prove to be the case.

JC: *Was there another option?*

TC: That is an excellent question – was there another option? We could have relied on the US military but that would have involved deploying more military forces into the region.

JC: *And that simply wasn't an option, politically at least.*

TC: Definitely not, no.

JC: *Another issue you were involved with was de-Ba'athification. This must have been a major initial problem and still seems to be so.*

TC: First of all it was basically a good idea. But it needed to be looked at very carefully; and, as I wrote in *Time* magazine, you shouldn't throw the baby out with the bathwater. I told them not to use the quote, but they did anyway, it is too cute. But it is also accurate. Basically Bremer went rampaging, didn't have a large staff, didn't know how large the Ba'ath was and basically didn't have a clue about the additional dimensions like the Iran-Iraq war prisoners being made senior party members just in time to lose their jobs. It just simply wasn't cleverly done.

JC: *And there was very little intelligence as to who these people actually were in the first place.*

TC: There should have been. Now maybe the Ba'ath was careful never to mention anyone's name publicly – I find that hard to believe, but I don't know Iraq. Some of them you have to get rid of, some of them were entirely too Ba'ath and zealous, incompetent and lacking labour relation skills for example. It is interesting that the initial policy was: 'You're out if you are Ba'ath and were involved in human rights violations, contributed to international terrorism or were engaged in producing weapons of mass destruction.' That was the policy from Washington. That changed with Bremer.

JC: *Why the sudden change? Was it just too difficult to identify the right people?*

TC: I think the reason for the change is that conservative group in Washington.

JC: *But again this is dictating policy from two continents and an ocean away . . .*

TC: You would need to ask the exiles as to what they told Washington regarding the Ba'ath party.

JC: *But any occupation policy, from past experience, shows that it is a bad idea to rely on exiles.*

TC: Absolutely. We certainly didn't in Cambodia.

JC: *The fact that you had to deliver hundreds of thousands of dollars around Baghdad, in your own car, does underline a sense of amateurism about the whole thing. Did the US army have any directive at all about how to deal with you?*

TC: It would be useful to recall two things. Firstly, the US army was doing that too. Wherever there was a US garrison or a coalition garrison near a factory they would provide the $20 emergency payment, and secondly we were delivering to finance officers in factories and facilities. The fact is, of course, that it is a socialist economy; the ministries had the state-owned enterprises and all of the employees around the country.

JC: *It does smack of a lack of forethought or the absence of enough people on the ground to do this in any meaningful way.*

TC: It was amateur. Handing out the payments actually worked surprisingly well. We handed the cash out to the finance teams in the enterprises, not the individual employees. It was still a big job, particularly when you were dealing with five and ten-dollar bills – I asked them at least to send twenties, but no!

JC: *It still seems very strange that so much forward planning had gone into fighting the actual war – and policy for Germany started in 1943 so that by the time the war was over a whole series of programmes and agencies were ready to roll. Yet you were pushed forward to the media as Jay Garner's team who are going to sort it all out; but it all goes horribly wrong. I can't understand why you were left unsupported.*

TC: I can't either! I think what it happened was that hope was leading analysis and believing that the collapse of the regime would be so quick that most of the government structure in Iraq would stay intact. Then, with a little bit of guidance, and a certain amount of housecleaning, policies that the coalition wanted to achieve would be achieved in a very short period of time. It was based on an incorrect analysis: events clearly did not fall that way, and were never likely to when you really looked at it. It was a totally inadequate way to prepare for the aftermath of the fighting.

JC: *When did you personally come to the realization that this was not going to be an effective way of operating?*

TC: When the museum was looted. When troops on the ground failed to protect it despite Garner's ORHA team attempting to communicate a list of priorities about institutions that needed to be safeguarded. There just were not enough men, and the military clearly gave no priority to that list.

JC: *So we are back to this division between ORHA and the US occupying forces. You would have expected that, because Garner was an ex-general, and the impression was that he had been put in place because he was an ex-general, and therefore would be able to liaise well with the US army.*

196

TC: More to the point he was an ex-general who had been leader of the effort to help the Kurds in 1991, but he was a *retired* general, he was not an active-duty general. The command structure put him subordinate to the combined forces land component commander and then in turn responsible to Central Command under General Tommy Franks. That was the wrong structure. He should have been in Iraq with the combined forces land component commander subordinate to him.

JC: *It would have been different if the US military commander had recognized the need for prioritizing civilian reconstruction. I always look at General Lucius Clay in post-war Germany as a military officer who fundamentally understood the security implications and the need for reconstruction. With military commanders unwilling to stick their neck out and reconstruct, and with the civilians under them, it seems like it was a recipe for disaster.*

TC: Yep. There is a need for new doctrine and I am working on that with some colleagues – what you do in so-called second echelon wars.

JC: *No consensus seems to have emerged from Washington as yet: now we see a desperate desire to get the UN involved – but with little idea as to how this is going to be a solution.*

TC: There has been a lot of time wasted. On the other hand if you go back and look at what I was involved with in Cambodia, which is the only UN mission that actually conducted an election rather than observed it, the UN was handed control of various areas of national life. I understand it is the nearest, inadequate comparison. It took us a long time to get our plans together for that Cambodian mission and it has been going for ten years.

JC: *Things have not gone well in Iraq. Certainly they have not gone according to whatever plan there was. Is there a conceivable exit strategy now?*

TC: I don't know. Certainly you have to arrest Saddam Hussein before you set up a provisional government.

JC: *You said when I first spoke to you that you found this to be a surreal experience, but when you look back on it how do you feel about your role in it?*

TC: First of all we had to do it, there is no doubt about that. I find the debates in the US and the UK about 'Did the government lie?' misses the point. Saddam Hussein had built weapons of mass destruction, had used weapons of mass destruction and was clearly prepared at some point in the future resume those programmes. We had to go for it, there is no doubt about that at all in my mind. The question, then, is: how do you

197

go about building a twenty-first century Iraq? That should really have been planned and thought through thoroughly with the active participation of Iraqis.

JC: *Do you think the policymakers in Washington DC understand the social and economic complexities of tackling a job like Iraq?*

TC: They don't have a clue, except on the most extreme theoretical level and it cannot be controlled from Washington. There is a need for far more initiative to be given to the people on the ground.

FOUR

The Broader Middle East Conflict

Sudan: the bin Laden connection – Paul Moorcraft went to Sudan in January 2002 to talk to key military and intelligence leaders about the expanding war on terrorism. Here he outlines the debate about Osama bin Laden's connections with the war-torn country.

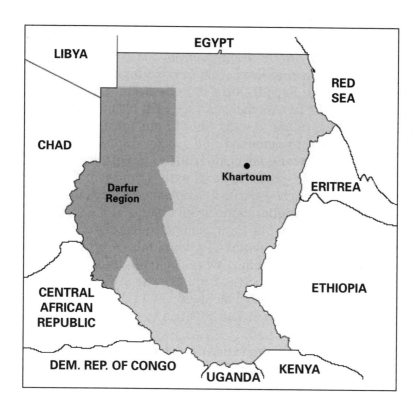

Sudan has been at war with itself – except for brief periods of peace from 1972–83 – even before it emerged from colonial rule in 1956. From 1983 the war had been fought between the government in Khartoum and the Sudan People's Liberation Army (SPLA) and its ever-changing allies in both the south and the north.

There have been numerous ceasefires and peace plans. The most recent [during my visit in January 2002] was in the Nuba Mountains. This area is not part of southern Sudan, which some rebels want to make into a separate state. The war has been exacerbated by external meddling by the great powers as well as by some of the nine states which border Sudan. The conflict also stems from the way deep-seated religious, tribal and ethnic differences have been inflamed by politicians and warlords. The military government in Khartoum is dominated by Muslim Arabs from the north, although it contains a sprinkling of southern Christians and animists. The rebels in the SPLA are predominantly black animists and members of the Christian minority. The SPLA says it wants a secular democracy in the whole country, but it has also espoused separatism. The Islamic government opposes both options, not least because of the large oil deposits in the south. The government, however, said that under the 1997 Khartoum Peace Agreement it will allow further federalization and even a referendum on the future of the southern states.

US peace envoys have advocated 'one country, two systems': an Islamic government in the north and a secular one in the south. The government points out that *Sharia* law is not enforced in the south. Many southerners argue, however, that the government has dishonoured far too many agreements and self-determination is the only option. Despite America's support for the rebels, outright secession would incense Egypt, Washington's key ally in the region. Cairo does not want multiple states controlling the Nile.

What the south desperately, needs is development. Foreign oil companies, particularly the Canadian group, Talisman Energy, are building schools and clinics in the southern oilfield. While tens of thousands of southerners have fled the fighting, others have migrated to new population centres attracted by oil company facilities and aid agencies' feeding centres. According to John Ryle, a leading British expert on the region, many of these centres constitute 'a counter-insurgency programme; they are not a sign of munificent government'. A regular visitor to the southern war zones, he confirmed the frequent reports that helicopter gun-ships sometimes fly from oil company bases. The government's air force conducts 'random terror bombing', Ryle said, to display their supremacy over the SPLA rebels. Neither side can win a military victory, but a political settlement has proved elusive.

Media backwater

Despite being the largest country in Africa and the most tribally complex, as well as enduring the continent's longest civil war, Sudan's travails were largely unreported. Nor did the alcohol ban entice many foreign correspondents. Osama bin Laden, however, made Khartoum his base from 1991 to 1996 and this – much later – became a major international story.

Sponsor of terrorism?

Once a US ally, Sudan increasingly fell out of favour with Washington, especially after the 1989 installation of a revolutionary Islamic regime which the Americans put in the same box as Iran (even though Sudan adheres to a Sunni model of Islam, unlike the more radical Shi'ite creed espoused in Teheran). Washington also damned the Sudanese as being too pro-Saddam in the Gulf war. In 1993 the Clinton administration listed Sudan as a state sponsor of terrorism. The Islamic government was also accused – by Cairo, Ethiopia and the UN, as well as the US – of complicity in the attempted assassination of President Mubarak of Egypt, though Khartoum insists that there is no evidence to prove this allegation. UN and US sanctions were imposed and the American embassy in Khartoum was closed in 1996.

The CIA accused bin Laden of being the mastermind behind an international terror network, yet the Sudanese government insists that, during his stay in Sudan, he was involved in purely civil engineering and charity projects. Bending to mainly US and Egyptian pressure, Sudan ejected the Islamic warlord on 18 May 1996. According to a Sudanese government minister who knew him well, bin Laden was 'very angry'.

Bin Laden told him: 'The Saudis and the US didn't even pay you – you are throwing me out for nothing.' Nor was bin Laden paid the large amount of money owed to him by the Sudanese government for his construction projects.

An embittered bin Laden returned to Afghanistan. Denied an opportunity to engage in more constructive enterprises, he turned to terrorism. This is the official Sudanese line (espoused in particular by the former head of *Mukhabarat,* the Sudanese Intelligence Bureau). Western intelligence sources, however, have indicated that bin Laden had been politically active in the Sudan, coordinating what became the al-Qaeda network.

Lieutenant General Gutbi al-Mahdi, former head of the Sudan's powerful *Mukhabarat*, denied this: 'When he was here he was under surveillance. We were watching him. He was busy. He was preoccupied with his business . . . Kicking him out was a big mistake.' The same phrase was used by the London *Sunday Times* recently when it quoted Bill Clinton's self-assessment of his refusal to accept the Sudanese offer to hand over bin Laden as the 'biggest mistake' of his presidency.

This miscalculation, according to Khartoum, led directly to the abominations of 11 September. Clearly, the success of the strategic attack on America was the result of a massive failure of Western intelligence. The agencies have since put up a smokescreen of disinformation to cover their embarrassment. There is even an argument that bin Laden was not directly responsible for 11 September and that the Saudi exile is just a convenient hate figurehead for a large international Islamic terrorist conspiracy, which will continue regardless of whether bin Laden and al-Qaeda, fashionable media shorthand, are crushed. But, if the conventional wisdom of al-Qaeda guilt is accepted, a central issue remains: could bin Laden have been stopped before his terrorist spectacular?

Khartoum claims that in 1996 it offered bin Laden on a platter to both Washington and Saudi Arabia. Both turned down the opportunity, and so the future 'most wanted man in the world' decamped to Afghanistan and helped to bankroll the Taliban and plot the war on the West.

There was ingrained scepticism in US intelligence about the ruling National Islamic Front in Khartoum, partly because nearly 100 bogus reports from unreliable agents in Sudan had created a distorted assessment of the country's sponsorship of terrorism. The CIA reports were later dumped as useless, but they had reinforced the negative response to Sudan's overtures to the West. On the other hand, opponents of

Khartoum insist that the ruling regime was too implicated in al-Qaeda to ever give up bin Laden to the CIA.

Perhaps Washington and London should have tested the 1996 offer because, if Khartoum was genuine, this was a missed opportunity of cataclysmic proportions. Elements in the FBI and CIA wanted to take the Sudanese at their word; meanwhile others, in the State Department, argued that there was not enough evidence to convict bin Laden in US courts, that the Sudanese offer was a bluff and that, even if it were not, intelligence dialogue would weaken the sanctions pressure on a 'rogue' state that the US was trying to isolate.

In 1998 bin Laden was held responsible by the US for the embassy bombings in Tanzania and Kenya. Two of the terrorists involved (as paymasters) were arrested in Sudan by the *Mukhabarat,* but the FBI was apparently prevented from interrogating them by the State Department. Eventually, the two extremists were deported to Pakistan, where they disappeared. In response to the embassy bombings, the US launched cruise missiles against Sudan and Afghanistan. Unfortunately, the target in Sudan turned out to be Khartoum's al-Shifa medical factory, which produced anti-malaria and veterinary products. The factory had no proven connection with bin Laden nor has the innocent owner yet received compensation from the Americans.

In 2000 the terrorist attack on the USS *Cole* was blamed on an increasingly mobilized al-Qaeda network. After 11 September the worldwide manhunt for bin Laden reawakened interest in his old connections with Sudan.

Diplomatic conundrum

The bin Laden issue is at the epicentre of a much larger diplomatic conundrum. Khartoum has argued that Washington has demonized Sudan because it doesn't like the Islamist government. The Americans have been real terrorists, Khartoum says, because Washington has, at different times, encouraged Uganda, Eritrea, and Ethiopia to support guerrilla and conventional incursions against the government in Khartoum. (The Islamic regime has also dabbled continuously in its neighbours' affairs.) Because of lobbying by the US black congressional caucus and by the religious right, Washington has consistently supported with diplomacy and money (most recently $13 million of overt, 'non-lethal' aid) the 'secessionist' rebels in the south, led by Colonel John Garang. Such lethal meddling along a Christian-Muslim fault line could plummet Sudan into anarchy, a second Somalia, and create further breeding grounds for international terrorism.

Khartoum insists that it has bent over backwards to satisfy American demands. The government arrested Carlos the Jackal and extradited him to France. Then Khartoum expelled bin Laden, his wives and 'several hundred' of his associates. (Critics, however, argue that some members of al-Qaeda remained in the country.) But it is true that the Sudanese government has repeatedly requested US inspections of the alleged chemical weapons factories at al-Shifa and elsewhere in Sudan. As one Sudanese diplomat explained to an American audience: 'You guys bombed Iraq because it blocked UN weapons inspectors. We're begging for a UN inspection and you're blocking it.'

Washington finally took up the invitation: in May 2000 a joint FBI-CIA team arrived in Sudan to investigate the alleged terror connections. At the same time, US intelligence was actively seeking to assassinate bin Laden in Afghanistan (although some of the leaked stories of thwarted derring-do and near misses smack of US agencies attempting, after 11 September, to suggest that they had always been on the ball, but were just unlucky). The visiting US team was given carte blanche in its search for any terror infrastructure – camps and banking networks – in their country. It would appear that the Americans were sufficiently satisfied with the team's progress not to oppose the lifting of UN sanctions. According to Khartoum, by the end of the first year of investigation, the joint FBI-CIA team was prepared to 'sign off' – dismiss – the key terrorist allegations.

Curiously, senior Sudanese security sources also indicated that, at the beginning, the top American intelligence experts showed little interest in the 400 major files on al-Qaeda which were stored in intelligence head-quarters. Intelligence sources in Khartoum also point to the Western failure to collect valuable data when the Northern Alliance captured Kabul; the Russians soon moved in and took much of it. The response by Western intelligence agencies is that the Sudanese were much more protective of their information and Islamic connections than they now pretend. A group of US counter-terrorism experts still remained [in January 2002], at Sudanese request.

Khartoum had also turned to the former colonial masters in London. The Sudanese government dangled the prospect of intelligence co-operation as far back as 1997. But MI6 officials, said Khartoum, showed little interest in the al-Qaeda files, although they displayed some curiosity about the alleged Hamas and Hezbollah cells in Sudan. In December 2001 a team of senior British intelligence agents was expected in Khartoum, but at the last minute the visit was rescheduled to March 2002.

A charm offensive

After 11 September Khartoum's charm offensive went into overdrive. Even though Khartoum immediately arrested, interrogated and (quietly) deported 'a handful of remaining Islamic undesirables', Sudan was frequently mentioned as a target for retaliation. The al-Shifa debacle could be repeated, senior defence officials feared. In January 2002 this writer was conducted to the centre of the Sudanese intelligence headquarters to meet Dr Yahia Hussein Babiker, whose role is equivalent to the deputy head of MI6. Sitting in a deep grey-green leather seat, he conceded that the possibility of US attack was 'low', but 'suitable preparations' had been made. As the intelligence boss was conducting his personal briefing, a TV screen to his side showed an American NBC programme with a prominent map of the world's potential counter-terror targets, which included Sudan.

More encouraging for the National Islamic Front government is the fact that EU-Sudan relations have been normalized and UN sanctions had been dropped, without US opposition; the country was slowly emerging from its diplomatic purdah. President Bush, well-versed in Texan petro-politics, is more inclined to be pragmatic, not least about the vast oil potential in Sudan.

Why did the US turn down the golden offer?

There is a flaw in the Sudanese version of events, however. Why didn't the resident CIA-FBI team ask to see the al-Qaeda materials, especially as they had expended millions of dollars on electronic surveillance of bin Laden's network in Afghanistan? The Sudanese explanation is that 'US intelligence was too politicized'. The Minister for Peace, Dr Ghazi Salah al-Din al-Atabani, explained that 'US policy had been ideological not pragmatic. There was no way to break the barrier.' This may have been an unconscious display of irony by the Surrey-educated physician because Khartoum has indulged in intensely ideological politics.

The Sudanese rationale may have been partly true of sections of the State Department in the Clinton administration, but it cuts no ice in interpreting the Bush administration. 'The Americans see the world differently now,' conceded the Peace Minister. Western intelligence sources, however, insist that the Sudanese are not as open as they pretend to be. 'They have skeletons in the cupboard, and they don't want us to get too close,' warned a senior UK Foreign Office official.

Eventually, about a month after 11 September, the US requested access to some of the crucial files. Photographs and important biographical details were copied and taken to Washington. It is unclear how much was shared with its major ally in the coalition war, the UK. Initially, the Sudanese may have been politely rebuffed by MI6, but recently they have found more willing partners in other UK security agencies, which have dramatically beefed up their resources in the hunt for Islamic extremists based in England. Perhaps the unofficial Sudanese jibe to the Americans – 'If you want to bomb a country with Islamic terrorist cells you should try hitting London – or Saudi Arabia' – had found its mark.

A very manipulative government?

In contrast, many critics say the Khartoum government's charm offensive is just spin. Gill Lusk, deputy editor of the London-based *Africa Confidential*, argued: 'The National Islamic Front government is trying to delay as long as possible any US military reprisals because Sudan is perceived as a poor third-world African country by Western and Arab governments and the longer the government is seen to be appeasing Washington, the worse the international backlash will be against an American attack.'

She added: 'This is not so much a charm offensive as a form of diplomatic deterrence by a very manipulative government in Khartoum. The Sudanese anticipated all this as a response to 11 September. They are chess-players — always several moves ahead.'

Khartoum's many opponents in the US and the domestic opposition insist that the government is still a centre of Islamic extremism (although a middle-ranking al-Qaeda extremist was arrested by the Sudanese authorities in February 2002). The regime has also been charged with tolerating, or practising, slavery and bombing civilians in the civil war. According to Amnesty International, nearly 2 million people have been killed in the civil war since 1983 and a further 4.5 million have been internally displaced. Not all the blame rests with the Islamic government: many, perhaps most, of the fatalities have been caused by internal faction-fighting in the south. Southerners explain this is partly a result of Khartoum's divide-and-rule policy of arming factions. Amnesty said: 'All parties to the conflict committed gross human rights abuses against civilians living in contested areas including indiscriminate bombing [only the Khartoum government has an air force], abduction, enslavement, forcible recruitment, torture and killings.'

President al-Bashir's government is arguably a disguised military junta. The original coup leaders in the military were heavily influenced by the National Islamic Front, which then proceeded to purge the anti-Islamist elements in the army. Whatever its current complexion, the government has tried hard to change its image, partly to capitalize on the growing oil bonanza. Khartoum, though, has been accused of planning to spend the new petrodollars on a big defence programme, including the purchase of Russian Mig-29s. The Sudanese Defence Minister, General Bakri Hassan Saleh – a towering man sporting imposing sunglasses indoors - gave his first-ever media interview to a foreign journalist. He told this writer: 'Oil does allow us extra revenues which permit some modernization, but if we modernize we are accused of militarism. This is a dilemma for us. But we have to be concerned with modernization because there are nine countries around us and we need helicopters, for example, to guard the pipelines.'

In military terms, the Sudanese army and its allied militias have performed relatively well by African standards. The equipment is often poorly maintained, but their generals have managed to conduct, simultaneously, a regular, semi-conventional and counter-insurgency war over many years. Their battle-hardened neighbours have on occasions provided brigade-level fully armoured forces to support the SPLA. The largely conscript government forces have confounded regular predictions of their imminent collapse. But General Bakri Hassan Saleh did concede that there was definitely a sense of war-weariness in the country.

Peace to exploit the oil and political reforms to counter its pariah status are key pillars of the government's image-building. It organized presidential and parliamentary elections in December 2000. 'Both UN and European Union monitors turned down invitations to monitor the elections which were widely believed to be seriously flawed,' stated Amnesty International. 'Arrests of journalists, political opponents and humans rights activists intensified ahead of the elections.' Ironically, most of those arrested were Islamic activists. President al-Bashir even placed under house arrest the leading Islamic radical in the government, Dr Hassan al-Turabi, who in turn branded Sudan 'a police state'.

From Western perspectives, Sudan appeared to be shedding some of its Islamic fundamentalist baggage. Western business interests were also attracted by the rapid improvement in the economy, fuelled in part by the oil windfall. Government statistics – although analysts often suggest that Sudan is a twilight zone for hard facts – claim that the country enjoyed an 8.3 per cent rise in its GDP in 2001. The boom in luxury cars and mobile phones is evidence of the new prosperity, at least in the capital.

Nevertheless, US economic sanctions on Sudan remain in place for the time being. The US listing of Sudan as a state sponsor of terrorism has not been removed, although Afghanistan, for example, was not listed even when US intelligence was focussed on al-Qaeda operations in the two years prior to 11 September. As with Iraq, which has been on and off the list since 1979, (it was conveniently de-listed in 1982 when it went to war with Iran) what matters more is political expediency and not so much the level of state-sponsored terrorism.

Afghanistan mark 2?

Political expedience is also a factor in ditching Clinton's human rights agenda. Russia's onslaught on the Chechens or China's crack-down on internal Muslim (and other) dissidents have been ignored, even encouraged, in the Western crusade against terror. In this context, Sudan's re-branding may succeed.

The demonstration effect of Afghanistan has worked well. Some US strategists were arguing that John Garang's rebel movement could replicate the victory of the Northern Alliance. This notion is based upon proxy forces' hold on distinct territory. Anti-Khartoum groups are not based only in the south – there are significant areas of opposition not just in Khartoum but also in the Nuba mountains and in the east of the vast country.

The Bush administration, however, seems to be engaging more with Khartoum as part of a general realignment of political allegiances in the region; one goal is to restore some stability, especially in Somalia. Uganda may also be pressurized into reducing its military support for Garang's Sudan People's Liberation Army and its allies. In September 2001 the US named a special peace envoy in the region, a former senator, John Danforth, and reinvigorated its diplomatic presence in Khartoum.

During a highly symbolic visit to Khartoum in January 2002, Clare Short, the UK Minister for International Development, told this writer: 'Any objective observer in the world can see that the government of Sudan has moved. Turabi has been removed from power. They have cooperated since 11 September. Sanctions have been lifted by the UN. There's been progress.'

Progress on ending Africa's longest war, though, has taken far too long. Khartoum, however, has achieved much in its PR blitz. It is no longer the pariah police state it was, for example, in 1996 when this writer was personally arrested, on the first day of his first visit to Sudan, by the Justice Minister himself.

208

A stubborn fact, however, skewers the charm offensive: bin Laden was an honoured guest of the National Islamic Front, which still rules in Khartoum. Fashions change though – bin Laden was once a US-backed pin-up boy in the 1980s war against the Soviets in Afghanistan; in 1994 he was even allowed to spend time in the UK. Despite the current official 'bash bin Laden' line, members of the government and business elite recall 'Osama' as gentle, intense, courteous and caring; the kind of man who asked after their children and enjoyed talking in fine detail about heavy construction equipment. Even his Khartoum travel agent fondly recalled the warlord paying with an American Express gold card. Dr Ghazi Atabani, the Minister of Peace, articulated a view common in the Islamic world: 'I still believe the group involved in 11 September was autonomous, not linked to bin Laden.' Conversely, some of bin Laden's closest former fundamentalist allies, such as the deposed Hassan al-Turabi, now complain that bin Laden was a bore: in their conversations, they say, 'He talked nothing but *Jihad, Jihad, Jihad.*'

A wider war

So is Sudan a terror state or simply the victim of mistaken identity; a future target for the US or a potential ally in the expanding war on terror? A Canadian diplomat in Khartoum said: 'I can say that the Canadian government has no evidence that justifies a major armed attack.' As an afterthought, he added mischievously: 'But there have been lots of claimed sightings of Osama – about the same number as the sightings of Elvis, in fact.'

11 September was a tragic wake-up call for US diplomacy, but the initial – convenient – focus on one holy warrior has now given way to a much wider strategic perspective. The construction of a new Muslim coalition in the forthcoming war on the Iraqi regime may well mean that Khartoum's friendship with bin Laden, no matter how culpable, will be sacrificed on the altar of realpolitik.

Although Secretary of State Colin Powell recently criticized the Sudanese armed forces for their bombing campaign in the south, he conceded that 'The Sudanese have been helpful with respect to intelligence sharing and shutting down some of the terrorist activities that were at least . . . headquartered in Sudan . . . ' And yet the Sudanese connection with bin Laden is more than a footnote in a widening war; it may have highlighted important intelligence deficiencies.

American politics rather than Sudanese realities have sometimes influenced Washington as it vacillated between constructive engagement and isolation, between military assault on the Islamic government or grabbing some of the oil bonanza, which has been dominated by European, Canadian and Asian interests. The Sudanese government has a point when it says that US intelligence has been corrupted by received wisdom rather than informed by hard facts. Nevertheless, Khartoum has been a past master of grey propaganda, mixing truth with clever disinformation.

Madelaine Albright, former Secretary of State, Samuel R. Berger, the former National Security Advisor, and others have insisted that on numerous occasions between 1996 and 2001 senior US officials met with the Sudanese and nothing of significant operational value was offered. The State Department did not block FBI involvement. They argue that the Sudanese before and after 1996 aided and abetted Islamic terrorists, including bin Laden. A senior US intelligence officer told me: 'Do you really think we would turn down any information on bin Laden, especially from an organization like the *Mukhabarat*? We would look at it, carefully. It just doesn't make sense just to say no.'

Whether Khartoum would really have handed over bin Laden in 1996 remains an open question. Khartoum would have been condemned by the Islamic world, but the Sudanese might just have done it in return for the lifting of its pariah status. At the very least, bin Laden's ejection could have provided an opportunity for a US special operation. The bombing of the al-Shifa factory in 1988 was undoubtedly a major intelligence blunder. The intelligence failures regarding Sudan should be heeded, and applied, as the war against Saddam Hussein looms ever closer.

[Since this report major strides were made in establishing peace in the south, but in mid-2004 the civil war and refugee crisis in the Darfur region of the west prompted renewed international political pressure on the Khartoum government.]

The West Bank: can there ever be peace? – Paul Moorcraft
travelled through the West Bank during the height of the Israeli military incursions in May 2002.

Israel's former image as brave underdog has long been tarnished by the arrogance of occupation and the harsh response to the first and second intifadas. But the American war on terror has evoked fresh sympathy for the Israelis, despite the continuously provocative behaviour of the settlers in the West Bank. Israel's very existence seemed imperilled by the firestorm of Arab anger symbolized by Islamic suicide bombers.

For decades the received wisdom had been that there could never be a military solution to the Arab-Israeli problem. But secular and religious right-wing opinion in security circles in Israel, and crucially the US, has been suggesting a radical solution. In early January it was mooted that Israel would launch a lightning attack on the leadership of the Palestinian Authority's security apparatus and that of Hamas and Islamic Jihad. Israeli troops would stay long enough to decapitate the intifada, evacuate the more far-flung Jewish settlements, and then build, right along an adjusted border including Jerusalem, a dirty great high security wall, stronger than Jericho's and longer-lasting than Berlin's.

From the Israeli perspective, the Palestinians had lost their chance to swamp the Israelis by demography or a war of gradual attrition. Draconian as this seemed, it would have been better than another all-out war between Arabs and Israelis. Such a conflict could spark an Armageddon in the arc of Islamic instability from Kosovo to Saudi Arabia and Egypt.

In March and April 2002 at least part of this plan appeared to have been put into operation as an Israeli response to increasing Palestinian suicide bombings. Prime Minister Ariel Sharon said he was determined to 'uproot terrorists'. Arabs said it was to destroy the Palestinian Authority and to enforce submission from civilians and insurgents alike.

Massacre in Jenin?

The Israeli Defence Force (IDF) sent its troops into a number of major West Bank towns, but it was their action in Jenin which aroused the most international concern.

Staying in empty hotels in Jerusalem was a bit like emulating Jack Nicholson in *The Shining*. I was practically alone except for an Arab Israeli businessman who confided: 'Both Sharon and Arafat are crazy old men. They hate each other – this is personal. They are stuck in history. They both must go before we can move on.'

Did Sharon commit in Jenin a major war crime, on a par with the massacre of Palestinians in the refugee camps of Beirut twenty years ago? Or was the devastation in the West Bank town an inevitable consequence of a pitched battle against entrenched terrorists in a crowded urban setting? What is the truth amid the storm of conflicting propaganda claims?

The IDF invaded the town on 3 April. For eight days Israeli Merkava tanks, armoured personnel carriers and Cobra helicopters, firing wire-guided missiles, waged war on Jenin's inhabitants. On 9 April, thirteen part-time Israeli soldiers were killed in an ambush in the narrow winding streets. Ten other Jewish soldiers also fell in the battle of Jenin. This triggered fear and anger in the besieging forces; bulldozers – giant armoured vehicles the size of a double-decker bus – were brought in to demolish the centres of resistance; some of the houses were destroyed with civilians still inside. About 25 per cent of the camp was flattened.

Israeli armour encircled the town. During the five-day curfew, bodies were left to rot in the streets. On 14 April a trickle of international aid got in, but journalists were barred. With great difficulty, travelling partly across country in an armoured Land Rover crewed by Channel Four TV, and guided by friendly Palestinians, I entered the town, after dodging around Israeli tanks determined to stop interlopers.

On 18 and 19 April, amid the awful choking stench of decaying flesh, I spoke to scores of survivors. The landscape was more like an earthquake zone. Indeed, Palestinians claimed this was their 'Ground Zero'.

Casualties have been inflated by the Palestinians and minimized by the Israelis. I counted twenty-one bodies being buried amid Israeli machine-gun fire, although it was not aimed at the burial party. Elsewhere I saw remnants of six people, small pulped lumps, with bits of clothing and the odd bone; the result of being pulverized by tons of debris. Lost children wailed on mounds of crushed stone which were once their homes. People were digging with their bare hands to find survivors or recover possessions.

'This is Sharon's fault. And Bush's,' lamented one Palestinian woman who had lost most of her immediate family. (A few inhabitants, realizing I was British, also harangued me, blaming Foreign Secretary Arthur Balfour for his pro-Zionist declaration in 1917; like the Irish, the Palestinians have long memories.) One young boy, aged about eleven, told me his mother and brother had been killed by the soldiers. 'When I grow up I want to be a suicide bomber too,' he said.

Palestinian propaganda claims that 500 were killed; Israelis suggest about 100. What was odd was the lack of wounded; I went to the three nearest hospitals and encountered only a few men with minor war wounds. In such wars, the figures are usually three wounded for every fatality. Perhaps many of the wounded were taken into custody along with the thousands of fighters.

In my opinion, this was no planned massacre to avenge the hundreds of Israeli civilians killed by suicide bombers. There is evidence, however, that Palestinians were used as human shields, and families were taken hostage as Israeli troops secured individual houses as their bases within the town – called a camp, but in fact an elaborate maze of large brick and breeze-block structures. Such actions are violations of international law and the Geneva Convention.

On doors and in alleys the Israelis faced numerous booby-traps – many of which I saw still intact; and so the soldiers used civilians to knock on their neighbours' doors, or detonated or hammered their way through basement walls of houses to avoid street-level booby traps or ambush.

Bulldozers were used as a new and terrifying weapon of war, and clearly some women and children were trapped in the buildings, too fearful to come out when Israeli troops used megaphones to tell them to escape.

'The fighting was the fiercest urban house-to-house fighting Israel has seen in thirty years,' Major Rafi Laderman told me. This part-time officer – a marketing consultant in civilian life – explained how he personally had led hundreds of women and children out of their camp at the height of the fighting. 'Jenin was a capital of terror – 50 per cent of the suicide bombers came from here. We have cleared out this nest of terror.'

Numerous posters – extolling the heroes who had died in battle or in suicide explosions – were still in evidence, along with vengeful graffiti in Hebrew. I also saw Palestinian fighters removing light machine guns from ruined houses.

Jenin's numerous Hamas and Islamic Jihad armed fighters were a justified target for Israeli retaliation, but the court of world opinion will damn the excessive use of force against civilians. In urban warfare – especially where women volunteer for suicide missions – separating combatants from the innocent is often impossible.

Israel (especially its highly professional armed forces) is often very sophisticated in its dealings with Western journalists. This time, trigger-happy – or plain nervous – troops treated the press aggressively. One Italian journalist had already been killed by an Israeli sniper. I was detained on my way out of Jenin, along with senior journalists from Channel Four TV and the *Sunday Times*. Our detention, arrest and threatened deportation, I pointed out to the Israeli officer holding us, would be bad publicity for an already beleaguered country. 'Good PR,' he said, 'doesn't stop a single suicide bomber.'

Normally, I would disagree with the officer, but the suicide bombings have indeed dramatically increased American support for the beleaguered Jewish state; they have also showed that Israeli military response only compounds the anger and the action-reaction cycle. But the US is the only nation powerful enough to act as a deus ex machina. Washington is seen, by the Palestinians, as hopelessly compromised. Yet it may be the only show in town.

Towards a settlement?

In May 2001 Senator George Mitchell published his report advocating a ceasefire, a resumption of bilateral negotiations, a complete end to new Israeli settlements and a complete crackdown by the Palestinian Authority on terrorism. In return Israel would stop incursions and ease economic sanctions. Since then George Bush has accepted a two-state solution to the problem. A key will be an interposition force made up largely of US soldiers, but also involving other nations. The UK is also considering a contribution, should a settlement be reached.

Termination of the conflict probably requires the exit of both Arafat and Sharon. Both are part of the problem. Sharon is loathed by all Palestinians and seems inflexible to many Israelis. Arafat's administration is utterly corrupt. Many of the foreign donations have been spent on his personal security force – twelve separate agencies, all answerable to him. It even included a miniature navy, of which he is admiral. A great deal of this security apparatus has been destroyed by the Israelis. This destruction is used as an excuse not to rein in the suicide bombers, but much of Arafat's security apparatus has been busy jailing his opponents. While Sharon has a number of obvious successors, Arafat has tended to eliminate or remove rivals.

New leaders, however, could return to an old solution; almost as far back as 1948 or at least 1967. In February 2002 Saudi Arabia revived the possibility of a grand bargain – land for peace. Recognition of a secure Israel by all Arab states would come in return for a Palestinian state in a slightly revised 1967 border. There is surprisingly broad agreement, based upon the details evolved at Camp David and Taba (twice) and President Clinton's proposals of 2000. Jerusalem may have to be shared and partly internationalized with foreign troops.

Only Washington has sufficient clout to bang heads together and take a lead in sending a (not necessarily large) contingent of troops to monitor the buffer zones; the US would not find it hard to work with an IDF it has helped to arm and train. The Saudi plan, if implemented, could provide that rare influence: an array of benign neighbours. This happened in Afghanistan, because the US had the will. And like the Afghans, both Israelis and Palestinians are very war-weary (as well as angry). Could a deal on conflict resolution mean ISAF 2 in Jerusalem?

Israel's 'War on Terror' – Brigadier General Eival Gilady,
Head of the strategic planning division of the Israeli Defence Force General Staff, talked to Paul Moorcraft, following the siege of Jenin in May 2002.

PM: *There's a perception that Jenin was seen as both a strategic and PR disaster. Fair comment?*
EG: Absolutely not. On the ground there were many achievements in Operation Defensive Shield. At that time [March] we lost 131 Israeli civilians and about 700 injured [in suicide bombings and other attacks]

so we had to launch the operation. We stopped the wave of terror by deploying our troops in Jenin and other cities. We prevented the physical movement of the terrorist groups, weapons and bomb-making material into civilian areas of Israel. Secondly, the terrorists learned that we can get them wherever they are. For a few years, no section of the Palestinian security apparatus had ever entered the refugee camps. The terrorists had build up whatever infrastructure they wanted to. So once we got into the refugee camps we could collect a lot of illegal weapons and destroy the terrorist infrastructure, especially the laboratories, as well as arresting some of these people. Thirdly, during the fighting, we would prefer that the terrorists – if they have to use weapons and explosives – use them against soldiers who are better protected and trained than civilians. Previously about 75 per cent of our casualties had been civilians; during that operation about 3 per cent of casualties were Israeli civilians killed [by terrorist action].

At the strategic level, there was a positive level of deterrence. Two weeks after Jenin, some people in the Gaza Strip wanted to launch a Qassam missile, but a senior Palestinian official warned: 'Do you want them to devastate us as they did in Jenin?' So deterrence works.

Yes, there are some bad pictures in Jenin of APCs [armoured personnel carriers] and the military force ranged against terrorists who were hiding behind civilians in civilian neighbourhoods. On the other hand, if you consider the impact on the perceptions of the Palestinians they now perceive that they will never achieve anything via terror.

PM: *You have said previously that there can be no military solution to the Palestinian problem.*

EG: There will be no military solution, but there will be a big contribution from military operations, along with steps in other spheres – economic, legal, diplomatic, PR etc. We can minimize the terror level by the application of force and create conditions conducive to dialogue.

For the Palestinians, after two years of trying to find every possible crack in Israeli society – trying to use the left wing who ask tough questions about why we have to be in the territories, and why don't we get out of there etc. – they have unified Israeli society. The Palestinians have lost the peaceniks and unified Israeli society to fight against terrorism. They have discovered that even a prosperous Western society is willing to fight if it has to; that a Western society is prepared to sacrifice both economy and the lives of its soldiers, if necessary.

They made a strategic mistake by forcing us to fight terrorism rather than taking their own initiative to do so.

216

PM: *Do you see this as an example to President Bush's war on terrorism?*
EG: Partly. We are in the vanguard of fighting terrorism. Both President Bush and Prime Minister Blair are fighting terror in general. Their global campaign is very sensitive to what level of success we achieve. If suicide bombers succeed here, soon they'll be all around the world.

PM: *If there is a war on Iraq, Israel will have to show absolute restraint. Otherwise, Saddam might survive. How do you cope with that paradox?*
EG: There is no coalition as there was in 1991 . . .

PM: *But if Israel gets involved in the war with Iraq it could destroy 'Western' war aims.*
EG: We will do whatever we can to remain out of it. It is not our war against Iraq and we have no interest in being involved. If we are not attacked, we will not take part in this war. But we might find ourselves forced to respond. If Saddam Hussein launched long-range missiles against Israel, we may have to respond. And that depends not only on the level of casualties. It also depends upon the intention of these possible attacks. For example, if Saddam launches chemical or biological missiles: even if they miss and fall into the Mediterranean Sea, then we may have to respond because it was a non-conventional warhead . . . even if we had no casualties.

PM: *How prepared is Israel for chemical or biological attacks?*
EG: Israel is the best-prepared country in the world, for different levels of missile threat. It also depends on the duration of the alert, the time we have to prepare our population. This campaign is going to be a long one . . . a few weeks or months. If this is the case we will have to take appropriate steps to maintain the collective protection of the population. It would be difficult, without people going to work or children going to school for a long period. Just sitting at home waiting for the siren, getting into the sealed room and putting on their gas masks.

So the US forces will have to start this campaign by trying to minimize the risk of Saddam being capable of launching missiles against Israel. If they can entirely prevent, or at least minimize, his chances of launching missiles against Israel, this will increase the probability of our staying out of it.

PM: *Do you think there is a clash between Judaeo-Christian traditions and the Islamic world?*
EG: In a way, although I would not describe it as bluntly as you have. President Bush feels that he's not only fighting against terrorism throughout the world but also for the society he wants: democracy, the free markets scientific education etc. not the kind of totalitarian society

with no civil rights, ignorance and poverty that breeds terrorism. What happened on 11 September was not only the terrorists not accepting the Western way of life, but their active attempts to destroy it. In a way, it is a cultural struggle, though not exactly Jews and Christians against Islam. I'm certainly not saying that all Muslims are on the other side of the hill.

PM: *The IDF has always deployed a highly manoeuvrist offensive strategy, but in the new asymmetric static warfare you have to shift from a large-scale armoured strategy to small-unit tactics. How are the intifadas changing your doctrine? Will the IDF be restructured?*

EG: There have been two major changes in the last decade. One is the maturity of new technology, the revolution in military affairs, with all the communications and command and control systems, precision-guided missiles and so forth. Israel is very advanced in this area. But the second change is in the nature of conflict, not just in Israel but around the world; Bosnia, Kosovo, Rwanda, Chechnya . . . intrastate, wars waged by organizations, not states; militia groups fighting among civilians, the presence of the media and the sensitivity to the number of casualties, not only on your side but on the other side too. This influences the way you use your forces. In our conflict now with the Palestinians, or previously with Hezbollah, we have adapted to these changes.

PM: *Critics of the IDF say it is over-equipped with advanced technology, and there are problems with the training, education and discipline of the ordinary soldier. And morale has suffered as the IDF has been sucked into a no-win struggle in the cities.*

EG: Let me answer on a tactical level. I have been travelling around these Palestinian towns very frequently. For example, if you come one day to an IDF checkpoint and you see the soldiers standing there with their helmets on and holding their guns at the ready, I could say: 'Why can't you be more polite? Take your helmets off, put your guns down. Smile. Everything is OK. Let them [the Palestinians] go.' Then the following week there is an attack on the same checkpoint. Then I come along and say: 'Stand to attention. What about your guns? Put your helmets on.' Sometimes the troops don't understand what we [senior officers] want, because procedures change on a day-to-day basis. Every day we have eight to twelve alerts. Somebody, for example, is trying to plant a car bomb in Tulkarm, and we need to find that car. It's urgent. But still we have developed over time the correct way to deal with civilians with terrorists among them and civilians at large. We use more Arabic speakers, more non-lethal weapons. We are not 100 per cent, but we have made some big steps forward.

PM: *You say the 'peaceniks' have been undermined, but 400 reservists have refused to serve in the West Bank and one or two have even refused to serve on the Israeli side of the Green Line.*

EF: This is a marginal problem. Prior to Operation Defensive Shield we had fifty officers signing a letter of concern – this is a signal we should be aware of. We look carefully at the norms and values of Israeli society and, in line with these, will never go beyond a certain threshold. The number of people actually refusing to serve is marginal.

PM: *There is a revival of the peace movement within the Labour Party – articulated by former senior officers, who argue the settlements [in the occupied territories] should be abandoned as a precursor to a peace agreement.*

EG: I am trying to avoid the political debate.

PM: *In Clausewitzian terms, I am attempting to get you to define the military goals . . .*

EG: The military will never say whether a specific settlement needs to be removed or needs to stay where it is. The government has to take this kind of political decision. Our job is to advise them on the security implications of their decisions.

Everybody understands that a final status agreement is not achievable in one step. We understand that the two sides need to agree to make progress; the problem is we don't have a partner to do so. As long as [Yasser] Arafat is there, there is no way to move forward. He is a disaster for his people. I have been personally involved in many of the negotiations [local and international] including [US] General Zinni's effort to implement the [CIA Chief]Tenet plan . . . whatever we tried to do we couldn't move forward because of Arafat's strategy. The frustration was also felt by the Palestinian leadership and others such as the Egyptians and EU representatives. Large sections of the Palestinian people and leadership understand this and recognize that he must be removed or sidelined.

PM: *You are creating facts on the ground with your new defensive wall. It moves in places away from the Green Line to include Israeli settlements on the West Bank.*

EG: This is a security fence, not a political solution. We want each side to work and live in peace on each side of the fence. We want to reduce the friction and increase security.

PM: *Won't you create a Maginot mentality behind this line and further reduce the famed mobility of the IDF?*

EG: Yes, in a way, that might happen, but the operational concept rests on technological means and mobility. What we really need is a political counterpart – a negotiating partner among the Palestinians so that we can make progress. But meanwhile we have to take action to minimize the risks, to stop the terrorists coming in to Israel.

PM: *Overall, do you think that Israel is winning its war on terror?*

EG: Absolutely yes. The Palestinians have realized that they cannot further the achievement of their goals by the use of terror and violence. And since the world has decided to fight terrorism, it's much easier for us. Our restrained policy comes from Israeli values and norms, which are the same as Western ideals. The Palestinian people and leadership have realized that, despite all this terror, they were much closer to achieving their independent state two years ago.

PM: *Is Israel weaker than it was in 1975–76, after it had recovered from the Yom Kippur war?*

EG: No. Not militarily or our society in general. Our democracy and independent judiciary still flourish. For example, today the military wanted to demolish the houses of terrorists and also expel terrorist sympathizers from the West Bank to Gaza. But we couldn't get approval from the Supreme Court. This has annoyed some of my colleagues, but I think this indicates the strength of our democracy.

Battles in a twice-promised land – Brigadier General Gershon HaCohen on the impact of recent operations on Israel's approach to urban warfare. Brigadier HaCohen, the Head of Doctrine and Training for the Israeli Defence Force's General Command Staff, was interviewed by Paul Moorcraft in August 2002.

PM: *What are the main lessons of the battle of Jenin (April-May 2002) in redefining your urban doctrine?*

GH: We need to differentiate the physical engagement from the symbolism of Jenin – for both sides. It was quite different from classical examples of urban warfare, such as Stalingrad or the capture of Jerusalem in 1967 or Suez in 1973. In those cases the main mission of the military commanders was to secure positions inside the cities. In places such as Stalingrad or in Caen in the Second World War, the main aim was to enter and secure the cities. In 1967 in Jerusalem the mission was to connect the old city, especially the Western Wall of the Temple, with west Jerusalem. This was a territorial definition . . . And if the enemy withdrew, then this was an advantage. In Jenin – and it was similar in Grozny in Chechnya –

220

there was no interest in the territory itself. What we wanted was something else: terrorists hiding among the general population. We had no interest in the refugee camp, to hold the territory. This is an entirely new phenomenon.

PM: *Would you concede that there were major errors in Jenin, perhaps similar to the mechdalim [fundamental errors of the 1973 Yom Kippur war]? Can lessons be learned?*

GH: It's the same as in football: there are always lessons to be learned. But when you refer to *mechdalim*, perhaps you are referring to political issues rather than professional military matters? May I continue what I was saying about the military mission, which was to capture the terrorists, in this special strategic environment? It was very sensitive because of the dangers of what is known as collateral damage – either to civilians or infrastructure. This is a new problem for military commanders. They must engage the terrorists without the capacity to isolate them from the civilians. In doctrine (US doctrine for example) the civilians are not supposed to be in the area. And British military doctrine defines the activities of civilian-military support staff officers whose main mission is sometimes to help civilians leave the city, so that inside the city there can be a 'pure' military engagement.

The main difference between fighting in the hills and urban areas is normally just the terrain. But in Jenin we were in a difficult situation. In a way it was similar to what the Americans found in Mogadishu. Every conflict is unique, of course, but the general name of the game for the terrorists is creating confrontation among the people who are living inside the city. What was a forest for partisans in Eastern Europe during the Second World War, and what was the jungle for the Viet Cong, is now the city. And you can't separate the civilians from the warriors, who seek shelter in not identifying themselves as soldiers. They are both civilians and warriors.

This deserves the title of 'post-modern war', because post-modernism is exemplified here as the well-established conventional distinction [between civilians and combatants] being made irrelevant. The notion of the separation of civilian and soldier is not working because they [the Palestinians] are not obeying one of the main rules of the Geneva Convention – that soldiers must be identifiable.

PM: *From my own observations of the battleground and interviews in Jenin of both sides, I got the impression that there was element of unprofessionalism – perhaps some panic, anger even revenge – among some reservists in the Israeli Defence Force.*

221

GH: Of course, we used reservists but also special forces. The main fighting was guided by the Golani Battalion who are highly experienced in this kind of warfare. The battalion was sent on this mission, because it was operating in Jenin one month before. In the whole brigade, there was one battalion of Golani troops, another battalion of *Nahal* ordinary infantry, and elite units, including marine commandos. All of these units worked under the command of the Reserve Brigade Commander. That is a very good example of the new challenge for officers that they have to organize the force for tailor-made necessities. It was not an ordinary mission where you take an infantry brigade into familiar conventional fighting. You have to create a specific task force.

PM: *I appreciate that it is difficult to separate civilians from combatants – especially when young girls may be suicide bombers – but the IDF appears to have breached some of the rules of war in Jenin. For example, making civilians knock on neighbour's doors, in case the entrances are booby-trapped.*

GH: If that is true . . .

PM: *Yes, that happened.*

GH: The general staff declared that it is absolutely against our norms, so we learned from our experience that we shouldn't do it.

PM: *One of the novel aspects of the battle was the use of the massive armoured bulldozers, the D-9 . . . The Israeli engineering corps seems to have taken on a new importance. Is the deployment of D-9s part of a new doctrine?*

GH: It's true that the role of this [engineering] unit was necessary in every engagement. The unit also used charges to enter houses or to detonate booby-traps that the enemy had put in the streets and in the houses. Their special expertise was absolutely necessary.

PM: *The use of charges (and hammers) to enter basements – to avoid booby-trapped alleyways – is a fairly standard infantry tactic, but this was not effectively explained. You could argue that the IDF failed completely in the media ops aspects of the battle, and indeed the whole Operation Defensive Shield.*

GH: I am not avoiding the question, but can I emphasize that we found the engineering units very useful to help the troops' entry into fortified buildings. Not just in Jenin but also regarding [Yasser] Aafat's HQ [in Ramallah]. The latter was originally a police station, built by the British with extraordinary wisdom. The strength of this structure was well known as a military problem since 1948. There was a similar problem in attacking Jordanian fortified police stations in the war of 1956. Now, with the protection of these armoured bulldozers, troops can enter these buildings. The D-9s are very versatile pieces of equipment.

PM: *Yes, but civilians were killed by these bulldozers in Jenin. I know that the IDF used loudspeakers to warn the civilians to get out, but the impact of these armoured leviathans crushing civilian housing was again part of the PR disaster for Israel, especially when journalists were kept out. The IDF appeared to be hiding something, perhaps a massacre almost comparable with the Sabra and Chatila camps during the [1982] invasion of Lebanon.*

GH: This media problem stemmed from two issues. Firstly, the anxiety that journalists would endanger their lives because there were so many booby-traps. So we closed the area for more than two days in order to evaluate the situation in the refugee camp. Secondly, we were also afraid that journalists would enter without permission. [The brigadier recounted the story of an Israeli Arab doctor who was told to stay out of a specific building. He ignored IDF advice because he thought they were hiding evidence of war crimes. The doctor entered and lost his hand to a booby-trap.]

PM: *You have been cut off from many of your usual sources of Humint [human intelligence] by the Palestinians' execution of so-called collaborators. Is this affecting your approach to urban warfare?*

GH: The main point about collecting intelligence in this kind of warfare is that all the technological superiority that Israel possesses – satellites etc. – was found to be irrelevant . . .

PM: *What about your UAVs? You have a tremendous range.*

GH: We use them a lot. We can have the whole picture of what is taking place in the operation. And we can investigate issues precisely, including the so-called failures you mentioned at the beginning of this interview. It's like watching a video replay in a football match; you'll find that sometimes the referee makes a wrong decision. There's wisdom after action.

PM: *But you need Humint for real-time intelligence or, better, advanced intelligence for pre-emptive tactics such as 'preventive acts' which in Hebrew is a euphemism for what we would call in English 'targeted assassinations'.*

GH: Of course Humint is very necessary. In every platoon or company we have someone who can speak Arabic and who can make rapid assessments in the field by collecting the appropriate intelligence. Otherwise the unit is almost blind.

PM: *Can we look at possible strategic and/or doctrinal changes since Jenin and Operation Defensive Shield? The dominant ethos of the IDF* *has been forward attacking movement. This is based on Israel's history of large-scale armoured warfare. Now in the era of asymmetrical conflict, perhaps you need to develop a fresh doctrine based on small unit infantry tactics. And this may be more difficult with an army that depends largely on reservists.*

GH: Asymmetric warfare is a very big concept. It ranges from tactical asymmetric physical engagement – the tank versus the stone-thrower – to the strategic issues of armed forces in the service of a state such as Israel. This is the notion of knowing the precise hierarchy, from the political directive down to the final military action. Israeli commanders in the field are committed to a well-defined and authorized mission.

On the other side you have a non-state entity. No one can really take responsibility. This creates a number of problems. How do you define 'the enemy'? And, coming back to the issue of intelligence, if you can access the enemy HQ and the formal chain of command, then you can react to, or pre-empt, the orders emanating from this system. Instead, we are engaging with an amorphous system.

PM: *The previous conventional wars were seen as wars of survival by Israeli reservists. Now in this much more unconventional asymmetric war you are having problems of reservists refusing to serve in the West Bank. Is this affecting the morale of the IDF?*

GH: It is perhaps a problem at the strategic level. The senior commanders have to be aware of this political sensitivity. But less than 0.1 per cent refused to serve.

PM: *But that's still around 400 soldiers.*

GH: No it's less. There is no reason to be worried about this phenomenon.

PM: *I've said that a new doctrine may be required which moves away from the war of tanks and rapid movement. Doesn't the new defensive wall – 'Sharon's Curtain' – imply a further shift from movement to static warfare, a Maginot mentality?*

GH: You would be right if the line were static, but we do not think that such an obstacle would be useful without a whole range of complementary activities – for example, a lot of reconnaissance troops on both sides. Take the case of Gaza: we are working on both sides of the fence. A single fence as a defensive obstacle is, in a way, an illusion. It is not sufficient on its own.

PM: *Has President Bush's recent policy statement justified the Israeli policy of undermining the authority of Yasser Arafat?*

GH: This relates to what I said earlier about the point at which the asymmetric strategy becomes a real threat to the state of Israel. The main idea of Oslo [the peace talks held in Oslo] was to take the nomadic terrorist activities of Arafat and his PLO [Palestine Liberation Organization] and to transform them and make a metamorphosis that would establish a state which would develop economically. It would have the ability to obey the law, both internal and international law. Bush's statement emphasized the necessity of establishing the process to create a symmetric situation between two state apparatuses.

PM: *It seems to me that Israel is much weaker today than it was after the Six-Day War in 1967. Would you agree?*

GH: Yes and no. The asymmetric strategy that the Palestinians are developing is a result of the power relationship between the armies of Israel's neighbours and the IDF. The Palestinians' strategy is an attempt to bypass our military and conventional superiority based upon our success in previous wars.

The urban environment is mainly a sociological and cultural phenomenon and not just an issue of terrain. The same is true about fighting in modern cities – it relates to a lot of cultural aspects. The urban warrior must take to the field equipped not only with appropriate weapons but also appropriate wisdom.

The Battle of Jenin

In response to suicide bombings in Israel, the IDF launched Operation Defensive Shield against key towns controlled by the Palestinian Authority. At the beginning of April 2002, 1,000 men of 5 Infantry Brigade entered Jenin refugee camp from four directions. Few of the reservists – unlike the regulars deployed – had received training in urban guerrilla warfare. During the ten-day battle, twenty-three Israeli troops and approximately fifty Palestinians were killed, with over 200 on both sides treated for wounds.

To avoid an international outcry, the Israeli cabinet decided not to use F-16 warplanes or artillery, even though they knew this would mean heavier IDF casualties. The task force commander, Brigadier General Eyal Schlein, did deploy, and use, Merkava main battle tanks and Apache gunships. According to UAVs and other intelligence estimates, the approximately 200 fighters, drawn from Hamas, Islamic Jihad and Al-Aqsa militias, as well as Palestinian police and security forces, had constructed very intricate defensive positions.

The IDF top brass had expected a swift victory, but the task force initially took three days to advance a few hundred metres because of the strong fortifications, extensive booby-traps and spirited Palestinian defence. On 10 April 2002, thirteen Israelis were killed in an ambush and another was later killed by a sniper. (This was the highest casualty tally in a single day since the 1982 invasion of Lebanon.) On that April day the IDF sent in the massive D-9 armoured bulldozers backed up by rocket and machine-gun fire from Apaches. The next day the surrender of forty Palestinian fighters – the site was dubbed 'The Alamo' – ended the battle.

The IDF had conquered the camp, but the death of so many Palestinian civilians – 500 was the number originally touted by Palestinian sources – led to unfounded accusations of a deliberate and planned massacre.

FIVE

The Global War on Terror

NATO: Modernization versus marginalization – NATO Secretary General **George Robertson** on the future of Western security. He was interviewed by Gwyn Winfield in July 2002.

GW: *Is it becoming harder to find a role for NATO?*

GR: No. NATO has never been busier in its whole fifty-three year history. We have three major peace support operations ongoing in the Balkans. We have a relationship with the European Union which promises to be one of the biggest projects that NATO will ever have embarked upon. We have a new relationship with Russia – this morning [19 July 2002] the NATO-Russia council, with Russia as one member out of twenty, took place. We have twenty-seven nations in the Partnership for Peace with the nineteen NATO nations. We are engaged with the seven North African Mediterranean countries in a Mediterranean dialogue. We have a Defence Capabilities Initiative. We have declared Article Five of the Washington Treaty and are heavily engaged in the war on terrorism. That is a pretty big agenda, and it leaves me with little time to worry about whether we've got a role.

GW: *While there is no denying that NATO is very busy, do these activities fit into the organization's original intended role?*

GR: It's a different world, and NATO has grown a different role. Its core mission is exactly the same: collective defence. We're a military organization, involved in making a safer and more secure world. This can be done in a number of different ways, from having the ability to send force packages, as we did to Bosnia, Kosovo and Macedonia, outreaching to Russia, Ukraine and the former Warsaw Pact Countries, and now to the Mediterranean littoral as well. We're highly relevant to a world that has

227

changed out of all recognition, and we build on our strengths for the new world.

GW: *As you build on your old strength, should we look for a rebrand, a relaunch – 'New, Improved NATO'?*

GR: Why change a brand name when we've got one of the best known in the world? We're the most successful military alliance the planet has ever known, and still have the reputation of being the best and the quickest. So the rebranding is taking place in terms of the product, but the name and the character are the same: a community of democratic countries sharing a collective responsibility for defence, but also a collective belief in values of democracy, liberty and freedom. NATO members are prepared, and willing, to defend these values if they're challenged.

GW: *But these values are not solely confined to the North Atlantic. As we see NATO expanding, shouldn't we be looking beyond those old geographical constraints?*

GR: Well, we already do, because we're in the Caucasus and Central Asia as well. I'm not sure if you should kill the brand just because it was formerly based only on the North Atlantic. That part of the title underlines the connection between Europe and the USA. The countries of the Caucasus and Central Asia (and indeed the countries of the Mediterranean) see themselves very much as being part of a single Euro-Atlantic space. I think it's what we do that matters, not what we're called.

GW: *You mentioned the fight against terrorism. Following the 11 September attacks, Article Five was invoked but nothing was done with it by the US. Is that a fair comment?*

GR: That's an incorrect view from the outside. The fact is that immediately after we declared Article Five, the United States asked us to do a number of things they considered vital: building blocks towards what the Americans were going to do themselves. One was access to airspace, which was given very quickly; access to ports, harbours and fuel dumps right across NATO countries - and indeed the Partnership countries as well. Standing Force Mediterranean was deployed to the eastern Mediterranean where, since 12 September, it has been involved in interdicting thousands of ships and creating a regime of protection from terrorists who use sea-lanes. And of course the Awacs (Airborne Warning and Control System) planes that NATO uses were deployed to the US to protect American mainland cities for the first time. These were things that were immediately done by NATO collectively.

NATO also facilitated cooperation in the central Asian republics, as part of the Partnership for Peace. The NATO-Russia relationship was advantageous when it came to the Russians clearing their airspace for combat planes. And of course the vast majority of troops who have fought alongside the US in Afghanistan against the Taliban come from that interoperability family that NATO has represented over the past forty years. All this was in the initial stages. We know the first chapter of the campaign against terrorism has been written, but the rest of the book is still there and NATO stands ready to help as and when it is required.

GW: *But these troops are of, but not from, NATO. When we look at what the US is doing in Georgia and the Philippines these are again outside of NATO. Has there been a sidelining of NATO in terms of importance?*

GR: No, far from it. Just as in the Gulf War, a broader coalition was required to take on the Taliban in Afghanistan. That coalition was going to include Pakistan and a number of south-east Asian and Gulf countries. Just as in 1991, it would have been inappropriate for an integrated NATO military command to be used at that stage. We also forget that there was a big debate at that stage about whether this was a 'clash of civilizations'. Therefore putting NATO ahead of what had to be a broader coalition may have sent out the wrong signal at that point. Afghanistan was only the first chapter – more will follow.

The political significance of declaring Article Five was huge, not just in the US, but, I would have thought, in the bunkers of Afghanistan as well. Al-Qaeda must have realized, by that signal alone, that they had crossed a very important acceptability threshold.

GW: *You have mentioned the expansion of NATO. Later this year, we expect the next tranche of new entrants. With Russia a lot closer, we seem to be choosing members for ease of interoperability rather than their strength. There seems to be no real threat that requires such a major increase in troop numbers. Why do we need NATO to get bigger? Is it just a political issue?*

GR: For a start, the alliance is a group of democratic countries that unite themselves together. There is no qualification limiting themselves to the original signatories in 1949. There is an open door to membership for those nations who want to be in, and who think they qualify under the military and political standards we laid down. We should enlarge because a bigger NATO has itself driven major changes within NATO. Territorial disputes and internal minority issues have been resolved. There is a character of democratic control of the military as well as democratic plurality – part of our civic standards that aspirant countries need to adhere to.

So we drive a process of change, we consolidate that change when it happens and we create a bigger, broader area of security and stability in a part of Europe that has known the opposite for generations.

GW: *While NATO is, in some respects, a very popular brand with some nations, the further east one goes in Europe and into Central Asia the more negative the image becomes.*

GR: Not in my experience. I've been to Uzbekistan, Kazakhstan, Azerbaijan, Armenia and Turkmenistan. Each of those countries has asked for a NATO information office to be opened in their capital city. They want NATO, not because it stands for a combatant in the Cold War, but because it stands for safety, stability, interoperability and democratic values.

The fact is we are a very attractive proposition. Those who write off NATO might care to look at the fact that there are ten countries wanting to join, with others waiting in the wings. We've never been busier and we've never been more popular.

GW: *You mentioned Uzbekistan, Kazakhstan etc. What can they offer that NATO doesn't have already? As NATO gets bigger, doesn't the problem of interoperability also increase, especially when you are looking at countries, such as Romania, with large forces? Interoperability problems are likely to make the whole of NATO move at the speed of its slowest member . . .*

GR: No, not if you're involved in specialization, and not if NATO is as careful at managing future armed forces as it has been. NATO doesn't need to move at the speed of its slowest member. We can move quicker than any other international organization in the world today. But Uzbekistan and Kazakhstan are not applying for membership of NATO – they're not ready. They are in the Partnership for Peace, however. Because these countries train and exercise with NATO troops, and are involved in a series of interoperability exercises with us, they are able to fit into peace support operations seamlessly and quickly. That's why you see a lot of these countries serving alongside NATO members in Kosovo, Bosnia and Macedonia. We're actually a force generator for peace-keeping and peace support operations, the like of which has never been seen before.

GW: *Connecting Central Asia and the war against terrorism, there is a body of thought that argues that the war against terrorism is being waged in Chechnya. We already have NATO members assisting the training of troops against alleged Chechen rebels in Georgia – could we see NATO troops in Chechnya?*

230

GR: It's highly unlikely the Russians would want us there. Chechnya is, after all, a wholly internal problem for the Russians. They've got enough troops to be able to handle it. What we must do with the Russians is look at the whole issue of global terrorism, and see where the areas of instability are, where terrorism, instability, ethnic conflicts and failed states are. This is as much of a threat to Russia as to the traditional Western countries. That's why the new NATO-Russia Council is important, and why it is likely to produce results.

There's a common enemy out there. Maybe it took 11 September to drive this message home, but now we are doing something about it.

GW: *Wherever there is a state providing succour to terrorists, there will always be this terrorist problem. Russian troops may well need specific technology or capabilities that NATO has. Shouldn't we try and help them deal with the situation?*

GR: I'm not a salesman – 'I'm George, fly NATO'! We respond to requests, as in Macedonia last year [2001]. It is unlikely, and almost certainly irrelevant, to imagine that Russia will ask for help within its own boundaries. It's got enough troops to handle Chechnya. We offer advice, some of it welcome, and we'll continue to do that. But we're not in the business of being a world policeman. We are engaged in responding where there is a threat to our members' values, security and stability.

GW: *There's been much disagreement over the International Criminal Court (ICC) and the American's decision to not be bound by it. How is this going to influence NATO members and NATO policy?*

GR: The argument was in the UN not NATO. The mandate for our troops in Bosnia is unaffected since the recent compromise. Obviously there is a disagreement between the United States and the other NATO countries about the ICC. But there was disagreement between the US and other NATO countries about the Ottawa Treaty on landmines. We are NATO, we are not the Warsaw Pact. There is no 'Big Brother' dictating policy, but a community of democracies who work out their problems and establish a consensus. I believe we will be able to do that with the ICC.

GW: *But couldn't this come back to the idea, expressed in several of your speeches, that European countries need to contribute more to NATO, to try and reduce reliance on America?*

GR: If people want to influence American foreign policy, it's easier to do so when you are sharing the burden. So, as I say to the Europeans and the Canadians, the choice is between modernization and marginalization. The European countries are beginning to put their hands in their pockets. The drop in defence budgets has now stopped. After 11

September a special tax from Germany has raised DM3 million extra for security. The British have increased their defence budget, and the French are saying they will match this. The new Portuguese government that came into power recently had to cut back on social expenditure but has actually increased its defence budget. So the signs are that the message is getting through. People want to do more and, after 11 September, they're doing more.

GW: *What would the impact on NATO be if the US acted unilaterally on Iraq and the UN deemed their actions unlawful?*

GR: That begs a number of questions that are nothing to do with me. But I would say that the US is briefing its NATO allies on its thinking about countries or groups which might have weapons of mass destruction. Among them is Iraq, which has shown in the past not only an appetite for these horrifying weapons, but even a readiness to use them against their own people. No doubt the Americans will make a decision on Iraq: they will either ask their NATO allies for help or simply inform them of their decision. But nothing happens in NATO unless it is done unanimously by nineteen countries. We have not reached that point and nor have the Americans (although they have identified Iraq as a threat)

GW: *But even some of America's closest allies feel strongly about Iraq. Could action in Iraq split the alliance?*

GR: Nothing splits NATO, because it is made up of nineteen sovereign countries who either agree or disagree unanimously. There have been differences of opinion, some characterized as splits, but nothing has fractured the alliance. Even something as fractious as the air campaign over Kosovo, on which opinion was divided, involved nineteen countries unanimously agreeing that they would stop an evil man doing evil things in part of the European continent. I'd simply say that there is genuine concern among all nineteen members of NATO about the proliferation of chemical, biological and radiological weapons. Proliferation has put them into the hands of people with fewer scruples than those people who had similar weapons in the past. Iraq is simply one of those countries that we know has, or had, weapons of mass destruction. It must be addressed in one form or another.

The Rumsfeld Question: Who is winning the 'war on terror'?
– Dr Paul Cornish, Director, Centre for Defence Studies, King's College, London, assesses the two years of war since the attacks on the US homeland. He drew up this scorecard in November 2003.

Within days of the terrible events of 11 September 2001, President George Bush launched the United States into a 'comprehensive assault on terrorism'. There was no ambiguity in Bush's declaration of hostilities: 'We're at war. There's been a war declared.' In a speech to Congress, Bush went further still, declaring the confrontation with 9/11-style terrorism to be a universal campaign: 'This is the world's fight. This is civilization's fight.' So began the US-led 'war on terror'. Together with the campaign against the 'axis of evil' of so-called 'rogue states' (or, latterly, 'states of concern') accused of sponsoring international terrorism and proliferating weapons of mass destruction, the war on terror has defined US foreign, security and defence policies for the past two years. In September 2003 Bush described Iraq, in all its post-conflict instability and with its uncertain future, as the 'central front of the war on terror'. The following month saw the announcement of a second front, in south-east Asia. During the summit meeting of the Asia Pacific Economic Forum (APEC) in Bangkok in October 2003, Bush insisted 'the war on terror goes on', and joined other leaders in repositioning APEC as a forum for global counter-terrorism.

In a controversial leaked memorandum of 16 October 2003, US Secretary of Defense Donald Rumsfeld posed a blunt question to senior Pentagon officials: 'Are we winning or losing the global war on terror?' Some media reports detected an admission of deadlock if not defeat, but Rumsfeld's memorandum was really little more than a call for a frank and balanced assessment of successes and failures in the war on terror, on the basis of which US policy and practice could be adjusted and improved. Rumsfeld's question was not unreasonable; after two years of intense political and military activity, it must be appropriate to ask who – or what – is winning the war on terror. More specifically, is the world now safer as a result of the US-led campaign?

Anti-Muslim crusade?

The difficulty, however, is that where the war on terror is concerned, balance and objectivity are commodities in very scarce supply. As the campaign has progressed, so the debate about the causes of 9/11, and the legitimacy and consequences of the US response to those events, have become more deeply entrenched. Bush's rhetoric – and particularly his 'with us, or against us' challenge to other governments – had a dramatic effect on international opinion. Close friends and allies of the United States (particularly those whose citizens had been killed in the World Trade Center) immediately closed ranks alongside Washington. In some of these cases, public support for Washington cooled as time went on, as governments sought a semi-detached, more critical relationship with their US ally. Other governments, in APEC and elsewhere, have become steadily more supportive of the US-led campaign, for a variety of reasons. But in many other parts of the world, disagreement with the US position has been trenchant if not openly hostile. For some, Bush's response was either incomprehensible (how is it possible to fight a war against a political method – terrorism?), or wrong-headed (witness Bush's inappropriate use of the term 'crusade' to describe the US response – a description that was subsequently dropped). But the more serious criticism has been that the US approach has placed an intolerable strain on the United Nations and the broader international system, has compromised the social and legal fabric of Western democratic societies, and has turned the containable conflict with al-Qaeda into a full-scale war between East and West, or even between Muslim and Christian.

Supporters of the US-led campaign see a balance sheet with a very healthy credit side, including two headline events; the US-led destruction of the Taliban regime in Afghanistan in October 2001, and the toppling of Saddam Hussein's regime in Iraq eighteen months later. There has also been a great deal of activity behind the scenes, largely out of sight of the world's media and public opinion. According to a paper published by the Bush administration in September 2003, efforts to contain and degrade al-Qaeda have been both sustained and successful. The paper claimed that some two thirds of al-Qaeda's principal leadership had been killed or captured, among them very senior figures such as Mohammed Atef, Zacarias Moussaoui, Abu Zubaydah, Ramzi Binalshibh and Khaled Sheikh Mohammed. As many as 3,000 al-Qaeda operatives have been jailed in over ninety countries, including those responsible for the October 2002 bombings in Bali. Efforts to identify and disrupt the financial networks supporting international terrorism have also been successful, with the seizure of bank accounts around the world. As well as attacking the infrastructure of al-Qaeda and similar groups, Western intelligence and counter-terrorism organizations also claim direct successes in the prevention of terrorist attacks by individuals and networks. In the United Kingdom, the Joint Terrorism Analysis Centre deals each week with about 100 intelligence warnings of a terrorist attack somewhere in the world, while the Federal Bureau of Investigation in the United States claims to have disrupted over 100 attacks since 9/11. Other, less tangible achievements are also listed on

234

the credit side. As a result of its military operations in Afghanistan and Iraq, the United States appears to be shifting from the intervention- and casualty-averse Weinberger-Powell doctrine, to a far more engaged and outward-looking foreign and security policy. And in spite of rhetorical differences, it seems the West is becoming steadily more coherent in the face of the terrorist threat. Most Western governments acknowledge the need to cooperate more closely to counter terrorism, and both NATO and the European Union have sought to establish their bona fides as leading organizations for counter-terrorism.

The debit side of the war

On the debit side, opponents of the war on terror present a long list of failures, false assumptions and unintended, uncontrollable consequences. In the first place, the two arch villains of the war – Osama bin Laden and Saddam Hussein – are still at large, with little indication (at least in the public debate) of their imminent capture. Furthermore, in spite of successes claimed by Western and other intelligence organizations, there has been a string of terrorist 'spectaculars' around the world since 9/11, including attacks in Islamabad, Karachi, Yemen, Moscow, Bali, Mombasa, Riyadh, Casablanca and Jakarta. In many cases, an explicit link with al-Qaeda has been formed. Another difficulty is that neither Afghanistan nor Iraq can yet be said to be settled and stable. Critics argue that US-led operations in these countries have all the characteristics of a quagmire, from which extrication will be difficult if not impossible, and claim that the Western presence in these countries is serving only to deepen the crisis, by providing a rallying-call for disaffected, would-be Islamist terrorists. Perhaps the West has jumped, all too willingly, into the trap set for it by al-Qaeda?

Other critics are concerned that the war on terror is based upon too many unverifiable or false assumptions. To claim 'victory' on the basis that there has been no repeat of 9/11 not only runs into the logical difficulty of negative proof, it could also amount to dangerous complacency; terrorism analysts point out that the planning cycle for major operations is often well in excess of the two years that have lapsed since 9/11. Another challengeable assumption is that in Afghanistan, Iraq and elsewhere, Western success is being impeded by aberrant organizations which can be isolated, bought off or destroyed, leaving the way clear for the triumph of the Western, free-market, liberal democratic idea. The unplanned, unintended consequences of the war on terror also weigh heavily on the debit side. Counter-terrorism measures can be counter-productive; the tightening of airport security, for example, might simply result in a compensating effort by terrorists to exploit weaknesses in maritime security. Terrorist organizations, well versed in asymmetric warfare, are not likely to hesitate before investigating new, unanticipated forms of attack. The broader consequences of the war on terror should also be borne in mind. However compelling the US need to secure a broad base of support, politically and logistically, might Bush's recruiting drive have provided an opportunity for certain regimes to repackage their repressive domestic policies as a contribution to the war on terror? Might civil liberties in Western societies be undermined by domestic security measures? Is the US policy of quasi-judicial detention in Guantanamo Bay a flagrant and persistent breach of international law and basic human rights? Could the Middle East peace process have been damaged – perhaps irreparably – by the US handling of the war on terror? And finally, does the war on terror indicate the wholesale militarization of international relations?

Winners and losers?

Returning to Rumsfeld's question; the merit of analysing the war on terror in terms of 'winners' and 'losers' is doubtful. By that approach, the only proper response from Pentagon officials could be 'on the one hand . . . on the other hand . . . ' While even-handed analysis of this sort might admirably describe the complexity of the war on terror, it would be less useful in policy terms. A better approach would be to divide the issues horizontally, rather than vertically. Below the line would be found the tactical and operational successes (and failures) discussed above. Above the line, however, lies the strategic uncertainty that ought to be the main concern of officials and analysts alike. Elsewhere in his 16 October memorandum, Rumsfeld acknowledges the problem succinctly and essentially answers his own question: 'Today, we lack metrics to know if we are winning or losing the global war on terror.' Traditionally, the metrics by which to judge tactical and operational achievements in war have been found on the strategic level. The problem for the campaigners in the war on terror, however, is that the strategic level is uncommonly unclear, unstructured and unpredictable. The task for policy-makers, in the United States and elsewhere, could scarcely be more difficult, in that the war on terror must be fought on at least two levels. On the practical level, the effort to contain, undermine and interdict al-Qaeda and similar organizations will no doubt be sustained. But the rationale for doing so, and the terms by which to evaluate achievement, must be sought on the strategic level. In the war on terror, strategy is no longer strictly a matter of territory, resources, alliances, the balance of forces, and even ideology. What matters instead is to deny the initiative to the aggressor, wherever and however necessary. The challenge for policy-makers and analysts, therefore, is to ensure they have a strategic framework that is as intelligent, coherent and responsive as possible, in order that the initiative, if lost, is quickly recovered, and in order to rationalize and direct activity at the tactical and operational levels.

SIX

Homeland Security – the UK example

Battle of Britain Mark 2 – Paul Moorcraft, Gwyn Winfield and **John Chisholm.** In February 2004 the editors compiled an assessment of how ready Britain was for a 9/11 attack.

Ready for what?

Bombs, floods and pestilence: resilience experts in government constantly stress that they are ready for both terrorism and natural catastrophes. So how ready is the UK for a single al-Qaeda unconventional attack or a series of nearly simultaneous spectaculars? Apart from London, our assessment is that the country is disturbingly ill-prepared.

There are many in Britain who implicitly say: 'Well it hasn't happened here' or 'We'll deal with it when it comes.' Which of course will be too late. But is it worth spending billions on specific counter-terror measures, particularly against weapons of mass destruction (or effect)? During the Cold War, despite millions spent on civil defence in the 1950s and 1960s, in the event of a major nuclear attack the best option was probably 'kiss your rear goodbye'.

But al-Qaeda is different. 9/11 was a brilliant operational attack; it relied on an unconventional use of conventional artefacts – kamikaze aircraft. But much of the al-Qaeda infrastructure has been destroyed. Extremist Islamic fighters in Afghanistan in the 1980s (despite some Western training) were largely ineffective by modern military standards. They have got better, and some of the guerrilla attacks in Iraq have been well planned. Al-Qaeda and its motley alliances do pose a threat, but it should not be blown up into mythic proportions.

Still, WMD have spread and al-Qaeda has to get lucky only once to kill thousands of people in Britain. The prime responsibility of the British government is not to get the trains to run on time or to run efficient hospitals – it is the defence of the realm. But if government must prepare for the worst, is it doing it correctly and cost-effectively?

Dunkirk spirit

British history is littered with examples of being caught on the hop and then through sheer pluck and inventiveness fighting back. The ignominious exit from France in 1940 was of course a disaster, but the heroics of the retreat have transformed it into a national moral victory. This attitude still persists, according to Patrick Mercer MP, the Conservative spokesman on homeland security: 'We didn't have a Civil Contingencies Secretariat of any sort until the foot-and-mouth crisis hit us. Something has to happen first in this country before we take measures to ameliorate it.'

He likened it to Winston Churchill's warnings before 1939: 'Please don't you see what's about to happen?'

The government has, however, done a great deal – with far less money – to emulate some aspects of the US model of homeland security. Patrick Mercer insisted: 'This is not a party political issue; this is a national issue, which conceivably could be one of national survival.'

London

London is the most iconic target and its progress in resilience is considerably better than the rest of Britain. So any criticism of London's posture is likely to be doubly relevant in the wilds of Cornwall or the cities of Liverpool or Glasgow.

London has been the target of Irish extremists since the 1880s, and the victim of a concerted modern campaign after 1969. The capital is the centre of royal, parliamentary, political, economic, cultural and social life of the country. It is a magnet for tourists . . . and for terrorists.

Intelligence

London is also the centre of the intelligence community. The current furore focuses on the political interpretation of information on Iraqi WMD, but the vagaries of inter-agency coordination is more fundamental. Michael Smith's new book on British spooks, *The Spying Game,* describes a litany of cock-ups caused not just by the rows with the Americans, but also by the bitter infighting between MI6, MI5,

GCHQ, Special Branch and the various manifestations of military intelligence.

Take two recent cock-ups. There was an almost complete failure to move into Kabul quickly enough when the Taliban ran away. Both US and UK spooks had go to around asking journalists what they might have seen or photographed when they entered the various al-Qaeda establishments in the city. The Russians were a bit quicker off the mark. Much useful information was compromised or lost to the Anglo-Americans. Previously, both UK and US agencies probably missed a trick when Osama bin Laden's head was offered on a platter by the Sudanese government when the Saudi millionaire lived in Khartoum. The Sudanese handed over Carlos the Jackal to the more alert French agencies. Unfortunately, the many British intelligence successes cannot be trumpeted, but there is still a chronic need to bang heads together and end turf wars.

Homeland czar?

Patrick Mercer, the Tory shadow 'Minister for Homeland Security', was asked whom he was shadowing: 'I'm chasing my own shadow really,' he replied plaintively. There is a major reluctance in government circles to emulate the Americans who unified their approach in a single large department, and poured a fortune into it. Britain cannot replicate the money, but many in the security establishment want a unified command and control in this country; the notion that the Home Secretary – in charge of so many disparate matters – can also spend enough time on homeland security is nonsense. Sure, he has lots of able lieutenants such as Sir David Omand, but someone more senior is needed to trample on Whitehall egos. A whole range of ministers with different, and not always complementary, responsibilities proliferate. At one stage, John Prescott, the deputy Prime Minister, was in overall charge, as well as masterminding the regeneration of the British rail system. Patrick Mercer admitted that although more money and a larger and more centralized security establishment are required, that doesn't sit well with Tory notions of small government.

There is also much opposition in the Territorial Army to extending the military's role to homeland security as well as trying to plug the many holes in the regular forces overseas, Mr Mercer said. But the aspiring homeland czar does concede that it is 'remarkable' that only one person in the UK – a policeman – has been killed by terrorists since 9/11.

Communication

Communication is a problem, and not only within the central security establishment. The lessons learned in London are often poorly transmitted to the regions. It's getting better but it's still bad. And money allocated to resilience in local government is frequently not being spent on something that Devonians or Liverpudlians think is a Metropolitan hobby-horse.

Nor is the resilience message getting through to the public – even in London. It's not easy to inform people about terrorism without putting the fear of God (or Ken Livingstone) into them. Nicholas Raynsford, the minister responsible for resilience in London, summarized the main public safety message as 'Go in, stay in and tune in' in the event of a catastrophic terrorist incident. But, as he admitted, until recently his message was 'Go out, stay out and phone 999'. Since the Iraq WMD disaster, the general public, especially in cynical London, trusts politicians even less. Despite the tarnished image of intelligence experts, Londoners are far more likely to trust a mandarin such as Sir David Ormand, the Cabinet Office's Security and Intelligence Coordinator. Perhaps he should appear in public just occasionally – to explain how the public should prepare for an attack which the chiefs of MI5 and the Metropolitan Police say is inevitable.

That might spur some of the commercial fat-cats in London to beef up their business continuity plans. Even in security-conscious organizations such as the Ministry of Defence fire drills and other emergency procedures are regularly treated with disdain or annoyance (but maybe ringing the alarm bells at the same time early on Monday mornings could be varied).

Personnel

Better training and regular exercises of emergency drills require more money but it also requires properly trained personnel. More chemical, biological, radiological and nuclear (CBRN) expertise is required in the police, especially outside London. The intelligence services have been energetically recruiting since 9/11, but there is still a chronic shortage of ethnic minorities, especially people who speak Arabic, particularly in the police services. Better-trained people are needed to screen asylum seekers – not just against the (inaccurate) stereotypes of 'benefit-seeking gypsies, slave-trading Albanians or Nigerian con-men'. Ironically, it's the highly trained experts who could do the most harm – whether a maverick in a

Cambridge laboratory or computer hacker in the city. And staffing for sky marshals is currently a joke, as is the pay for many security workers at airports.

Protecting the skies

The USA currently has some forty sky marshals. Over 4,000 are planned by the US Transport Security Administration, but when the UK government requested forty volunteers from the Met, only twenty were forthcoming. Air France carried private security staff after 9/11, but there were scandals over employing murderers, ex-bouncers and people trained in the Middle East. This led to their replacement by between two to six gendarmes per flight to the USA.

But should the marshals pack heat? 'I am a bit worried about guns on planes. It's the last place you want guns. What if they are overpowered, what if they fall into the wrong hands?' Stelios Haji-Ioannou, founder of easyJet, asked. Others emphasize the calibre of the security officials, rather than the calibre of their weaponry: London has largely bent to US pressure, but Portugal, Sweden, Finland and Denmark have said they will ground aircraft rather than put armed men on board.

The US has twelve different lists operated by competing security and intelligence organizations and has failed to combine them into a single supra-agency list. The UK is better about centralized lists, but they contain those with criminal convictions; most al-Qaeda sleepers have clean records. Currently the US is spending billions on biometrics which is undermined by the cross-agency squabbling about identifying terrorists. So much for their centralized homeland security effort, UK critics will say. EU bureaucrats have helpfully declared ski poles and ice skates to be potential security risks on board in cabins and have banned their carriage, except in the hold. But, again, good personnel are vital: if airports continue to employ low-paid, casual labour and poorly paid security then all the laws and technology in the world will make little difference.

CBRN kit

The Iraq war showed up inadequacies in military kit, but a much larger issue is the lack of protection against possible CBRN attack in the UK. Admittedly, the Home Office has gone to great lengths to provide the emergency service personnel with the necessary equipment and training. Despite this, there are still major flaws in the system; many of these are procedural or logistical. For example, response time is likely to be in the order of thirty minutes before a CBRN-equipped civil responder turns up. This allows the incident to mature to such a level where, if a deadly chemical agent were used, the majority of people at the site would have died. It would also mean that the area affected would be measured in miles rather than metres.

Unlike the military, the emergency services have no 'surge-to-war' capability. The military keep expensive supplies down to a minimum, knowing that they will have the time – in theory – to build up to the necessary levels. The emergency services have to procure for the worst; this involves a vast initial outlay. The problem is also compounded by the fact that items, such as respirator canisters, once opened, lose their effectiveness and have to be replaced; this is especially demanding for the police. The military have spent millions of pounds on software to work out hazard warning and prediction for CBRN. Currently the civil responders have not invested in specialist software for this.

While core skills can be taught, and are being taught successfully, the procedures and tactics that are essential to the emergency services defusing these situations are only slowly being learnt. But the military have no specific tactics on dealing with a CBRN incident in an urban environment that they can pass onto the civil responders; any lessons they have are for military environments.

Currently chemical detection systems are also, at the lowest level, the Chemical Agent Monitor. Even though the police have bought the enhanced version, it is still a fairly basic detector and numbers are in shorter supply than preferred. Until the numbers are increased and prediction software applied, keeping the cordon, for example, becomes a hugely difficult task as the officers manning the cordon know when the agent has arrived only when people start keeling over. Radiological detection is more accurate. But detection of biological agents is the most dangerous threat; it requires the most rapid detection. And these machines are few and far between.

Collective Protection, or Colpro in the jargon, is a prerequisite for recycling tired officers into a 'clean' environment and to prepare them for re-entry into the incident area. Yet there has been no major investment in this field. The British Transport Police have one Colpro that they use for CS gas training. Without collective protection, the strain on officers will be phenomenal – should al-Qaeda finally get lucky.

To be fair, it is quite a balanced score card. The military, who are the acknowledged experts in this field, have a long way to go before they could claim to have covered the problem adequately. The emergency services have far greater public demands on their time and resources than the military. As the Assistant Chief Constable of Hampshire, Colin Smith, said: 'We have 125 demands of which we have the resources to fill 100.'

Meanwhile, CBRN experts are trying to explain to the media that these are not Weapons of Mass Destruction (WMD) but Weapons of Mass Effect (WME). The effects of a successful CBRN attack are not likely to be measured in the amount of deaths – the Sarin attack in Tokyo killed a dozen people – but in the financial damage that is done to industry. After such an attack, encouraging business confidence and repairing contaminated infrastructure will be the real challenge. The psychological effect of the disaster is likely to outweigh the physical damage.

Halabjah in London?

A CBRN attack in London is possible, even likely; images of 5,000 agonized corpses of Iraqi Kurds in Halabjah could be replayed in the British capital. Nick Raynsford has said: 'London in particular and indeed other parts of the country are much, much better prepared to cope with a very wide range of possible incidents and threats than we were in early September 2001.' True, but is it enough? For example, improvements are desperately needed in seaborne container security. The authorities have made great strides but, in our skies, on land and at sea, a new battle for Britain is being waged. God forbid that we need to repeat Dunkirk, 9/11 or Halabjah before the government gets its act together. Because it may not have even forty-five minutes' warning.

Chasing shadows – Patrick Mercer MP, the Conservative Shadow 'Minister for Homeland Security', examined the terrorist threat in the UK and the lack of vigour in responding to it. Interview in the House of Commons in December 2003 with Paul Moorcraft.

Who exactly are you shadowing?
PM: Well, I'm chasing my own shadow, really. I don't have anyone to shadow directly. If you asked the government, they would immediately say that I was shadowing Douglas Alexander in the office of the deputy Prime Minister [he is actually Minister for the Cabinet Office], and there's some truth in that, but there's no single minister who has responsibility for homeland security; there are a number of ministers who have

cross-cutting responsibilities, including Douglas, Nick Raynsford, who has responsibility for London resilience, the Home Secretary himself at the head of the pile, and Caroline Flint, MP for the Don Valley, who is in charge of domestic counter-terrorism exclusive of the security services. So they have a whole host of people . . .

John Prescott was in overall charge at one stage?

PM: Yes, he was meant to be coordinating all of them, but the answer [from the government] is: 'We have a Home Secretary who is extremely capable, and has a wide brief, and he can cope with all this.' There may be some truth in that. But, for instance, I was working on something this morning about maritime security, relating particularly to the containers trade. If you want to send police and customs officers to be stationed in France, who is in charge of that? Whose budget does that come out of, and what are they looking for? Clearly there would be a customs implication to such an exercise, but if there was a counter-terrorism aspect, which obviously there is going to be, who coordinates it? It's tricky. There is no single point of contact inside the government for these sorts of issues.

That leads on to my next question: Does Britain need a homeland security department?

PM: The Homeland Security Department in the USA is of course enormous, and terribly wealthy in comparison with us. My own view is that there ought to be a cabinet member who is exclusively responsible for this – that's the ultimate goal. I would be happier [than I am now] to see a government minister given direct and sole responsibility for this job. As for the size of his department, that's a different matter.

Why hasn't this happened?

PM: It hasn't been done because nothing substantial has so far happened, but the government's response seems to be not to take any measures which are very obviously counter-terrorist or homeland security-biased because, by so doing, we will terrify the public. So, why have we no department for homeland security? We didn't have a Civil Contingencies Secretariat of any sort until the foot-and-mouth crisis hit us; something has to happen first in this country before we take measures to ameliorate it.

Let me give you an example: if you are a suicide bomber and you wish to attack a target in London, the only target in London which is comprehensively defended, in terms of having concrete blocks in a stand-off position sufficiently far from the target, is the American embassy in Grosvenor Square. They have been allowed to block some of the traffic flow and to take measures against suicide bombing attempts – we haven't. The Houses of Parliament, which must be one of the targets, are not defended in a similar way. Why not? Because we haven't been through that experience yet. I have no doubt that if we get a suicide bomb this afternoon outside the House of Commons, even a failed one, someone will say that this proves that we need an apron of security measures in front of the House of Commons. Everything in this country seems to be reactive as opposed to proactive, as regards homeland security under this government.

Sounds a bit extreme to me, particularly regarding the House of Commons . . .

PM: No, I don't agree. My mum grew up in deepest rural Lincolnshire. She went to big school in 1939, the week war started. I asked her how well prepared she was for war, and she said that she definitely remembered travelling from her rural Lincolnshire home to school carrying her gas-mask. Before war started, my mother had, at the age of twelve or thirteen, been issued and fitted with a gas-mask, trained how to use it, and trained in what to do in the event of aerial bombardment and – and here's the point – trained what to do in terms of gas attack. Now Britain had never been attacked with gas, and yet we were prepared to deal with weapons of mass destruction in 1939, before the event.

Is there something ideological about the reluctance to have a unified department for homeland security in this country? Certainly in the MOD there was almost a ban on the term 'Homeland Security', as if it were one of the terms civil servants weren't supposed to use . . . I suspect it also has to do with the different system of government, as well as ideology.

PM: If you ask government ministers why we have no department of homeland security, they will answer that it would follow the presidential model of government in America, whereas the system we have in place of cabinet government is better reflected by the systems we have here, and that there would be a mismatch.

I don't know [why we don't have one]. It is a cheap and easy shot to say that it's complacency, but you need a Hoare Belisha or a Winston Churchill to say, 'Please, don't you see what's about to happen. Let's start taking measures proactively rather than reactively.' And it is worth studying that period of time, from about 1935 onwards, to see what huge political risks certain ministers, and senior civil servants and indeed armed forces officers were taking, by sticking their neck out and saying, 'We have to do something, because the inevitable is just around the corner.'

The inevitable being a terrorist attack using weapons of mass destruction?

PM: I don't know about weapons of mass destruction, but mass unconventional attack. I don't want to split hairs, but the Twin Towers was a conventional attack, or was a conventional weapon used in an unconventional way. I can only take the words of such luminaries as Eliza Manningham-Buller [the Director of MI5]; if she is telling me that a terrorist attack is inevitable, as is the Assistant Commissioner of the Met; if these people are saying these things, then who am I to argue?

Let's say the Tories are in power next week, would you establish a homeland security department?

PM: This is not something that's going to happen overnight, but I would like to see a ministry, or a funded and staffed department within another ministry, in order to establish a coherent system, preparation and warning. This goes on to your domestic agenda question – 'Should the UK get in on the duct tape market?'; that is, useful preparations by Joe Public. I am hoping that we'll be able to demonstrate a series of very pragmatic policies, whereby we can warn the public of what is likely to happen, train the public in how to deal with the problem, equip the public so that the effects can be mitigated, and raise the level of expectation in such a way that understanding dispels part or all of the fear involved.

How are you going to do all this without putting the fear of God into people?

PM: Well, I think that's relatively simple. Let's just look back to the 1930s again; there was an understanding of what weapons of mass destruction can do, you might have veterans who have experienced gas attacks in combat, for example. The public aren't stupid; the advantage we have now that they didn't have in the 30s is that people have watched the effects of weapons of mass destruction on their televisions. They have watched the effects of terrorism in Northern Ireland for the past thirty years; while the problems we are discussing are not identical to the problem of living with terrorism in Northern Ireland, there are parallels to be drawn.

In the 30s, one of the measures they took – and if you think about it for a few moments, it is clearly risible – they painted red pillar boxes with gas-sensitive paint, the idea being that, when tiny concentrations of gas came wafting down Orpington High Street, the pillar boxes changed colour, say from black to green – clearly that is complete nonsense. There might be some chemical thought behind this, but what

247

it is really doing is reminding you that there is a threat: here is a totem of everyday English life, which is going to change. In the same way, there are no rubbish bins in railway stations, a consequence of IRA fire-bombing in train stations.

There are little things we can do: there are signs in the corridor saying 'This way in event of fire', there are instruction panels, and there are extinguishers located around the office. We don't come in each morning and have a fit in case we might perish in an inferno; surely it's not such a big leap of faith to tell people that they need to know what to do in the event of a conventional bomb attack, or in the event of a chemical attack? We can do this without scaring the pants off people, because if we don't we are doing the terrorists' job for them. Another analogy is AIDS; at first, it was a great scare, but when the government devised programmes for the promotion of safe sex, the panic levels fell. Knowledge dispels fear.

The London Resilience Team seems to work quite well, but how can that be applied as a model for wider use?

PM: Is it beyond the realms of possibility that we could legislate that firms do not just need to practise fire drills, but also bomb and contamination drills? I'm not suggesting that everyone should get gas-masks like my mother did, but in the same way that building regulations, for places like schools or other public buildings require a design that allows quick evacuation, should we not also demand that these buildings can be sealed. These things will not necessarily be excessively expensive.

We could also introduce First Aid tests as a mandatory concomitant of driving tests, as is the case in several other countries. We could introduce NVQs in First Aid and firefighting. The trouble with this is that I am meant to be practising 'less government', not more, but this does not sit comfortably with Conservative Party policy, or a party of fewer taxes.

What about the Territorial Army programme, the Civil Contingency Reaction Force?

PM: I think the government has snatched defeat from the jaws of victory. The TA – and you're talking to a long-serving TA officer – exists not on a strict disciplinary code, but on goodwill, drive and initiative. I have no doubt that much more imaginative schemes could have been devised to make use of the TA; the one thing that is clear to me about the TA is that they don't want a homeland security role, but I deeply resent the creation of this extremely modest force via double-hatting. There's been a tiny expansion in the TA establishment to allow this to happen. If this was to be couched in different terms, we could easily recruit something like the old Home Front army, with different commitments. The sad thing is that a great number of the CCRF tend to get called up – I think you will find that many of them are currently in the process of defending Kabul and Basra.

Do you think that the government hyped the terrorist WMD threat for political purposes prior to the Iraq war?

PM: This time last year, I identified four main arguments, for and against the war on Iraq. Firstly, that there were troops in place and they needed to be used, and something had to be done before Iraq became more capable on the ground than it already was; that's a pragmatic argument, but has little moral cohesion. The second argument is that, every day that Saddam Hussein is in power in Iraq, more people die at his hand; that is an extremely powerful argument that is irrefutable – the removal of Saddam Hussein was a good thing for the people of Iraq. However, how many countries could you say the same thing about? A lot. The third argument was the WMD argument, and the fourth was the terrorist argument.

I was never convinced by the WMD argument, and I was even less convinced after talking to people like Hans Blix, Kofi Annan, and so forth, in my capacity as a member of the Defence Select Committee. However, my abiding worry about this was terrorism, and I think this has been borne out by what has happened in Iraq during and following the war. Many non-Iraqi fighters who you may care to class as terrorists died in the war, and now there is little doubt that Iraq is proving to be a focus for international terrorism. This is a fairly pragmatic argument, and perhaps has little moral element, but if these terrorists are being drawn to Iraq, rather than to the streets of London or New York, then it must be a good thing – there may be something in that. I strongly believe that there were connections between Iraq and international terrorism that led to things such as the establishment of a group called Ansar al-Islam, the work of Ansar al-Islam in the Kurdish autonomous zone, which was manifested in the ricin plot that seems to have originated in Baghdad. If I had been in government, I would have deployed those four arguments, with WMD being third or fourth.

It seems to me that the Hutton Inquiry and the failure to find WMD in Iraq have shown up the inadequacies of our current intelligence systems.

PM: I'm not going to comment on the JIC [Joint Intelligence Committee], other than to continue to pay tribute to the work of our intelligence services. It's a little bit like saying, 'Have you ever seen an elephant on a billiard table?' Of course I haven't, because they camouflage it. We

249

haven't been attacked in this country, and yet a number of attacks have been interdicted as a result of covert and competent intelligence operations. Now part of the skill of the intelligence operative is that he or she does not trumpet their successes more than their failures, so it's a thankless and difficult task working in the intelligence agencies. The fact remains that, inside the shores of Great Britain, as far as I'm aware, only one person has been killed since the beginning of the war on terrorism; that's remarkable.

However, finding, fixing and striking in Iraq, we seem to find the wrong enemy; we found the conventional army, we found the Republican Guard, we found the Special Republican Guard, and these people didn't fight, it wasn't they who were causing the problems. It was the Fedayeen, the foreign volunteers, etc., who were never going to be detected by radars and surveillance techniques – this should have been indicated by intelligence. Where did the intelligence point to the fact that a successful military phase would then be followed by a popular insurrection? It didn't. Is there a popular insurrection – not yet, but it could go that way. I would hesitate to say that our intelligence was faulty, but I do wonder how much false intelligence we were fed, and I wonder if that was fed to us by our enemies, or by otherwise friendly countries who wished to push in a particular direction. I think the government is guilty of taking intelligence and canting it, twisting it, and turning it from intelligence into propaganda.

Have you any comments from a security perspective about the blackout problems in London resulting from power shortages?

PM: I would refer to what I said earlier about suicide bombing – no really effective preventive measures will occur until something happens. I would remind people that the most daring and successful terrorist attack during the IRA campaign was of course the Mk 10 mortar attack on 10 Downing Street, so the government complex has not been immune to very sophisticated aerial attacks in the past, and we should bear that in mind.

I have no comment about blackouts in London, but I feel very strongly about airport and airline security; why are we dragging our feet on this, why are we allowing the Americans to legislate that their airliners in future will have to have electronic counter-measure suites fitted? Some of them already have sky marshals. We are going to have to get with the programme on this, because if we're not careful, we're going to lose the business advantage – if you have the chance to fly to America on a safe aircraft or an unsafe aircraft, clearly you will choose the safe one.

Is there any other general political message you would like to add?
PM: It's not my job to take cheap shots at the government on this particular problem; my ambition is to provide sensible, proper, principled opposition. Rather than just calling them a bunch of complacent layabouts, I want to provide proper and sensible ideas which will help the government. This issue is not a party political issue, this is a national issue, which conceivably could be one of national survival.

Eternal vigilance – Nick Raynsford, the Minister for Local and Regional Government, also had special responsibilities for civil resilience. In January 2004, he talked to Paul Moorcraft about the state of British resilience.

PM: *What impact will the new Civil Contingencies Bill have?*
NR: It's very important. There has to be an updating of arrangements that go back to the 1940s that are no longer entirely appropriate, but also to ensure more effective coordination. The Bill does clearly build upon the work we have been doing, not just in London and nationally, from within the Office of the Deputy Prime Minister [ODPM}, but also the experience of the Civil Contingencies Secretariat over the last two years of pulling together a large number of different strands.

The Bill is inevitably controversial; anything of this nature is likely to raise concerns about civil liberties. And rightly so. We think we've got appropriate safeguards in place to make sure that the extensive powers to cope with real emergencies will be used only in those circumstances. It has been and will be extensively scrutinized in parliament.
PM: *The opposition spokesman, Patrick Mercer, insists that a solution is a minister devoted solely to homeland security. Do you think that would improve coordination?*
NR: No, I don't. The Home Secretary performs that function at the moment. He asked me immediately after 9/11 to oversee the arrangements in London, which we've done. That coordination has worked very well. And we are using the experience of London to build similar arrangements throughout the rest of England – with the regional resilience forums that we have put in place. Whatever framework you've got in place, and whoever's responsible at the centre – whether it's called Home Secretary or homeland defence minister – there has to be liaison between them and other departments. That is the very nature of the process. Ensuring effective liaison – that's the key to successful resilience.

PM: *The Home Secretary has lots of others things to do; resilience requires the entire attention of a very senior minister.*

NR: I see no sign whatsoever that the Home Secretary is not giving his full attention to this and he's got a very large team of ministers and civil servants who are supporting him. And Sir David Omand [head of security and intelligence at the Cabinet Office] is able to give absolutely full-time attention to this. I genuinely don't think there is a problem here.

The main question is: Are we doing all that is possible to safeguard against a very wide range of eventualities? I believe we are doing everything that we reasonably can do. This is a very difficult area, where all the time you have to test, question, check, and all the time you can spot areas where you can do better. It's a continuous process of plugging gaps, dealing with unexpected potential risks, developing the technology and linkages, bringing more people into partnerships that are necessary. We have been doing that for two and a quarter years, very intensively in London.

PM: *It's sometimes said that, until a catastrophic attack hits the UK, there won't be enough political energy and above all cash put into resilience.*

NR: There's a huge amount of cash been put in. For example, the £56 million that's gone into the mass decontamination kit some of which was used in the Bank underground station exercise in London. There's a further £132 million going into urban search and rescue. We are commissioning a new Firelink system to ensure that the fire service can communicate with the other emergency services. That's a major capital procurement exercise. All the evidence indicates that cash has not been an obstacle to ensuring resilience.

PM: *The London Resilience Team may be doing a good job, but it has not been effectively replicated in the regions.*

NR: London came first for obvious reasons, but the whole framework of resilience forums in each of the English regions is building on the London experience. We learned incrementally as we went along. [Not long after 9/11] the nucleus of the London team began mapping out what was in place in different parts of London and we are now gathering in the evidence from every region in the country. We are following a very similar pattern and learning from the London experience. London is most likely to be a target, so it was right and proper that it was initially the main focus. There will be inevitable variations between the regions as to what the main risks are.

PM: *Some of the money specifically allocated to local authorities is not* *being spent on resilience, precisely because there is less threat awareness in the regions.*

NR: I am often asked this question, from two different perspectives. Local government spends all their time criticizing us for, quote, 'ring-fencing' sums of money. Their argument is that if they don't have a degree of discretion in how they can deploy resources, it causes inefficiency and unnecessary pressure on the council tax. It prevents their making linkages between different services.

Conversely, I get individuals from individual local government departments who say, 'My chief executive won't give me enough money until you tell the chief executive you have got to give this money to me.' In the centre of this debate about local government finance, I do not know any areas where the lack of finance has inhibited local government from responding where essential.

PM: *There is some unhappiness in the TA with their involvement in civil contingencies. Any comment?*

NR: The biggest worry I had was the exercise we did a couple of months ago, which was designed to test their availability to help civil authority. It was planned to happen on the day of the rugby World Cup final. The commanding officer had to arrange a 'tactical pause' for two and half hours that morning in order to ensure that they did turn out. And it was a very good turnout. Both that exercise and the deployment of the regulars – because of the standby arrangement to secure immediate support from the regular army as well as provision for the Territorials – have been better than expected in terms of participation and the linkages.

PM: *Can we return to the Bank exercise? There were very few actual 'casualties' processed. Could London cope with a big CBW attack'?*

NR: We have made an enormous advance. We've now got the mass decontamination kit out to all fire authorities throughout the country. We've got the interim vehicles which are now being replaced with the permanent ones. It has been tested and certainly met the requirements. There are still details which need to be worked on – for example, the difficulty of communicating with members of the public if you're in a gas-tight suit. There were handouts with pictograms. That can be refined. But the kit worked. There was a huge worry a year ago when the Health Service procured personal protective equipment which leaked. Now the kit appears to be absolutely robust.

But there are still huge difficulties with fire-fighters working underground in that kind of restraining equipment. One of the clear lessons is that if you've got an accident in the Underground you must, wherever possible, get the train to the nearest station. London Underground and the emergency services are aware of this issue and have contingency plans in place.

PM: *If you go into some fire stations in the more rural areas and ask what CBW kit you've got, you may well be shown a very empty cupboard.*

NR: Every region, as I said, has now got the mass decontamination kit. And the urban search-and-rescue equipment is beginning to be supplied. We have said in our fire White Paper that we are moving towards a regional organization, and the fire Bill will be published next week. Those things that need to be organized on a regional basis, including all the anti-terrorist work, will be done on a regional basis to ensure we are capable of deploying in all parts of the country.

PM: *In London, what do you advise Joe Public to do in terms of preparation and training for resilience?*

NR: The short practical message is: 'Go in, stay in, tune in.' The range of possible eventualities is so large that if we give people an indication of how to react against one particular set of circumstances, they could do exactly the wrong thing. Advice on how to respond to a CBRN incident is likely to be totally different from other kinds of incidents, whether they be aircraft or more conventional explosions. We need to communicate as quickly and effectively as possible after an incident and to ensure that people can be told and reassured as quickly as possibly. That's why we've been developing the fast time communication pager system; that's why we've got arrangements for local authorities and police to be contacting vulnerable people who may need to be told what happens in certain circumstances.

But if we were to set out in advance certain dos and don'ts and they turned out not to be the right ones or people were to misinterpret them and to behave in an inappropriate way, I don't think anyone would forgive themselves.

PM: *Since the failure to find WMD in Iraq, there is a certain scepticism of what the authorities, particularly politicians, say about CBW threats in the UK. How do you counteract that?*

NR: Everyone knows that events such as Bali have been happening. Everyone is aware of what happened in Istanbul. I don't think the public are unrealistic. You are right [when you spoke earlier] about the balance between informing and not alarming. We agonized over this regarding the Bank exercise. Some of my colleagues were very nervous about engendering a degree of public panic or serious anxiety. All the evidence is that it didn't. If anything, the public felt reassured that that kind of detailed planning was taking place. And the public do seem to appreciate – and we have done research on this – that there is a need for confidentiality because we are certainly not in the business of informing terrorists of what steps are being taken to safeguard against any threats. In my view, the public *don't* expect detailed information; they *do* expect to be told honestly and effectively if there is a serious and imminent threat. They also need to be told how to respond after an incident.

PM: *Meanwhile, they are staying in and tuning in . . .*

NR: The irony is that one year ago I was trying to put across exactly the opposite message. Because when the fire dispute was taking place, we had to tell people: 'Go out, stay out, and phone 999.' That indicates the problem. In a conventional fire you get out of the building. In the event of a major terrorist incident people need to be informed of what's happening. That's why the 'stay in, tune in message' is of benefit.

PM: *Talking again of tuning in, you could argue that the authorities have not fully adapted to the psychological paradigm shift from the anti-IRA campaign to the war against Islamic extremism.*

NR: There has been a shift, not only in government and the intelligence community, but in the public as well. The biggest single thing we learned about London after 9/11 was that while the emergency services were well prepared to cope with a conventional attack, we simply didn't have arrangements in place to deal with a much larger-scale attack. There was a need to build effective partnerships with a wide range of other agencies. Ultimately, that's what London resilience has been about – the partnership involving not just emergency services but the local authorities, the utilities, the transport operators and wider grouping including business and the voluntary sector. So that you've got a really good network of people, all able to make their contributions; helping with detailed planning on individual issues, such as mass casualty and mortuary facilities. There were real lessons learned from New York. That's highlighted the need for work not just from the local coroners but a range of others as well. That kind of partnership is the biggest change that has happened since 9/11.

As far as the intelligence services are concerned, they know there is a very different environment and a much more serious threat. I am not privy to much of their work, except when there is a realistic threat that could affect London. There have been some of those in the last two years. They have shown they are alert and able to respond.

PM: *The intelligence chiefs have hidden behind a wall of secrecy. Now with the Hutton inquiry many have come out into the open. Would it make sense for a someone – not a politician – someone like Sir David Omand to occasionally address the public on resilience, especially at a time of high threat? It would have more credibility.*

NR: There is a real difficulty here. The language of security and intelligence is of necessity not as sharp and clear-cut as the language in which politicians are expected to speak. Many problems have resulted from people trying to interpret information that has got into the public arena as a result of Hutton and even before that in a way that is not entirely appropriate because of necessity intelligence sources are drawing inferences from a range of information with different levels of credibility. In many cases, it's shades of grey, rather than black and white. In the political arena everyone is always trying to get facts into much sharper focus.

PM: *Your argument applies less to an internal audience within government. There is also a serious communication problem within the resilience community, particularly outside London.*

NR: There is always a tension between giving the public appropriate information which doesn't endanger intelligence sources and processes, and to give information which ensures the public knows what's happening, and that they are aware how to get information if they need it in an emergency.

There is a separate issue of communicating with those who need to be involved. I talked about the partnership within London resilience, and we are replicating that in the regional resilience forums. It was the case in my first meeting with the local authority chief executives in London that they did feel they were in the dark. We now have regular meetings and confidence is building up as a result of their involvement in London resilience. But there are bound to be people within local authorities who are not within the net, who have not been informed by their chief executive or emergency planning officer. If they are interviewed, they will say, 'I haven't got the foggiest idea of what's going on.'

PM: *You seem very upbeat about resilience countermeasures.*

NR: There is no complacency. We are constantly checking and exercising and probing to find where weaknesses are. We could be caught out any time by something that hasn't been anticipated. You have to be constantly on the alert. Why I am positive – I won't use the word upbeat – is because I am conscious of the huge amount of work that has been done. I am very well aware that London in particular and indeed other parts of the country are much, much better prepared to cope with a very wide range of possible incidents and threats than we were in early

September 2001. So I am conscious of the improvements, hard work and the effective partnerships that have been forged.

PM: *So what's your key message?*

NR: Resilience is a task that continues twenty-four hours a day, twelve months a year, year on year. There is no let-up; it's continuing hard work to ensure that we are as well prepared as we can be.

Heart to Hart – City of London Police Commissioner **Dr James Hart** talked about security in the Square Mile to Paul Moorcraft and Gwyn Winfield in November 2003.

Q : How successful has the Automated Number Plate Recognition (ANPR) system been?

JH: More than 34.75 million vehicle licence plates were read last year, resulting in 858 arrests, including offences such as armed robbery and murder.

Q: *Has the deterrence value of the system been as important as the actual arrests?*

JH: Most credible terrorist organizations conduct surveillance operations as a stock in trade. The presence of [extensive] CCTV coverage means that there is a very strong probability that anyone engaged in such reconnaissance would feature as a part of a CCTV image. We can conclude that it is a good deterrent.

Q: *What other technology is important?*

JH: There is a great deal we can do now in the detection field, for example crime scene examination. The way we use DNA and data recovery techniques, extracting information from workstations, etc. There is no single solution, say if we buy this piece of chem/bio-detection equipment which will enable us to make rapid assessment of suspect devices. It's making sure that technology is used as a seamless part of the police system. Technology has helped us all round – for example, secure communications. We are proceeding on many fronts. There are many gems in the crown – ANPR is such a gem.

Q: *You've upgraded your communications for local businesses from your former pager system to email, instant alerts and so on.*

JH: One doesn't replace the other – they are very much complementary. We're working with the Metropolitan Police on a pan-London system.

Q: *How much cooperation are you getting from businesses on the resilience front?*

JH: We're plugging away at it. Getting chief executives and managing partners interested in security is terribly difficult. It's like staff development; if it's not adding value, it's one of those things you put in the corner. If you're making lots of money there is a tendency to forget about it.

But we've had remarkable success in trying to encourage senior commercial, financial and industrial figures to listen to the story we have to tell about security and business contingency planning. Once the senior people start to get involved it becomes very much easier to energize their business continuity managers and security directors. We are trying to work at all levels, trying to stimulate an interest in every aspect of business security management – whether that's encouraging shift workers to make sure that tapes are changed in CCTV and VCRs, wiping the lenses of the cameras – this sort of low-level stuff, but vitally important to us – right the way through to making sure that evacuation plans and other contingency plans are as good as they possibly can be.

We are sharing as much information with the business community as we can. What are the accurate threat assessments? What do they need to be protecting themselves against? How do they need to appraise their business in the context of what is going on worldwide? Not only in relation to headline terrorism, al-Qaeda and the rest of it, but in relation to, for example, eco-terrorism and organizations which have really brought protest against corporations to the top of the agenda.

We get a lot of help from Corporation of London and London First. We haven't done nearly enough [to work with such organizations] but part of my agenda in the next year is to do much, much more. I keep saying this: policing is not something you do *to* people – it's something you do *with* people. That's as much the case with security policing – counter-terrorism – as it is about dealing with the yob culture. I can't protect the City of London on my own. We need partners – we need the public to help.

Q: *In terms of the asymmetric CBW threat, how do you interface with businesses, especially regarding the question of detection?*

JH: Are you suggesting that companies and individual buildings should have their own detection equipment?

Q: *There could be a network of such devices tied in with police systems.*

JH: That's an interesting idea. The truism about assessing the merit of any suspect device – whether it's an improvised high explosive or some chem/bio device or white powder – is not only in the nature of the device itself but an assessment in terms of the wider threat context. Where it's come from, who's got it, how did it come to our notice – the whole plethora of questions we need to ask in the early period of the discovery. That requires an in-depth knowledge of the likelihood of some threat perhaps made against a particular individual or company. We need to share more relevant threat information with potential victims, but there comes a point where it's just not sensible to do that because it would either compromise a source or information that other people had. The need to know cuts in fairly abruptly.

I would certainly encourage a greater knowledge among individual companies as to the nature of the likely threat that they are exposed to. As far as the fast-time deployment of chem/bio detection equipment is concerned, we would have to be careful about how we grade our response. I would be more comfortable if my officers were on the scene as soon as possible to assess the hazard.

Q: *Once the incident has occurred, the information could come much more quickly if the companies' detection systems could piggyback onto your own procedures. It would expand your capabilities.*

JH: I would want to know a lot more about how such a system could work. As a comparison, we use a lot of CCTV and share companies' own CCTV product to make both of us safer. Perhaps there is some benefit in being able, to use your expression, to 'piggyback' information. I would need to know more, especially in terms of issues such as evacuation. Would we want people hanging around to gain data when what they should be doing is evacuating themselves? It may be the best advice is simply to shut your front door and stay there. There could be much benefit in having the information about the drift of a chemical cloud.

Q: *Can we take a practical example? Were you happy with the recent exercise centred on the Bank station?*

JH: Oh, yes, pretty happy. We had a comparatively minor part to play in that – we policed it . . . I thought it worked pretty well. I have a story from the exercise which illustrates the value of community policing in a counter-terrorist environment. A gentleman approached one of our cordons at the perimeter of the sterile zone. He was very distressed because he couldn't get his luncheon party to a restaurant to celebrate his wedding anniversary. The officer kindly escorted his party through to the restaurant. He later sent a very nice letter saying: 'He was familiar with the role of the police in escorting people away from licensed premises, but never *into* licensed premises.' We are not an army of occupation. London has to get on with things – people have to feel comfortable about their lives. We can't have the Monty Python boot approach to security.

Q: *What percentage of your time do you spend on counter-terrorism? Your predecessor told me he spent roughly 50 per cent of his working day on this issue.*

JH: If you include worrying about it, then it is about 50 per cent. I have a police force to run so I do do other things. Since I've taken over, we've restructured ourselves internally so I have senior officers who run bits of the business which are key to such priorities. We now have a chief superintendent who runs our counter-terrorism/public order section. We have better management oversight than we had hitherto. That takes some of the day-to-day pressure off worrying about the tactics.

Q: *You've had great success with your Fraud Squad. Does that run into your ability to prevent money laundering from al-Qaeda?*

JH: Yes. Much of the income of terrorist groups around the world comes from fairly low-level fraudulent activities: misuse of credit cards, misuse of fairly straightforward banking instruments. The police capability to get in and understand how these frauds are committed – perhaps a fairly low-grade, but high-volume fraud such as credit card cloning – is very important. We put a lot of effort – by high-grade officers with the right background and skills – into tackling these crimes. Our financial investigators do a very good job.

Q: *I take your point, but what about shifting large sums of money around for terrorist purposes?*

JH: We have got some new legislation in place which will help us enormously – the Proceeds of Crime Act. Suspicious Activity reports have to be made by people in the banking and professional sectors which are sent to the National Criminal Intelligence Service and then farmed out to local police forces for enquiry. We are getting a much stronger grip on money which is used for fraudulent purposes. Senior officers in our Economic Crime Department enjoy significant support from the banks and financial services community. They fully appreciate the need for vigilance with regard to the international movement of funds. That relationship helps to ensure that we, as well as the National Criminal Intelligence Service (NCIS), receive early warning of any suspicious transaction and can quickly respond to a request for assistance in establishing its legitimacy or otherwise.

Q: *There has been speculation recently that terrorists could deploy ships – either an oil tanker to ram a coastal port, or in London's case a ship coming into the City with containers full of explosives or worse.*

JH: There are all sorts of doomsday scenarios which one could come up with. My job – in collaboration with colleagues in the Metropolitan

Police and British Transport Police – is, as far as I can, to ensure that we have generic contingency plans for as many of these things as possible. We do an awful lot of work with London Resilience, and other groups, to make sure that the whole civil contingencies agenda is fulfilled. It's enormously difficult to second-guess what the terrorist is going to do next. Some would say there is not much point in doing that. The best we can do – as we were saying about CBRN – is to have generic contingency plans which will hopefully stand us in good stead across the whole range of prospects.

Q: *There is a problem of preparation and warning, and yet not scaring the pants off the public – that happened to an extent with the recent scare stories in the media about plans to evacuate large swathes of London.*

JH: That's what we're here for. You pay us to soak up a certain amount of the hype here. To use our information sources and experience to make judgement calls on how far we need to excite or energize a community in relation to a particular threat. I am not in the business of withholding information from the public where they have a legitimate need to know for their own safety and protection. As the Prime Minister said at the Lord Mayor's Banquet last year, if we were to share every piece of threat information that came across our desks in a working week the entire population would be completely paranoid. To some extent, that's what you pay me for – to soak up some of this stuff, but also to make sure that the information that does get placed into the public domain isn't going to compromise any other agencies or any work that's ongoing, and is going to be positively helpful to the public. For example, if I can say something that is reassuring to a group of bankers, to give them a bit more confidence to go on and do what bankers do, that's positively helpful. But, if I need to say, 'Look chaps, your corporate headquarters is vulnerable because there are people who wish you harm,' then I hope they will find that helpful as well.

Q: *Because of the failure to find WMD in Iraq, there may well be a tendency now to be sceptical about terror warnings in London.*

JH: We have to be very cautious to avoid wild supposition about the CBRN threat getting really out of hand. There are colossal difficulties about the dispersal of some of these things, as well as the technological difficulties about putting some of these together in the first place, let alone transporting them from one place to another. It's perhaps okay if you are in the USA, but it's much more difficult if you're working out of a garden shed wherever. A bit of a reality check on some of this stuff is the sort of thing I can do.

261

Q: *How many of your officers are fully trained in CBW?*

JH: We have a 24/7 coverage.

Q: *Do you believe in the inevitability of a major terrorist attack?*

JH: If the levels of sheer hatred and the anti-Western feelings that have been developed – as evidenced by the attacks on the USA on 9/11 – then it's not unreasonable to assume that that level of hatred is still there and if it happened once it will happen again. That's not on the basis of any intelligence – that's pure supposition. To try to put yourself in the mind of terrorists, to try and plan and execute that sort of attack, you would need to ask why they did it in the first place. Presumably to send a very strong signal to the American people. And, for counter-terrorism purposes, for America read United Kingdom.

Q: *You were very involved with diplomatic protection. Although we talk about big indiscriminate attacks, how do you rate the possibility of more targeted attacks on individuals – assassinations – as in the case of the IRA mortar-fire on No. 10 Downing Street?*

JH: The prospect of personal assassination has always got to feature in any counter-terrorist strategy. Here in the City, protecting visitors, guests and dignitaries from the whole portfolio of potential terrorist attacks is something we try to consider. Personal close-quarter assassination or indeed remote assassination by a whole variety of means is a very credible threat.

Q: *And the royals?*

JH: It would seem logical that terrorists would go for what the nation stands for. The Twin Towers, White House, the Royal family, Palace of Westminster, the City as a symbol of capitalism.

Q: *There's a general acceptance that resilience coordination in London is reasonably good, but that it is a shambles nationwide. How do you educate the regions in better coordination? Especially as a terrorist attack could be more likely outside the relatively well prepared London?*

JH: We do need to take the subject seriously outside the capital. The IRA had a history of attacking targets around the country. There is no reason why London should be the only target, although it is target-rich. You mention coordination. Responses to mass casualty attacks do not happen by chance; it happens with thorough planning, exercising, understanding each other's standard operating procedures, knowing who the key players are . . . I am sure my colleagues around the country will be more than familiar with exercise scenarios. It may not be possible to devote sufficient resources to exercises similar to the ones we have here.

Making a comparison with military conflicts – the relations between air, sea, army power – command and control across that purple interface is absolutely vital. It's exactly the same coordinating any major incident that civil authorities are in control of. The complexity is multiplied many times. It goes across police borders, or regional and administrative borders, involving various utilities – water, railways, police, ambulance. Someone has to be in command, and know how each of those organizations is going to react. It's hugely complicated. We need people who are skilled in taking command of those situations, and can also work with the military.

Finessing the terrorist threat – David Veness, Assistant Commissioner, specialist operations, in the Metropolitan Police, is in charge of intelligence, protection, anti-terrorism and security. He is one of the UK's foremost experts on the threat from al-Qaeda and its affiliates. Interview with Paul Moorcraft in January 2004.

PM: *How has the Met performed since 9/11, as far as counter-terrorism is concerned?*
DV: There is a sense of achievement. There has not been an attack against UK interests within the UK. There has been an enormous investment in preventative and disruptive strategies which we are confident have prevented terrorist activity. Over twenty-eight months – that is a significant achievement. However, there are no grounds for complacency . . . There is still a great deal to do . . . for example, in understanding the nature of the threat and the methodology of international terrorism. Secondly, getting skilled people in the right numbers in the right places. Thirdly, the force multiplier of technology. All those areas need to be pursued vigorously. Although much has been achieved, remorseless effort is essential to maintain defences.
PM: *Would you give a precise example of where you thwarted an attack? Was the big deployment of police and army at Heathrow a success in stopping an alleged al-Qaeda shoulder-launched rocket attack?*
DV: The difficulty of precision is not being able to know the exact outcome of terrorist planning and activity. It *is* justifiable to claim that what has been stopped would otherwise have led to terrorist activity.
PM: *Have recent arrests dented al-Qaeda's capacity to launch a spectacular in London?*
DV: There are no grounds for that judgement.

PM: *There was an expectation that there could be a major attack over Christmas and the New Year. It didn't happen. Was that good policing or maybe the original intelligence was not that sound?*

DV: We need to look at what the enduring threat is and what the fluctuations of threat level over weeks and months are. The enduring challenge still encompasses a simultaneous spectacular terrorist attack that could result in mass murder. That 9/11 model remains the unequivocal intention of al-Qaeda and its top echelons. You also have the menace of dire attacks. Examples such as Bali, Mombasa, Casablanca and, most recently, against British interests in Istanbul, where you have groups affiliated to al-Qaeda who are mounting car- and lorry-bomb or comparable attacks, which are not on the scale of the intended spectacular. At the third tier, you have semi-autonomous groupings or those who appear to be acting as individuals, who are conducting other forms of attack. All these remain constant. That will be with us for years and years. Within that we will have periods where the threat is perceived to be greater or lesser. In the American context, that is a period where we have just passed through. They had grounds for forming a view on 22 December [that there was a higher threat] and which was reduced [at the end of the first week of January].

PM: *Do you think this war on terror will last as long as the Cold War?*

DV: The threat from terror if you encompass all its forms will not be eliminated. We are going to have manifestations of terror in various pockets of conflict and that will be enduring. The realistic mission for those of us who are operationally engaged in counter-terrorism is to seek to eliminate the capacity for international terrorists to perpetrate mass murder on the scale of 9/11. That provides a focus in terms of the groups who have the capacity and the intent to conduct those forms of activity or who aspire to do so. This is the war aim of the focussed counter-terrorist effort which has the outcome of reducing harm to the public.

PM: *But how do you focus on such a wide spectrum of threat: from the unconventional use of conventional transport – aircraft as flying bombs – to the dangers of a CBRN attack, maybe a dirty bomb?*

DV: The significant different factors of al-Qaeda and its affiliated groups are:

1. It's a global enterprise – that's beyond the previous British experience of counter-terrorism.
2. The unequivocal intention to cause mass murder – almost on an agenda which is politically unachievable. There's no scope for negotiation.

264

There's no political solution. This is a destructive and malevolent agenda, which finds its expression in murder.

These two factors are strategically different.

Within that strategic framework, how are the tactics different?

1. The intention to cause simultaneous spectacular events, which have traditionally had a focus on aviation. That threat continues, as indeed do other forms of transport threat: for example, the USS *Cole*.
2. The suicide bombing – seen by the terrorist as an effective means of committing murders with fairly limited logistic demands. From their perspective, it's a logical choice, if your intention is murder.
3. Then there's CBRN. We need to distinguish between them. Clearly, there's evidence particularly in the CB category that al-Qaeda and its affiliated groups are committed to engage in this if they can achieve the practicalities of delivery. That's a realistic threat.
4. Then there's man-portable air [attack] systems, linked to aviation again. It's a real threat. We saw that in Mombasa, we're seeing it regularly in a slightly different context in Iraq.
5. Series, no-warnings bombs. That happened in Istanbul in November. Istanbul is significant because that was the first attack against Western interests in a European city, in this case delivered by multiple suicide bombings.

PM: *In my own experience of fundamentalist fighters in Afghanistan and elsewhere, they were often much more cautious than the average British soldiers in battle. Nor, despite Western training in some cases, were they very effective. I wonder whether sometimes we exaggerate the threats until they become almost mythically dangerous?*

DV: That's a fair question. What is the real capability of the enemy? The ability across the spectrum to consistently deliver a whole range of meticulously prepared and inexorably successful operations is a question mark. But if you look at the operational environment – particularly in the Western cities – if you achieve, out of ten attempts, one successful impact in the heart of the city, and the casualties are completely innocent civilians, then the terrorist will achieve his goal. So it's not a question of gauging the military efficiency of our opponents, it's the consequences that would result – the fear created in a Western environment.

PM: *No matter how bad they are, if they keep at it they will succeed.*

DV: Compare it with our thirty-year experience of effectively dealing with car and lorry bombs. Lorry bombs even with warnings, when delivered with consistency, had the ability to significantly affect city life. For example, [the IRA attack on] Bishopsgate. And look what was happening in Paris in 1995–6 – relatively low-level bombs, but significant casualties. Attacks by the GIA on Metros and markets, but no warnings at all; completely clear intention to commit murder. From an urban counter-terrorist point of view, we have to consider what the consequences will be in major Western cities.

PM: *The police deemed the major terror exercise at the Bank station in London a success, but very few 'casualties' went through the decontamination process. You can't really relate this to a major CBW attack by al-Qaeda.*

DV: This exercise was a small part of a much larger endeavour. We did learn valuable lessons. Everybody recognizes that there is more to be done. There's greater opportunity for coordination between the emergency services. More to be done on equipment, and, yes, the scale of the activity.

PM: *You mention coordination. But there is still too much turf warfare in Whitehall, let alone in the regions.*

DV: Everybody who is involved professionally takes this point very seriously. There is a recognition that the significant advance needs to be sustained in order to have a response that the public would have confidence in.

PM: *So do we need a homeland security minister?*

DV: That's for the government to decide.

PM: *OK, let's approach this from another angle: do your police counterparts in the USA say that they are achieving greater coordination because there is a Department of Homeland Security?*

DV: We work very closely with the Department of Homeland Security, and they are going through a very challenging phase at the moment. Because it is still evolving, we have yet to see the benefits which will clearly flow from it. Where the American experience may teach us a great deal – and if our analysis of a long war on terror is correct, as I am sure it is – then in two to three years' time, the Homeland Security model might be an even more compelling one.

PM: *What can Joe Public do in the counter-terror war? And how do you inform him (or her) without causing panic?*

DV: We are confident that an engaged debate with the public would be completely productive. Everything that has been achieved over twenty to thirty years – in a different category of terrorism – has demonstrated that an effectively informed public is remarkably responsible. They form balanced judgements and they conduct a whole range of extremely useful activities – such as spotting bags on the underground, or reporting suspicious vehicles during the Irish extremism era. I am completely confident that there is a good basis for that dialogue to happen again. The way it is practically valuable is to give specific information on which people can act. So that they can do something useful. There is more to be done to add that practical advice.

PM: *In the late 1930s through to the civil defence measures of the early Cold War a great deal of practical dialogue took place – from gas masks to stocking up on food stuffs. But there is very little of that now.*

DV: Clearly there is scope from moving beyond the threat warning phase into systematic practical advice. The other factor is creating an understanding that the nature of this threat will be with us for a long time to come. Over this Christmas, for example, people were aware there is an enduring challenge to transport security. Then we can all approach these issues in a more constructive frame of mind.

PM: *How has the Met progressed with staunching money laundering to terrorist movements?*

DV: We have here the national focus for police endeavour against terrorist finance and we are vigorously supporting the government policy on this. The Chancellor has taken a key role in engaging with the financial institutions. Following the money is vital, not only because relatively small amounts of money lead to deadly terrorist attacks – literally thousands of pounds can be the difference between a terrorist attack occurring and it not occurring. But even more the money takes you into the intelligence and planning processes, both for deterrence and disruption and for the intelligence which may result – even though you haven't recovered a dollar.

PM: *How important is the military contribution, especially the TA units committed to support civil contingencies?*

DV: We regard this as extremely valuable. An important early win was enhanced linkage at the brigade level. Here in London there is a remarkably good linkage with the emergency services and London [military] district in terms of the availability of regular forces. That was one of the ingredients which was often forgotten in the New Chapter [of the Strategic Defence Review]. The second was the Civil Contingencies Reserves. There is a great deal of effort going into the contribution of the London district. That's part of the need for reinforcement in an emergency. Any of the UK resources – public or private – that can assist us in this regard, we think is helpful. We are not critical of the TA role.

Anybody can contribute, if we need to deal with a dire emergency, which is affecting the life of the city, then a formed body of individuals with effective communication and good leadership is going to be extremely welcome.

PM: *The TA is pretty overstretched in war-fighting, not least in Iraq, and many territorials are not keen on the homeland security role.*

DV: Of course the volunteer reserve is never going to provide the complete response to a dire emergency in a British city. But it might be one of the means of reinforcement of the civil power which would be particularly valuable. We might need to get back to normality over a forty-eight to seventy-two hour window where effectively a city has become frozen in terms of its services. The TA's leadership and communication skills etc. could be vital. There are other reinforcing options as well – the private security industry, the charitable sector, and our own special constabulary, for example.

PM: *Do you need more resources – equipment and men – for the re-inforcement roles?*

DV: The way we have been able to expand the previous model of counter-terrorism – designed for a different challenge in the car bomb era – has been stretched in the last twenty-eight months and it may lead us to ask: Is that degree of stretching sustainable, without continual re-inforcement? The answer to that would be no. We are at the point where serious reconsideration is justifiable overall – not just for counter-terrorism, but for consequence management and resilience. Yes, there is a structural challenge for the UK, and certainly for London.

PM: *Not enough men to fight crime and terrorism?*

DV: It's a broader issue. It's certainly true of the police service, but also of the agencies which come together [on the resilience front]. One of the UK's strengths is teamwork, but we have stretched the previous model. The time is right to reconsider whether a new and expanded scale of response is necessary.

PM: *The structure might need changing, but have the psychological demands of shifting from thirty years of anti-IRA counter-terrorism to an Islamic extremist threat been fully recognized as well?*

DV: Within the European context, including the UK, I don't think that understanding is widespread. You only have to sit down with American colleagues to see the difference of perception. That's understandable. We have not moved to a position where there is widespread understanding of the true menace of the threat.

PM: *How many Arabic speakers have you recruited into the Met?*

DV: Skilled people are regarded as one of the main planks of the scale of the reinforcement I have referred to. Within that, familiarity with the enemy, understanding of the culture and linguistic skills are absolutely key. We are investing heavily in that.

PM: *Will you be specific: how many Arabic speakers do you have in the Met?*

DV: We have a significant number.

PM: *Ideally, how should we proceed in this war against terrorism?*

DV: The most grave end of the challenge – spectacular attacks – we must treat very seriously. We need to recognize that challenge for many years to come. The response to make London and the rest of the UK safer would be to work ever more vigorously not only with the agencies which are at the heart of counter-terrorism but a whole range of supporting mechanisms – health, local government etc. - and to recognize that they are also a vital part of the solution. That includes not only those who work here but also those who visit London.

SEVEN

Future Shock

Paper Tiger: real teeth – The future threat from weapons of mass destruction by **Gwyn Winfield.**

Iraq and Afghanistan were said to be powerhouses of research and development for weapons of mass destruction, but has the non-appearance of their nuclear, biological and chemical weapons downgraded the threat?

The fall of the twin towers predicated the start of a new conflict as much as the fall of the Berlin Wall presaged the end of an old one. This new conflict was likely to be asymmetric (small terrorist forces versus large conventional ones) and to utilize weapons that would put the advantage in the terrorists' hands – the perfect example of these weapons are chemical, biological, radiological and nuclear (CBRN or NBC) devices. The synchronicity of 11 September and the anthrax letters was such that it immediately became apparent that, if these two events could have been linked, the death toll would have been much higher.

The world had become used to the threat of mutually assured destruction (MAD), the reality of a nuclear attack was so horrible that it was easier to live in a state of denial and not worry about it. The relative mundanity of chemical, biological and radiological weapons, however, despite their likely use on the plains of Germany during the Cold War, makes the threat seem more likely and therefore far more frightening. Countries or states are made up of a government that is keen to remain in existence, and as such can be bargained with; fundamentalist terrorist groups who are happy to die leave no such avenue. WMD ensured death to the dealer as much as to the recipient and it was this threat that maintained the balance. If a user of CBRN is happy to die the same death as his victims then there is no such balance. In a world of smart bombs and surgical precision the twenty-first century was not supposed to be threatened by poison gas and biological clouds.

Radiological weapons are probably the easiest to make of the three (chemical, biological and radiological). While nuclear is a threat, the chances of rogue states or terrorists being able to build a nuclear device are slim (theft and black market purchase are not impossible, however). Chemical or biological agents often have their life measured in hours or days. In contrast, radiological agents are hardy and remain as virulent as they were on the minute of release for years afterwards. They are also relatively easy to find, caesium 137 is commonly used in medical radio-therapy (and has a half-life of about thirty years) and as such is readily available. Plutonium (half-life of 80–6,500 years) or uranium 235 (700 million years) can be stolen from any number of nuclear reactors in eastern European countries and turned into 'dirty bombs' (an explosive device surrounded by radiological material). The effects of radiological poisoning are varied and depend on what isotope and how much of a dosage the individual received. This means that, compared with the more lethal chemical or biological weapons, radiological weapons, as a 'weapon of mass destruction', leave a lot to be desired.

As a 'weapon of mass effect' (WME), however, because of their long half-life, there is nothing better – while casualties may be low, damage to property and buildings will be enormous. We know that radiological weapons are of interest to terrorist organizations: there were concerted attempts to steal radiological sources from Afghanistan; Grozny (an attempted theft in 1999 of a container of radiological material); Ukraine (most recently in 2004 but the Ukraine is chock-full of the material); and the rather innocent theft of some strontium 90 by wood-cutters in Abkhazia (they stole it because it was warm!). Thankfully, despite many thefts and many warnings, there have been only a couple of attempts to use this technology in an offensive way, and both times the Russian police have been able to detect the Chechen terrorist device before it was exploded. Radiological weapons are a threat to property and a limited threat to life, but are (in the right circumstances) easy to make. While their effect is low, their probability is high and there is very little that states can do to be able to stop this. The rot in Eastern Europe has gone on too long and the prevalence of material is such that the only way to deal with the situation is crisis management.

Chemical warfare agents (CWA) are probably the second most prolific weapon out of the three. The US and USSR built up huge

271

stockpiles of chemical agents (to be dispersed via artillery and mortar rounds) throughout the Cold War and are now spending large amounts of time and money in disposing of their chemical arsenal. While this provides a potential pool of weapons for the enterprising terrorist/thief, it is far easier for any country, or large terrorist group, to manufacture their own. They were largely written off towards the end of the Cold War for political reasons (neither East nor West Germany was keen on being uninhabitable for thirty years) and were a mixed blessing for the user. Chemical weapons force both sides into obstructive and physiologically draining individual protective equipment (IPE, which consists of respirator and vapour- and liquid-proof suits). NATO policy would have been for large amounts of agent to be put down to slow the Soviet advance while the Soviet policy would have been to cause disruption in NATO's command and control to allow them to punch through.

Chemical agents are split into blood (cyanide), blister (mustard), nerve (VX, Sarin etc.) and psychotropic (BZ). All of these can be manufactured by a good laboratory (though VX does take a level of specialist knowledge) and there is evidence of their use in the world. Sarin was used by Aum Shinrikyo in their Tokyo subway attack and was also one of the agents suspected to be used by Saddam Hussein in his Halabjah attack. Mustard was also used by Iraqi forces in the Iran-Iraq war, cyanide has been used by Farc insurgents in Colombia, and BZ was suspected of being used in the retreat from Srebrenica. The effects of these agents vary depending on the quality, quantity and form (whether liquid or vapour) but all of them are unpleasant. The population's terror comes from their lack of knowledge of these agents and this translates into political fear and military caution. It used to be noted that all that was needed to hold up a military convoy for hours was a sign that said mines (regardless of whether there were any mines there), now one mustard shell would stop a military advance until the politicians can agree on what an 'acceptable risk' would be.

Biological agents are the last and most unpleasant of this unholy trinity. They were mainly spurned by the Cold War forces because of their inability to control them – many virulent agents once released could make their way back into friendly lines. They were also unwieldy, needing beneficial environmental conditions (low light, moderate temperature range) and often requiring specialist distribution methods (being sprayed from aircraft, for example). Some, such as anthrax, which are more resilient and able to fit into this restrictive niche, were seriously considered, but the military desire for these weapons was not

272

as a weapon of mass destruction, but as a weapon of mass effect – in this case destroying the enemy's logistic and support structure by flooding it with casualties. Despite the Russians agreeing to be bound by the Biological Weapons Convention (1972) the defection of Biopreparat scientist Kanatjan Alibekov (among others) proved to the world that a great deal of biological weapon research had been done in recent years using sophisticated technology. The collapse of the Soviet war machine and the subsequent non-payment of wages meant that a great deal of the scientific research that had been developed went to the highest bidder. This has been a real concern to the West. While many biological agents can be simply manufactured (tularaemia, ricin), many require a dedicated team and a hefty research bill so the migration of these scientists was a welcome bonus for any country that wanted to develop a major biological agent programme. As opposed to chemical weapons which have an instant affect, biological agents can be surreptitiously delivered and the only realization that it has been released comes after a significant amount of people have died. The vast majority of biological detectors require there to have been a major event – an over flight by a spraying aircraft, an artillery barrage etc. – for them to alarm. The release of vector transmission (mosquitoes and rats) or a more covert release of something virulent can circumvent these devices. Syndromic surveillance, the means by which the medical records and notes are monitored for unconventional symptoms, does provide a better way of judging a covert release, but this still requires GPs or medical officers to realize that what they are seeing is not flu but anthrax. Releases of biological agent are thankfully limited. A major accident occurred at a Russian lab in Sverdlovsk which killed a number of people (exact details are difficult to corroborate but was in the region of sixty-four) and there have been some small-scale biological attacks, either to attack co-workers or, in one case, to influence local politics (the attack by the religious sect Bhagwan Shree Rajneesh in Oregon). The anthrax letters in the US are the most well known of any biological event, but the mystery of who sent them and why makes them a difficult template for expected use. The lessons that rogue states and terrorists will take from this, however, is that – even though the body count was low – the press coverage and cost of clean up was huge. Biological weapons are a 'win' for terrorists. Even if they don't kill many people, the publicity they gain the group and the pressure that it puts on the state are out of all proportion to the small amount of money necessary to create them.

A full appreciation of the results of the Iraq Survey Group [ISG] and Unmovic would require volumes. But some key points can be made about the capability of Afghanistan and Iraq.

The al-Qaeda network in Afghanistan had made some low-level progress in the search for radiological, chemical and biological weapons. Afghanistan has some high-grade radiological sources left over from Russian rule and these, combined with the paper research that was found, could have been used to create an effective radiological dispersal device. There had also been some work done on chemical weapons, (cyanide but also research into nerve agents), but this had been on a very low scale and required a lot more work. While there were significant amounts of agents that could have been turned into effective biological weapons (strains of veterinary anthrax) the necessary technology and disciplines were absent.

Iraq was at the other end of the scale. It was known that the Iraqis had huge stockpiles of chemical weapons (nerve and mustard) as well as a sophisticated biological weapons programme. Suggestions were rife that Iraq was also keen to buy or build a nuclear device and there is a lot of sound rationale behind this. Iraq had used chemical weapons to try and turn the military tide in the Iran-Iraq war (against soldiers and civilians) and was likely (despite persistent suggestions that it was an Iranian accident) to have attacked its own population at Halabjah. The vast majority of the facilities which created these weapons were effec-tively destroyed in the Desert Storm and Desert Fox bombing missions and many of the Intelligence reports that were generated before the war were based on how much could have been salvaged and how much could have been rebuilt. It is important to remember that Iraq had one of the world's most efficient intelligence services and was extremely efficient at ensuring that information didn't leak out into the West. Without hard information, a lot of the 'evidence' was necessarily built on informed speculation.

Why was there such emphasis on NBC or WMD in Iraq and Afghanistan? Part of the answer to this is based on realpolitik: it was only the possession of WMD (when linked to the 11 September attacks) that could form the casus belli necessary to wage war. WMD had to be there otherwise there would not be the trigger for war, so the intelligence put forward was coloured (either passively or proactively) with that aim in mind. Part of the reason why this was possible is that all of the experts are agreed that it is very easy to hide a small-scale chemical or biological weapon facility. A great deal of the necessary machinery and components of a chemical weapon can be found in an agro-chemical factory – the sort that would produce perfectly legitimate fertilizers. Biological agents can be created with the same sort of technology that is required for brewing or for legitimate pharmaceutical research. The single-use sites that Iraq had used previously had effectively been destroyed by allied action, but the sort of amount and facilities that Iraq needed, to have a base level capability, could be fulfilled by these dual-use facilities. It is also worth mentioning that these weapons are relatively easy to create. It is not difficult to build a bad chemical or biological weapon; they would be crude and not particularly effective but the capability is there. For many Iraq-watchers the question was not whether Saddam Hussein had chemical or biological weapons but whether he had a pure enough form to be effective and an efficient distribution method. This can be summarized as Saddam had the capability to launch a chemical attack, but not the ability to threaten anyone outside of a tactical range in forty-five minutes.

Even now questions persist over what happened to Saddam's stockpile. The Iraqis claim that, in line with UN resolutions, they destroyed all their munitions and facilities, yet this doesn't chime with the obstructions and difficulties that Unmovic inspectors had, even up to the end. There are significant gaps in the paperwork that the Iraqis need to corroborate their claim, and these are either blamed on poor filing or being destroyed or moved during the conflict and subsequent looting. The fact remains that large stockpiles of chemical munitions can be buried and remain undetected for years – there are still chemical munitions from the 1950s being found on the UK mainland. There is no reason to doubt that the same, in limited numbers, didn't happen in Iraq – that a number of shells were saved for a rainy day. If buried correctly the shells should be able to weather a number of years and still have a degree of efficiency. The same cannot be said for the biological agents which would have to be destroyed or moved out of Iraq: and at least one inspector (Richard Spertzel) has suggested that large amounts of Iraq's capability were shipped to Lebanon.

The challenge with NBC weapons is not whether countries have them, it is whether countries think that they can use them – the intention rather than the possession. Did Iraq prove to any country that if it has these weapons that it is better to give them up? Some would point to Libya's recantation of its non-conventional arsenal and show that as a direct link to Iraq. There may be some truth in that. This would, however, downplay a lot of good diplomatic work that has been done over a number of years to try and bring Libya back into the fold. What the Iraq scenario has done is show 'rogue states' the fear that Western powers have of these weapons. We are living in a time when desperate men with a knife and a camera are able to force a sovereign nation out of Iraq. What lesson will they take from the potential of chemical, biological and radiological weapons? If they were not doing so before, the froth of fear that has been whipped up in Western countries has given them a clear indication of the power even a limited supply of these weapons could have.

Hopefully one lesson that they will also take from Iraq is that these NBC weapons are a use-or-lose proposition. Once the US knows that you have them it will stop at nothing to take them away from you and render your force useless. For terrorists, who like to boast of their capability, this makes them a twin-edged sword – if you have them you'd better use them, because once it becomes known wheels will be put in motion that may destroy your organization.

The final lesson from NBC weapons and their usage has yet to be relearned – that they are not that bad in reality. Cold War training has provided NATO troops with the ability to sustain (literally) gallons of VX, anthrax and mustard and fight through it. Chemical weapons, for all their current terror cachet, are no different from any other weapon. If you take the right countermeasures they can be defeated. It is this return to an earlier age that makes them seem terrifying to members of the public and the politicians, but with the protective clothing and detectors that the armed forces have, and the training they endure, they are far less lethal than a bullet. Lethality is a major component that is lacking in NBC. These agents are very good at wounding and slowing an advancing force but they are very poor at stopping it. Casualties can be high among the unprotected, but lethality (with the exception of the nerve agents) is often low – unless in very high concentrations. Often these weapons have to rely on very inefficient dispersal methods, explosive, meteorological or vector, that can either destroy the agent or send it in a harmless direction. This is not to suggest that NBC weapons do not pose a real threat to our way of life. The greatest damage that these weapons do is to our infrastructure. An epidemic of botulinum toxin could be controlled, but the strain on the health system would make the annual flu epidemic look very puny indeed. Post-incident counselling and therapy would also tear great chunks out of any governmental budget and secondary infection (for things such as mustard gas) is high – ensuring long stays in hospital beds that can't be used for other patients. Legal and insurance claims would also loom for many governmental departments and large corporations, forcing many into severe financial difficulties.

The NBC arsenals of Afghanistan and Iraq that we had heard so much about turned out to be smoke and mirrors. What needs to be taken from the experience is the realization that these weapons are not difficult to create and, thanks to the emphasis that has been put on them politically, their 'stock' has risen exponentially. The fact that they can be built in small quantities without the backing of a military-industrial complex has made them of inestimable worth to organized terrorism. Until enough NBC attacks have been put in and defeated – and these weapons' true worth ascertained – then the threat of radiological, chemical, biological and nuclear weapons will continue to unnerve Western society.

Conclusion

A new Hundred Years' War? – Paul Moorcraft

For nearly three years the Anglo-American-led coalition has been fighting a global war on terrorism. For President Bush there could be no shilly-shallying – 'either you are for us or against us'. But can this war be won? If not, could some kind of settlement with the al-Qaeda network or at least its hosts be negotiated?

What kind of war?

Is the global war on terrorism (GWT) merely a convenient substitute for hawks who lusted after a replacement for the Cold War? Will it end up as 'another Hundred Years' War', a phrase used by Jean-Louis Bruguière, the French judge and counter-terrorism expert. George Bush clumsily talked of a 'crusade'. Are we indeed facing – or creating – 'the clash of civilizations', prophesied by Professor Samuel Huntington, a continuation of centuries of Muslim v Judaeo-Christian conflict? Although equally numerous historical examples of cooperation between these civilizations exist, the GWT could make Huntington's forecasts self-fulfilling.

Terrorism is a political method; how do you fight something that is universal and timeless? Above all, Islam is a belief system – how do you fight an idea? Hawks will say, however, that communism was an ideology that was fought and beaten.

Take a narrow military definition of the GWT: a small and loose coalition of dedicated Islamic extremists is fighting an asymmetric economic and armed conflict against a hyper-power. The war is vastly different from other terror campaigns. Strategically, it is global with no apparent chance of political compromise. Operationally, the terror planners aim for simultaneous spectaculars, without warnings, with volunteers who embrace death. Is there room for compromise with someone who sees it as his religious duty to acquire and use weapons of mass destruction (WMD)?

Who is winning this war?

As US Secretary of State for Defense Donald Rumsfeld confessed: 'We lack the metrics to know if we are winning or losing.' But some assessment must be made.

These are the positive developments for the West. Since 9/11, mainly because of the war in Afghanistan, more than one-third of the senior al-Qaeda leaders, as well as roughly 2,000 rank and file, have been killed or jailed (although these figures exclude the unknown number of foreign *jihadists* killed in Iraq). That leaves, from those who went through the Afghan training camps, about 18,000 trained al-Qaeda personnel at large. But mostly they are men concentrating on survival. At the beginning of 2004, over $125 million of suspected terrorist assets had been seized or frozen. And Muslim countries such as Pakistan have supported the US, thus proving this is not a war on Islam. Despite Pakistan's WMD proliferation, its government has been persuaded by Washington to launch major operations in the lawless tribal regions which harbour the Taliban and al-Qaeda. Libya has renounced WMD, and there are glimmerings of democratic unrest in Syria and Saudi Arabia. And there is at least a hope of constitutional democracy in two Islamic lands – Iraq and Afghanistan. Despite the turmoil in both countries, growing domestic lobbies are demanding democratic elections. The relative success of the Afghan elections in October 2004 surprised experts. Although many Arabs feel humiliated by Saddam Hussein's treatment in captivity, the novelty element of seeing a classic tyrant being tried for his crimes is encouraging to many modernizers in the region.

Losing?

What is the downside of these successes in counter-terrorism? The military attacks on the Taliban and Iraq have intensified radical Islamic resentment. Iraq, often seen as a detour in the terror war, has sucked in al-Qaeda supporters where few existed under the profoundly secular Saddam Hussein. The *madrassas* (religious schools) are daily churning out far more *jihadists* than the West could ever catch or kill. Al-Qaeda operates as a virtual entity in loose alliance with supporters in ninety countries. Its cells function within a flat informal trans-national infrastructure, whereas counter-terrorism is nationally based and hierarchical. And intelligence agencies are hampered by frequent turf wars.

Much of the terror money circulates through the informal Islamic *hawala* system – conventional banking systems are largely irrelevant, except as avenues for fraud. Thanks to modern technology and the multinational allure of the *jihad*, it is very difficult to deter such a hydra-headed monster. Since 9/11, constant worldwide attacks, most dramatically in Madrid, have demonstrated the resilience of al-Qaeda. It is only a matter of time before spectaculars are repeated in London or the USA.

To some Western critics, the Bush administration is riding roughshod over Arab sensibilities; for Muslims, the war on terror has been portrayed and widely accepted as a war on Islam. The Americans are quagmired in Iraq and Afghanistan, and the divide between the US and Europe was exacerbated by Spain's defection from the coalition in Iraq. Spain's election results have proved that terror works – and creates rapid regime change. The message was: hit London and Tony Blair will go the way of the former Spanish premier. In short, al-Qaeda is about creating a climate of terror and fear in the West. Growing anti-war sentiment, especially in the USA, is playing into the hands of those who want to cut and run from foreign adventures. Moreover, the public inquiries into massive intelligence failures in both the US and UK have undermined confidence in politicians, not least their ability to wage wars.

A draw?

So what is the counterweight to this negative assessment? The Americans have led a global effort to kill and arrest terrorists, while fostering an internal homeland security model. They have improved multinational law enforcement along more horizontal lines. And they have led efforts to curb the proliferation of WMD in rogue states and their seepage to the likes of al-Qaeda. But, so far, Osama bin Laden (or his body) has not been found and the threat – on the evidence of actual attacks, not intelligence assessments – is clearly growing.

A fair-minded conclusion could be that – thus far – the war is a draw, though not a stalemate. Catching bin Laden would be a tactical success, but his martyrdom could well boost his adulation for generations to come.

Constant terror alerts, especially in the US, have afforded al-Qaeda the oxygen of publicity. All sorts of lone screwballs as well as unrelated but committed Islamic extremist groups have latched on to the al-Qaeda label. The decimation of central command in Afghanistan disrupted but also dispersed trained commanders. This is good and bad. Highly organized spectaculars on the 9/11 model may be less likely, but localized atrocities may well increase. This redirection of Islamic terrorism encourages more concerted counter-terrorism in a larger number of states. This process appears to be happening in Pakistan, for example. It may also be true of the UK.

'Londonistan'

So there may perhaps be a score-draw internationally, but what of the domestic factors? Take London, for example. Determined and much more joined-up UK counter-terrorism has thwarted a number of attacks in the UK, most publicly the danger of a surface-to-air missile launch near Heathrow airport. The vast majority of the British Muslim community views al-Qaeda with some distaste; Muslim moderates have helped law enforcement agencies extensively. The two UK suicide bombers in Tel Aviv and Richard Reid, the shoe bomber, are very much in the tiny minority, but there could still be hundreds of 'sleepers'. As Eliza Manningham-Buller, the head of MI5, succinctly put it: 'We do not see the Muslim community as a threat; in the same way that we did not see the Irish community as a threat. Our focus is terrorists.'

The French intelligence agencies, though, used to refer to extremists in the UK capital as 'Londonistan'. The Paris spooks alleged that an unofficial concordat existed – *jihadists* were allowed to operate at the political and fundraising levels, provided there were no attacks on British soil. (Allegedly, a similar understanding was reached that the Irish Republican Army would not hit targets in Wales and Scotland, fellow Celtic countries.) In 2004, the round-ups – though not convictions for Islamic terrorism – have increased dramatically throughout the UK, while also exacerbating Muslim indignation.

Yet 9/11 was the single largest loss of British lives in a terrorist attack. And the MI5 chief said that 'we are faced with a realistic possibility' of some form of chemical, biological, radiological and nuclear (CBRN) attack in the UK.

It may be, however, that a CRBN attack is more likely from a non-Muslim maverick within the existing Western scientific establishment. Take the anthrax attacks in the US. Or consider domestic right-wing violence: the Oklahoma bomber in the US, or the neo-Nazi fanatic who killed three people in the Admiral Duncan pub in Soho, London, in 1999. Despite all the alarms, however, in the three years following 9/11 just one person – a policeman – has been killed in Britain by Islamic extremists.

A new empire?

9/11 displayed a challenging juxtaposition of the invincibility of the US hyper-power and yet also its absolute vulnerability. The old rules of Cold War deterrence are gone, because al-Qaeda *apparently* cannot be deterred. The impossibility of deterrence has encouraged the logical use of a US pre-emptive military strategy. But, morality aside, successful pre-emption relies totally on excellent intelligence. The failure to find WMD in Iraq has floated a huge question mark over fighting other rogue states, and the very basis of the war on terror.

The US has not relied solely on hard military power. European diplomacy in Iran and careful multilateralism over North Korea have brought, it seems, rewards – perhaps – on curbing nuclear proliferation. The demonstration effect of Iraq, plus subtle backstairs haggling by the UK Foreign Office, has removed Libya from the list of rogue states. True, Kashmir still festers. And the Beslan school massacre in September 2004 displayed the intractability of the Chechen struggle. The US has, however, helped to curb Indo-Pakistan nuclear sabre-rattling, while al-Qaeda support for the stubborn Chechen rebellion has corralled the Russians into the US anti-terror camp. Likewise, Chinese concern at Uighur Muslim separatists in Xinjiang province has also muted Chinese criticism. But, in Central Asia, US backing for dictatorships such as in Uzbekistan could fire up enduring resentment among the *jihadists*. The vast energy wealth of some of the 'stans' will prompt further Western engagement and Islamic counter-reactions.

Doing a deal?

The fanatical regime in North Korea is arguably the greatest threat to world peace, but a brokered compromise is on the cards. Could a similar deal be cut with al-Qaeda? What does Osama want? Washington should know: he was once the CIA pin-up boy in the war against the Russians in Afghanistan.

Jihadism is fuelled by a large number of causes, including low levels of economic development, a population time-bomb allied to a sense of political impotence among the young educated elite of undemocratic regimes, and Western support for these regimes. Terrorism is inspired and led not by denizens of absolute poverty, but by the wealthy middle class. Osama, remember, is (or was) a Saudi multimillionaire. Look at the educational background of the sixteen Saudis involved in the 9/11 bombings.

The mass-casualty aggression is aimed at the 'far enemies' – the US and the UK in particular. There is also anger at the 'near enemies', especially Egypt for making peace with Israel, and at Saudi Arabia for allowing US soldiers near the two most holy sites in Islam. Above all, despite an intrinsic belief in the superiority of Islam, many Muslims feel a sense of cultural humiliation imposed by decadent Western imperialists.

Tactical remedies

Durable solutions equate to massive social engineering. Meanwhile, the West can proffer immediate remedies. It could be summed up by adapting the UK Labour Party's mantra on crime: tough on terror, tough on the causes of terror. After the fall of the Soviet Union, the crazy or corrupt Cold War dictators in Africa, Asia and Latin America were largely dumped, but not in the Middle East. Why should the Anglo-Americans have bombed Iraq into democracy but support the fundamentalist dictatorship in Saudi Arabia? Secular Iraq, for example, was light years ahead in its treatment of women compared with the Saudis. America is beginning to disengage from Saudi Arabia. This exit could accelerate regime collapse and possible partition of the country.

A serious attempt to *enforce* a settlement between Israel and the Palestinians would be a massive step forward. Only Washington can make the Israelis withdraw from some of their settlements in the occupied territories, while guaranteeing the security of the Jewish state. Apartheid walls will not work in the long term. America could dictate a two-state solution with far fewer troops than used in Iraq, and to much better effect.

In short, even though al-Qaeda's methods are abhorrent, some of its demands may be reasonable. Osama will never get his pan-Islamic caliphate, but that is an issue for Muslims themselves.

America can set the stage, especially in Saudi Arabia and Palestine, by pulling the rug from under the extremists centred on Osama's fanatical Wahhabi brand of Islam.

So far, the pan-Islamic threat is largely a myth – far too many divisions rankle even within the extremist groups, ranging from Shia backing for Hezbollah in Lebanon to Muslim groups with local, often nationalistic, agendas in Asia. In this popeless religion no single authority can resolve centuries-old disputes, intensified by the chasm between modernizers and democrats versus autocrats and traditionalists.

Despite the stereotypes, many Islamic leaders are not medieval throw-backs – with the Afghan Taliban being an exception rather than a rule. Muslim fundamentalism is only one part of Islamic attempts to modernize their societies by removing the nepotistic, unstable status quo. Many Islamic religious leaders want to cooperate with the West, but without being swallowed or denigrated by it. They are important because the mosque is one of the few relatively uncontrolled institutions in the more repressive Arab states. So political fundamentalism has tended to be weaker where some toleration and opposition have been allowed – Morocco and Turkey are examples.

Withdrawal of support for anti-democratic systems throughout the Middle East will do a great deal to lessen the tension. The Arab percep-tion of Western support for the nominal Muslims in Kosovo (against bloodthirsty Orthodox Christian Serbs) was a start. Withdrawing completely from Saudi Arabia is a necessary step. Nudging Egypt towards democracy is another.

In early 2004 Arab leaders acted predictably to a leaked draft of Washington's 'Greater Middle East Initiative'. The US was trying to secure support from its partners in the G8 nations, but it will have to overcome the not-invented-here outrage of Arab states, whose leaders pay lip service to democracy in the abstract to appease Washington as well as their restive domestic audiences.

Democracy in Iraq, if it is ever conjured up, will be another major advance. Why should we assume that, unlike Christians or Israelis, the Arabs are unfit for democracy? The West can provide some of the economic and democratic incentives, but individual Islamic countries, given the hope of democracy, should decide for themselves. They might initially opt for the Iran model and then claw back from the clerics more elements of Western democracy. But the Iranian revolution was primarily seen as an eccentric Shi'ite variation, not applicable to the vast majority of Muslims who are Sunni.

Instead of demonizing fundamentalist movements in many Arab states, why not encourage them with promise of a democratic voice? Even relatively democratic states such as Turkey could still prove to be awkward partners – note Ankara's truculence bordering on blackmail over the 2003 war against Iraq. But that is the point of freedom – the ability to disagree.

Backing off from oil-rich dictators in the Middle East might be dangerous for the West. But NATO did not argue that communism should be propped up because Orthodox autocracy or virulent nationalism might flourish in Russia and its former satellites if the Wall came down. Democracy may provoke unintended and unpleasant consequences, but not as many as support for the current bunch of nasty despots. As journalist and Middle East expert Robert Fisk wrote of the region: 'We like dictatorships. We know how to do business with the kings and generals – how to sell them our tanks and fighter-bombers and missiles.' That is, unless they renege on the Western embrace — as Osama and Saddam did. Washington has been battling democracy across the region in the name of stabilizing autocracies.

Democracy in Iraq terrifies the Saudi government as much as it does Osama bin Laden. Many of the Saudi Shias live in the oil-rich regions: no wonder Iraqi experiments in federalism and democracy, which could result in regional Shia ascendancy, frighten the royals in Riyadh. The current chaos in Iraq could spill over, as could the success of a Shia-dominated democracy. No Saudi Mandela is likely to ride in from the desert.

Short-term, George Bush and Tony Blair could follow the then Spanish Prime Minister, Jose Maria Aznar, if their electorates turn on them – although the British are more likely to respond to their own 9/11 with the same grim determination to fight back as the Americans. The Anglo-American leadership does not see Iraq as a detour on the war on terror. If it were, why are al-Qaeda and the whole Islamist-fascist terror network so keen to get coalition troops out of the country? Economic growth, political pluralism and religious toleration in Iraq and its demonstration effect elsewhere would undermine the appeal of Islamic fascism. That of course was the message of the US neo-conservatives who did so much to set the activist agenda in the Middle East. Their tactical ambitions have collapsed, but the strategy may well be valid.

Some hard-line Israelis regard Arab democratization as a pre-requisite for resolving the Arab-Israeli dispute. But a settlement cannot wait, even though democracy in Palestine could produce a radical Islamic result. Likewise, in Iraq, Washington's short-term interests and democracy may conflict: in elections, radicals – either Sunni, or more likely radicals from the majority Shia – could win power. Elsewhere in the Islamic world Washington has returned to its Cold War strategy of the enemy of my enemy is my friend; hence the friendliness with authoritarian regimes in Tunisia and Algeria because they have come out on the US side in the war on terror. This relates to the largely unreported growth of support for al-Qaeda-style groups right across the Sahel belt, which is playing a part in the mid-2004 international crisis in the Darfur region of Sudan. The Sahel and indeed the whole of North Africa could become the soft underbelly of Islamic extremist pressure on Western Europe.

Democracy, though necessary to displace the lure of al-Qaeda, could also unleash the demons of tribalism, sectarianism and more holy wars, as is happening in Iraq. By comparison, even secular Arab modernizers might regard the calcified status quo as temporarily attractive.

Islamic resurgence

Professor Huntington was right in at least one sense: Islamic resurgence is mainstream, not extremist, pervasive, not isolated. The West must accommodate the Muslim 20 per cent of the world, but bolstering the dismal band of dictatorships will guarantee more floods of refugees and more terrorism from the region. The tactics of *jihadism* must be fought by unified Western counter-terrorism, by hard military power, tough diplomacy and trade. Strategically, it is not, however, a war that can be won solely in military terms.

The GWT is as much about Western values as military might. Fighting a purely military campaign will mean the destruction of those values by the slow erosion of domestic civil liberties. It will also complement al-Qaeda's war aims — to create an Islamic-infidel divide. Persuading Islamic countries to understand and work with Western values is the only sustainable solution.

Washington's martial triumph in Iraq briefly shocked and awed the fundamentalists, but it has been accompanied by a dramatic reduction in the moral authority of America and Britain in the region. Democratic systems are the best guarantor of international peace – that was the lesson of the victory in the Cold War. Communism was a faith in terminal decline, Islam is resurgent. It might be better to work with it, not fight it; so far, only a minority in the Islamic world has become – to quote former CIA Director George Tenet – 'a global movement infected by al-Qaeda's radical agenda'. Al-Qaeda is a virus that can never be totally eradicated, but it can be effectively quarantined.

Hard US military power, while not to be discarded, is proving daily more counter-productive in Iraq. The European Union's more legalistic soft-power approach has some merits, but – except for the British example – lacks the bite and cohesion of US policy. Some analysts say the American approach is from Mars, while the EU's legalistic style derives from Venus (and the lessons of two world wars). The point: congress is needed between both Venus and Mars for consummation of an effective joint strategy. Sure, the intelligence agencies of the EU and US are working better together, but the rifts over the Middle East, especially Iraq, have dramatically undermined Western cohesion. In this context, al-Qaeda's targeting of the March 2004 Spanish elections was astute.

The war on terror will never be won in the manner of 1945 – with the total defeat of the enemy and victory parades. Nor will it be won by implicitly demonizing Islam or even explicitly diabolizing Osama bin Laden. The Saudi warlord is a hero to vast swathes of Muslims both in the Arab world and beyond. Many of these are young people.

Wilsonian compromise?

To prevail, the West has to coordinate both hard and soft power. The US needs to stand shoulder-to-shoulder with the EU, and compromise where necessary. Some will call this appeasement. Historically, appeasement until 1938 was based upon the most moral of liberal principles; the ideals of President Woodrow Wilson. The problem was that Adolf Hitler was insatiable and probably mad. He refused to play by the same liberal rules. Osama bin Laden – as some US generals will reluctantly concede – is a determined and clever opponent. His tactics may be abhorrent, but they are working. Not least that, in the West, Islam is now a serious issue; one that needs to be urgently resolved, by compromise, by trade and dialogue, and less by bullets and bombs. In short, Osama bin Laden may not be amenable to a deal, but many of his allies and followers could be.

This may be the message of the Democratic contender, Senator John Kerry, in the 2004 presidential race. John Kerry, the former war hero, may well increase US military power and the size of the armed forces, but he is less likely to use them in a unilateralist fashion. If Kerry wins, a more coordinated Western strategy of soft power could emerge. This may well do more 'to drain the swamps' of support for al-Qaeda and its numerous affiliates than all the Manichean rhetoric of President George Bush. President Ronald Reagan defeated Soviet communism, a giant with the feet of clay, partly by outspending Moscow in an arms race. Islam is a far more resilient creed than the brief reign of Soviet communism. The notions of the international community of Islam have been ingrained over many hundreds of years. This does not mean that the West must bow to a revived caliphate in the former Ottoman Empire;

what it does mean is that the West must understand that Osama bin Laden is not a crazy renegade. He reflects the desires and ambitions of millions of Muslims. These same Muslims may not espouse his methods, but what they do accept is the desire for more respect. Much of the history of Islamic-Judaeo-Christian relations has been one of mutual harmony, not of crusades, *reconquista* or clashes of civilizations.

The attacks of 9/11 were an unprovoked terrorist act which killed thousands of innocent civilians of all races and creeds. The retaliation against the Taliban regime was largely understood and tolerated in the Islamic world. Although Saddam Hussein was not a popular figure in the wider Arab world (outside the West Bank and Gaza), the ham-fisted occupation of Iraq has hastened the polarization of Islam and the West. In this context, both George Bush and Osama bin Laden share some of the blame for driving the cultures apart. Both men have been subject to widespread demonization. In microcosm, the same can be said of the blood feud between Yasser Arafat and Ariel Sharon.

After these four antagonists depart the world stage, new leaders may re-forge the dynamics of the conflict. If not, the war on terror, which has already lasted three years, might become another Hundred Years' War.

Index

Abdullah, Abdullah, 169
Abdullah, Crown Prince, 18–19, 191
Abu Ghraib, 1
Adenauer, Konrad , 187
Afghanistan, 135–6, 161–85
Africa Confidential, 206
Air France, 242
Alaa, Abu, 144
Al Aqsa brigade, 225
Al Atabani, Ghazi Salah al Din, 205, 209
Al Bashir, Omar, 206
Albright, Madelaine, 210
Alexander, Douglas, 244
Alibekov, Kanatjan (Alibek, Ken), 273
Al Mahdi, Gutbi Lieutenant General, 202
Al Qaeda 4, 6
  British readiness for attack, 238
  casualties, 279
  globalizing the conflict, 234
  in Afghanistan, 162–85
  in Baghdad, 20, 45
  in Sudan, 200–10
  maritime strategy, 91, 145
  money-laundering, 260
  NATO response, 229
  NBC research in Afghanistan, 274
  negotiations, 281–8
  pressure on Saudi government, 188
  structure, 151
  successes, 280
  threats to London, 263–9
  worldwide spectaculars, 235
Al Rashid hotel, 33
Al Sadr, Moqtada, 190

Al Turabi, Hassan, 207–9
Amiriya bunker, 34
Amnesty International, 206–7
Annan, Kofi, 249
Ansar al Islam, 249
Apaches helicopters, 128–9
Arafat, Yasser, 15, 16, 25, 26, 59,
  144–5, 212–15, 219, 222, 225
Armitage, Richard, 4
  interview, 141–6
Asia Pacific Economic Forum, 233–4
A-10, 123–4, 158
Atef, Mohammed, 234
Attah, General Mohammed, 169–70,
  172–3
  interview 175–9
Aum Shinrikyo, 272
Australian Defence Industry, 96
Automated Number Plate Recognition
  system, 257
'Axis of evil' 2, 20, 63, 233
Aziz, Tariq, 3, 22, 33–5, 54–5, 57
  interview 35–9
Aznar, Jose Maria, 285

Ba'ath party, 78, 142
Babiker, Yahia Hussein, 205
Baker, James, 34, 38–9
Balfour Declaration, 16, 213
Balkan wars, 45, 49–50, 144
Bank station exercise, 253, 259, 266
Barak, Ehud, 17
Barno, Lieutenant General David,
  interview 179–82

Barrons, Colonel Richard, 163
Basra, 72–7
Battle, John, 19
Beg, Rasul, 175
Berger, Samuel 210
Beslan massacre, 282
B-52, 46, 70
Binalshibh, Ramzi, 234
Bin Laden, Osama, 2, 4
  Arab hero 12, 21
  bringing to account, 32, 45, 135
  demonization, 287
  failure to capture, 280
  in Sudan, 201–10
  Islamic trial, 31
  not crazy renegade, 288
  Wahhabi influence, 283
  would fight in New York, 141, 145,
    180
'Bin Ladenism', 18–19
Binns, Brigadier Graham, 66, 70
  interview 71–9, 81
biological weapons, 56, 68
  US protection against 98–104, 272–7
Biological Weapons Convention, 273
Biopreparat, 273
Blair, Cherie, 16
Blair, Tony,
  comparison with Suez, 15
  debate on Iraq, 25
  fighting war on terror, 217
  impact of Spanish elections, 280, 285
  Iraqi presidential palaces, 38
  nature of his Cabinet, 21
  opposition to Iraq in his party, 14
  support for regime change, 36
  threat assessment, 261
  unintended consequences of Iraq, 187
Blix, Hans, 37, 249
Blunkett, David, 23
Bremer, Paul, 195
Brims, Major General Robin, 81
British Transport Police, 243, 261
Bruguière, Jean-Louis, 278
Bush, George, Snr., 33
Bush, George, Jnr.,
  assault on terrorism, 233
  attitudes towards Arafat, 15–16
  blame for clash of civilizations, 288
  fighting terror war, 217–18

following father's policy, 39
'for or against us', 278
impact of Afghanistan on US elections,
    171
impact of free Iraq, 190
long war, 146
 Manicheism, 1, 287
no-fly zones, 53
opposition in UN to his policy, 14
optimism about outcome of Iraq war,
    56
pragmatism about Sudan, 203
relations with Muslims, 20
road map, 144
Spanish election, 285
two-state solution in Palestine, 214
unintended consequences of Iraq, 187
views on Arafat, 224–5

Campbell, Menzies,
  interview 23–9
Caritas, 134, 135
Carlos the Jackal, 204, 240
Carney, Tim, 4, 78
  interview 192–8
Castro, Fidel, 52
Catholic Church opposition to the Iraq
    war, 15
Ceausescu, Nicolae, 55
Channel Four TV, 212, 214
Chemical Agent Monitor, 243
'Chemical Ali', 75
chemical weapons against Kurds, 11, 56,
    68, 98–104, 271–2
Cheney, Dick, 187
Christianson, General Claude, 66, 70–1
  interview 110–17
Churchill, Winston, 11, 239, 246
CIA 33,
  Sudan policy, 201–10
City of London Police, 257
Civil Contingencies Bill, 251
Civil Contingencies Secretariat, 239, 245,
    251
Clay, General Lucius, 197
Clinton, Bill, 28, 36
  human rights agenda, 208
  lies about Iraq, 38, 145
  Middle East proposals, 215
  views on Sudan, 202

Congo, 147
Cooperative Engagement Capability,
    108–9
Cordesman, Anthony, 187–8
Cornish, Paul, 4, 232–7
Corporation of London, 258

Dalyell, Tam,
    interview 20–3
Danforth, John, 208
Davies, Colonel Richard,
    interview 171–5, 181, 182
de-Ba'athification, 195
Department for International
    Development, 170
Department of Trade and Industry, 15
Dimbleby, Jonathan, 54
Dostum, General Abdul, 168, 170, 172,
    173
    interview, 175–9
Dutton, General Jim, 68–70
    interview 79–86

Eisenhower, General Dwight, 82
Eurofighter, 47
European Union,
    no monitors in Sudan, 207
    relationship with NATO, 227
    soft power, 286
Exercise Saif Sareea, 42, 87

Fahd, King, 19
Fahim, Mohammed, 169
Farc, 272
FBI, 203–4, 234
Feith, Douglas, 3
    interview, 6–9
Financial Times, 14
Firelink system, 252
Fisk, Robert, 285
Flint, Caroline, 245
Foreign and Commonwealth Office, 14,
    49, 170
    success in Libya, 282
Fox, Major Malcolm, 183
Franks, General Tommy, 82, 92, 197
Fraud Squad, 260, 267

Gaddafi, Mu'ammer, 190
Galloway, George, 3

interview 10–20
Iraq like Suez, 26
journey to Baghdad, 32, 35
partition of Saudi Arabia, 28, 64
travels with Tam Dalyell, 20, 23
Garang, Colonel John, 203, 208
Garner, Jay, 78, 193, 196
GCHQ, 240
GIA, 266
Gilady, Brigadier Eival,
    interview 215–20
Goislard, Bettina, 171
Greater Middle East Initiative, 284
Greenstock, Jeremy, 191
Griffiths, Colonel Mike,
    interview 183–6
Guantanamo Bay, 236
Guardian, 14, 15, 27
Gummer, John, 26
Guthrie, General Charles, 4
    interview 149–56

HaCohen, Brigadier Gershon,
    interview 220–5
Haji-Ioannaou, Stelios, 242
Halabjah massacre, 10, 11, 244, 272,
    274
Haldane, R.B., 61
Halliday, Denis, 12
Hamas, 204, 211, 214, 225
Harakat, 169
Hart, Commissioner James, 4
    interview 257–63
Hawala system, 280
Heath, Edward, 36
Hekmatyar, Gulbuddin, 162, 166, 167,
    183, 185
Henderson, Douglas, 19
Hezbollah, 204, 218, 283
Hilsum, Lindsey, 4, 186–92
Hitler, Adolf, 287
HMS Albion, 86, 91, 107
    Ark Royal, 87, 89
    Brocklesby, 96
    Bulwark, 86, 99
    Invincible, 88
    Ocean, 89
    Roebuck, 93–5
    Sandown, 97
Hobsbawm, Eric, 188

Ho Chi Minh, 52
Hogg, Douglas, 26
Holmes, Richard,
    interview 59–62
Homeland Security, Department of, 245,
    266
Home Office, 242, 249
Hoon, Geoff, 3
    interview 39–45, 50
Howard, Professor Michael, 154
Huntington, Samuel, 1, 20, 29, 31–2,
    278, 286
Hurd, Douglas, 26
    interview 49–52
Hussein, Saddam,
    attack on Israel, 217
    British support of, 10–11, 19
    effect of imprisonment, 279
    genius at survival, 33
    hiding WMD, 54, 275
    human rights issues, 193
    impact of overthrow in the region,
        191
    intentions, 24
    maintained unity, 153
    Muslim champion, 30
    need to overthrow, 187
    popularity in Iraq and Jordan, 21
    possible trial, 57, 145
    sanity, 25
    WMD policy, 197
Hutton inquiry, 249, 255–6
Hutton, Lord, 152

International Atomic Energy Authority,
    190
International Criminal Court, 231
Iran reform process 65
    impact of Iraq war, 190
Iraq Sanctions Monitor, 13
Iraq Survey Group, 143, 274
Iraqi National Congress, 51, 57
Irish Republican Army, 43, 250, 255,
    262, 266, 268, 281
ISAF, 27, 135, 136, 138, 162–85
Islamic Jihad, 211, 214, 225
Israel,
    threat from Iraq 34, 35, 39, 56–7
    possible settlement 59

Israeli Defence Force, 215–27
Istar, 46, 83, 127

Jalali, Ahmad, 173
Jamiat, 168–9, 172, 175–9
Jeambert, Chief Warrant Officer Stacy,
    interview, 98–104
Jenin, siege of, 4, 212–14, 215–26
Joint Intelligence Committee, 152, 188,
    249
Joint NBC Regiment, 99
Joint Strike Fighter, 46
Joint Terrorism Analysis Centre, 234
Jumbish, 168–9, 172, 175–9
Jumper, General John, 4
    interview, 156–61

Karzai, Hamid, 17, 21, 27, 163, 168
Kay, David, 143
Keating, Vice Admiral Timothy, 89, 92
Keetch, Paul 4, 146–9
Kerry, John 287
Keys, Lieutenant General Richard, 3
    interview, 118–24
Khan, General Ismail, 179
Khan, Milan Zafir, 183–4
Khan, Mirza Ali, 180
Khomeini, Ruhollah, 11
Kidd, Lieutenant Colonel Patrick, 99
Kilfoyle, Peter, 19
Kurds, 10, 11, 51

Labour Party,
    opposition to Iraq war, 14
    mantra on crime, 283
Laderman, Major Rafi, 214
Leaman, Commodore Richard, 87
Leaney, Lieutenant Commander Mike,
    interview, 94–8
Liberation of Iraq Act, 13
Livingstone, Ken, 241
Lloyd, Tony, 19
London First, 258
London Resilience Team, 248, 252
London Underground, 253–4
Lusk, Gill, 206
Luttwak, Edward, 188

Mackinlay, John, 4
    interview, 133–41

292

Mahon, Alice, 14, 25
Mail on Sunday, 14
Mandela, Nelson, 30
Manningham-Buller, Eliza, 247, 281
Masan, Abu, 144
Mattis, General James, 68, 100–1, 103
McColl, Major General John, 3
    interview, 165–7
Médicines sans Frontières, 134, 136
Megawati, Sukarnoputri, 52
Melvin, Bigadier Mungo,
    interview, 124–32
Mercer, Patrick, 4, 239–40
    interview, 244–51
Metropolitan Police, 24, 242, 247, 260,
    263–9
MI5, 239, 241, 247, 281
Milosevic, Slobodan, 25
MI6, 204–5, 239
Mitchell, George, 214
MOD (UK), 14, 148–9, 241
Mohammed, Sheikh Khaled, 234
Mossad, 33
Mother of All Battles Mosque, 34
Moussaoui, Zacarias, 234
Mubarak, Hosni, 201
Mukhabarat (Sudan), 202–3
Musharraf, General Pervez, 52

Nasser, Abdul, 52
National Criminal Intelligence Service,
    260
National Islamic Front (Sudan), 202–10
National Security Council (US), 194
NATO Article 5, 7, 8, 9, 27, 227–9
NATO-Russian Council, 227, 231
Netanyahu, Benyamin, 17
network-centric warfare, 46, 92, 108,
    119, 146
New Statesman, 31
no-fly zones (Iraq), 47, 53, 67, 157
Northern Alliance, 18, 163–5, 169, 204

Office of the Deputy Prime Minister, 251
Office of Reconstruction and
    Humanitarian Assistance, 192–8
Omand, David, 240–1, 252, 256
Omar, Mohammed, 178
OPEC, 189

Operation Desert Fox, 13
Operation Fresco, 81, 104

Palestine Liberation Organization, 225
Palestinian Authority, 16, 43, 211–15
Palestinians, 16–17, 26
Pentagon, 188
Peres, Shimon, 17
Perle, Richard, 3, 28
    interview, 53–9, 192
Pilger, John, 13
Powell, Colin, 26, 209
Prescott, John, 240, 245
Proceeds of Crime Act, 260
Provincial Reconstruction Teams,
    169–75, 179–82
Putin, Vladimir, 28

Qanuni, Mohammed, 169
Quinlan, Michael, 31

Rajneesh, Bhagwan Shree, 273
Ramiz, Gailan, , 187
Raynsford, Nicholas 241, 244–5
    interview, 251–7
Reagan, Ronald, 287
Reid, Richard, 281
'return of the tank' effectiveness of
    Challenger 2, 127–8
revolution in military affairs, 67, 218
Reynolds, Albert, 21–2
RFA *Sir Galahad,* 97
Rice, Condoleezza, 27, 194
Ritter, Scott, 12, 13, 23
Robertson, George, 4
    interview, 222–32
Robinson-Brown, Captain Roger, 67
    interview, 97–8
Rodman, Peter,
    interview, 62–6
Royal Anglians, 164
Royal family,
    possible attacks on, 262
Royal Marines, 3, 79–86
Rumsfeld, Donald, 3, 66, 145
    interview 179–82, 187, 194
    terror scorecard, 232–7, 279
    visits Afghanistan, 170–1, 178
Ryle, John, 201

Saladin, 12
Saleh, General Bakri Hassan, 207
Saudi Arabia,
   attitude to Iraq war, 67
   fear of Shias, 191
   instability, 58
   possible fall, 22
   possible partition, 18
   removal of US bases, 188
   US policy towards, 64
SAVE, 134
Sayyaf, Abdur, 167
Schlein, Brigadier Eyal, 225
Scud missiles, 56
Sea Harrier debate, 58
Sharon, Ariel, 17, 144, 191, 212–15
Short, Clare, 21, 208
Sierra Leone, 45, 50
Simonds, Miriam, 170
Siprnet, 85
Smith, Assistant Chief Constable Colin,
   244
Smith, Michael, 239
Snelson, Admiral David, 67, 69
   interview, 86–93
Special Branch, 240
Spectator, 49, 50
Spertzel, Richard, 275
Spying Game, 239
Squire, Air Chief Marshal Peter,
   interview, 45–9
State Department, 188
   views on Sudan, 203–10
Strategic Defence Review (UK), 43–6,
   146, 148, 267
Straw, Jack, 27
Sudan, 50–1, 192–209
   crisis in Darfur, 286
Sudan People's Liberation Army, 200–10
Sunday Times, 202, 214
Swain, Lieutenant Commander Andy,
   interview, 94–8
Swims system, 95–6

Tablet, 31
Taliban, 3, 4, 6, 18, 21, 31, 41, 162–7,
   185, 191, 229, 234, 279, 284
Talisman Energy, 200
Tenet, George, 219, 286
Territorial Army, 61–2, 240

Civil Contingency Reaction Force,
   253, 267–8
Thatcher, Margaret, 36
Thompson, Robert, 138, 153–4
Time magazine, 195
Torpey, Air Marshal Glen, 123
Treasury (HM),
   trims defence spending, 147–8
Turkey,
   northern front in Iraq war, 72, 80–1,
      111
   tolerant Islam, 284

UAVs, 158–9
Uighur Muslim separatists, 282
UK-US military relations, 7, 47–8, 84,
   105, 108
   air force cooperation, 157
   different approaches to peacekeeping,
      138–9, 142
UN,
   reconstruction in Afghanistan 163
   war on terror, 234
   weapons inspectors in Iraq, 37
UNHCR, 134–5
Unmovic, 274, 275
UN oil-for-food programme, 12
USAF, 46–7
   Iraq operations, 118–24, 156–61
USAID, 169, 170
US Navy Seals, 83–4
USS *Cole,* 203, 265
US Transport Security Administration,
   242

Veness, Assistant Commissioner David, 4
   interview, 263–9
Viet Cong, 221
Von Sponeck, Hans, 12, 13

Wahdat, 169
weapons of mass destruction, 3, 6, 23
   Iraq denies ownership of WMD 36–7
   US views on Iraq, 53–6
   hyping the threat, 249
   Iranian WMD, 63, 190
   Israeli readiness, 217
   mass effect, 244
   UK scepticism, 254, 261, 270–7

US protection against 98–104
use of, 61;
why none found there, 151–2, 191–2, 197
Weinberger-Powell doctrine, 235
Wellington, Duke of, 154–5
West, Admiral Alan, 69
  interview, 104–10

Williams, Rowan, 3
  interview, 29–32
Wilson, Woodrow, 287
Wingate, Orde, 154
Wolfowitz, Paul, 192

Zinni, General Anthony, 219
Zubaydah, Abu, 234